KU-536-082

THE HEART OF ETHIOPIA

By the same author

THE HEART OF NEPAL
THE HEART OF IRAN
THE HEART OF MALAYA
THE HEART OF INDIA
THE HEART OF GREECE
JOHNNY GURKHA

THE HEART OF
ETHIOPIA

DUNCAN FORBES

WITHDRAWN UNIVERSITY OF NOTTINGHAM

ROBERT HALE AND COMPANY
63 Old Brompton Road, London SW7

© *Duncan Forbes 1972*
First published in Great Britain 1972

ISBN 0 7091 2975 0

Robert Hale & Company
63 Old Brompton Road
London S.W.7

v

PRINTED IN GREAT BRITAIN BY
CLARKE, DOBLE & BRENDON LTD.
PLYMOUTH

CONTENTS

1	Hill Station Extraordinary	13
2	The Lion of Judah	16
3	Beer for Breakfast	24
4	Some Native Customs	41
5	The Historic Route	47
6	The Red Sea Land	64
7	The Holy City	74
8	Gondar and the Smoke of Fire	87
9	Getting Mobile	103
10	Christmas Eve in the Bishoftu Road	114
11	The Rock-hewn Epiphany	121
12	Journey to the East	134
13	The City of Arthur Rimbaud	146
14	Arnold in Ethiopia	167
15	The Way of the Cross	190
16	The Czar of Africa	212
	Index	218

ILLUSTRATIONS

facing page

Addis Ababa: listening to the Emperor's speech at the
Opening of Parliament   32
The contrasting styles of Addis Ababa: the old palace
church; Africa Hall, home of the Organisation of African
Unity   33
Axum: the fallen pillar and the Imperial Crowns   48
Gondar: Debre Berhan Selassie Church   49
Angels on the ceiling of Debre Berhan Selassie Church   49
Gondar: the empty bath of Fasildas   96
Lalibela: St. George's Church   96
Lalibela: at St. Mary's Church   97
Lalibela: the Tabot coming from Libanos Church   112
Lalibela: boys with genet sticks   112
Harar: the reputed house of Arthur Rimbaud   113
A Moslem girl from Bale   160
Gurage girls near Lake Zwai   160
Pilgrims on the road to Sheik Hussein   161
The author outside a Sidamo tukul   176
Derbaw, Said and the mules in Kundi on the Way of the
Cross   176
The gateway to Amba Gishen   177
Pages from the Holy Book   177

All photographs taken by the author

MAP

Ethiopia   *pages* 8–9

Land over 4900ft

SHOA Provinces

Rift valley

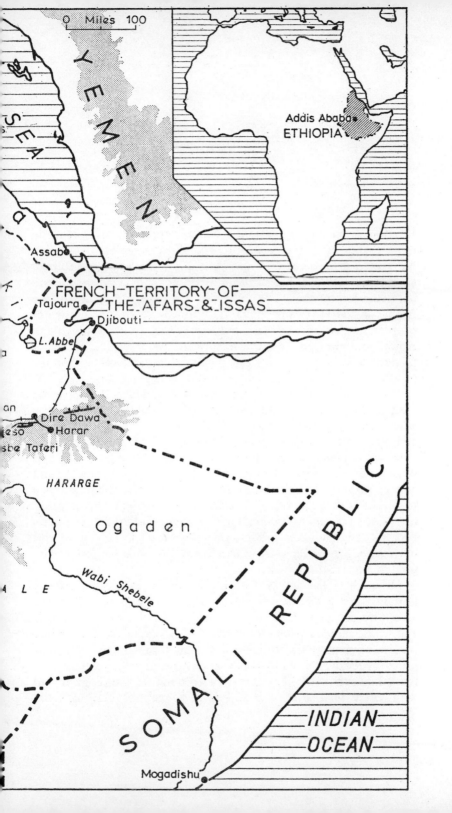

AUTHOR'S NOTE

Ethiopia is so vast and varied a country that it is difficult to do more than scratch the surface in one short book. Its population has grown from between 5 and 10 million fifty years ago to over 22 million today, yet it is still underpopulated in comparison with its natural resources. The highland Christians, principally the Amharas and Tigreans, have traditionally been the dominant peoples, and of these the Amharas, straddling the central highland region and the land known historically as Abyssinia, have in modern times imposed their government and their language on the people.

Yet Amharic, although it is the national language, is the mother tongue of less than a third of the total population. The Gallas, who are also a Cushitic race, are more numerous and spread far and wide in the southern hills, into which they poured from the dessicated plains of northern Kenya in the eighteenth and nineteenth centuries. Many of them, like the northern and eastern peoples of Ethiopia, are Muslims and make the pilgrimage to Mecca if they can afford it or to Sheik Hussein in Bale province, if they cannot go abroad. On the other hand the pagan Nilotic people of the Sudanese border, many of whom still go naked and unashamed, are even now the objects of the attention of the foreign Christian missions.

Although Gallas and Amharas have fought each other bitterly in the past, it would be difficult to distinguish one from the other except by language. Both live in primitive round huts made of mud and wattle and are primarily herdsmen. A homestead will simply consist of a group of these *tukuls*, standing on land which is probably legally owned by some absentee landlord. A village on a road, however, will have a row of rectangular buildings roofed with corrugated iron, which are less picturesque but more comfortable to live in. Higher standards are achieved by a growing number of town dwellers, who live more like westerners in villas and flats.

Although tribalism is officially discounted, many say that tribal consciousness has increased rather than diminished in recent years. Whether this is because of the interest that foreigners, including the large body of foreign-aid personnel, with their numerous demographic and linguistic surveys, always show in this aspect of African life, or because of the ever-increasing competition for good jobs as the educated section of the population increases beyond the capacity of the economy to absorb it, nowadays the words Amhara, Galla and Tigrean are always on people's lips.

For understandable reasons of national pride the Government chose Amharic rather than English as the national language, but others see it as a symbol of the dominance of Amharas in all the affairs of the country, typified most strikingly in methods of land acquisition which have had the effect of disinheriting many sections of the population, and in their colonization of the lower regions.

Ethiopia today receives as great a share of foreign aid in proportion to its population as anywhere in the world. The United Nations, Britain, Sweden, the U.S.A., Yugoslavia, the U.S.S.R., West Germany, France, Bulgaria, Israel, Italy, Australia, Japan and Holland all make their contributions, and each time the Emperor takes his begging bowl to a foreign capital some fresh contribution is added. However much of it trickles away in the sand, the total effect cannot fail to change the face of the country for the future. Meanwhile in Ethiopia today can be seen all the stages of transition from primitive tribal life through medieval feudalism to modern bureaucracy.

As with my book on Greece I have had to consider carefully the best way in which to spell Ethiopian names in English. For some time after 1940 the Italian system of writing place names in the Roman script prevailed, and on some maps it still remains. Then, a few years ago, the Imperial Ethiopian Mapping and Geography Institute produced a system of transliteration for the names of places, rivers and so on to be written on government maps. But if I had followed this system strictly, a number of well-known places would have looked unfamiliar to English eyes on the printed page. Addis Abeba and Asmera might have been readily comprehended, but Mitsiwa (for Massawa) and Mekdela (for Magdala) would have mystified many.

I have therefore retained a more traditional spelling and, in general, followed the orthography used in the English language daily newspaper, the *Ethiopian Herald*.

1

Hill Station Extraordinary

Some people told me I was a brave man to go to Ethiopia, and clearly it was a polite way of saying I was a fool. "The Emperor is old," they said. "When he dies, there will be bloody chaos. There is great tension between Christians and Muslims, which could break out into violence at any moment. Didn't you read the article in the Sunday paper magazine section? There are thousands of beggars there. The Eritrean separatist movement is dangerous."

I listened, but I was not unduly worried. I was coming from a country where, less than a month before, a man had been kicked to death in the street, and a few weeks before that hundreds of people had been burned out of their homes, all in the name of religion; where the separatist movement uses gelignite, petrol bombs and machine-guns; where the beggars strum guitars; where nearly a million people are said to be without adequate housing; where many of the weak-minded languish ill-cared for and unloved, committed to ill-found institutions.

I refer to the affluent society of the United Kingdom of Great Britain and Northern Ireland, and in particular to Northern Ireland and the death of Mr King in Londonderry in September 1969.

Besides, I had work to do in Ethiopia as one of the foreign advisers to the government of Emperor Haile Selassie I. As I boarded the Ethiopian Airlines plane at Rome's Fiumincino airport, walking past the green, yellow and red of the national flag painted on its tail, I hoped that the advice I might be able to give would be worthwhile.

And there was another thought that came to me too, as I looked at the pale wallpaper in the plane, with sketches of the great pillar at Axum, of a church cut into the living rock at Lalibela, and of a statuesque seated lion, repeated endlessly in the design, and as I listened to the soft music that was supposed to lull the passengers into a sense of comfort and confidence. It was a thought that took me back over half a lifetime to my life in Paris just before the Second World War, when I struggled through the magical French phrases of Arthur Rimbaud's poems, and they seemed to open a new door into my own mind. For Rimbaud, who seems to have never written another line of verse after he was 20, spent most of the working period of his short life in Ethiopia and nearly left his bones there.

When the plane took off, there were very few passengers aboard. A cluster of dark Ethiopians on the starboard side and half a dozen other passengers, scattered amongst the empty seats, were all that the coloured stewardess had to serve with the evening meal. But at Athens we were joined by a larger crowd, many of them Americans returning to the United States base in Eritrea, and at Asmara all the remaining seats were filled up by residents of Ethiopia doing the short leg down to Addis.

By this time it was light again, the midnight stop at Cairo only a blurred memory. It was a bright, clear light in a pale-blue, cloudless sky that I was to come to know well in the months ahead. And in the early morning light there stood a modest white airport building flying the Emperor's flag, which looked refreshingly simple and uncomplicated, reminding me of the little airports I had known up and down Malaya, where a passenger was something more than a piece of baggage to be fed on to the conveyor-belt. On the far side of the airfield a squadron of fighter planes reflected the rising sun in silvery flashes.

Many of our new passengers were speaking Italian, adding a third language to the English and Amharic that had caught my ear so far. But I was scarcely listening. When we took off again, I was too busy watching the Ethiopian countryside roll past below us to pay attention to what they were saying.

It was an open, untamed countryside, not of rolling hills and dales but of rough-edged mountains, flat-topped or rising sheer to rounded summits, cut by deep canyons and steep, crumbling valleys. There seemed to be no towns, or even villages, but simply small clusters of round huts, some thatched, some with corrugated-iron roofs flashing back the message of modernity to us. The huts were usually amongst clumps of trees. Outside these copses the better land was green, whilst the poor acres were a tawny brown, the lion colour of Africa.

This was the country into which Lord Napier of Magdala forced his way in 1868, and his soldiers said, "If this is a tableland, the table's upside down and we're climbing up and down the legs!" This was the country in which the Italians were defeated at Adowa in 1896 by the forces of Emperor Menelik II, with incalculable results. For the need to avenge the shame of Adowa was the emotional spur, which Mussolini used in 1935 to force through the conquest and annexation of the empire.

My neighbour kept asking me whether we were beginning to descend. I told her to be patient. She informed me that it was her first visit to Addis, where she was going to join her mother, who was married to an Ethiopian. It seemed that she was Greek.

"Are we coming down now?" she said for the fourth time.

And this time I was glad to be able to say we were, for the pitch of the engine noise had changed, and we were sinking towards a ridge of darker green, a rare forest in a land that was once richly wooded. Suddenly, as we came over the top of the ridge, there were flashes of light, not from one or two roofs half hidden in a copse, but from whole rows of them in streets and alleys, on the steep hillsides amongst the eucalyptus trees and on the flat land below, towards which we were heading.

Interspersed amongst the flashing corrugated-iron roofs, large creamy white buildings stood out—the palaces of tourism and bureaucracy. But there was no time to distinguish one from another. The general impression that I received in those few moments between skimming over the Entoto hills and landing at Bole on the other side of the city was of a hill station, like the ones I had known in India, swollen to extraordinary proportions.

2

The Lion of Judah

The impression of an enormous hill station, with a population of nearly half a million, remained with me during the following weeks. Nor was it an idle impression, for an Englishman ought to feel just as at home, walking the streets of Addis Ababa, as he does strolling down the Mall in Darjeeling or Mussoorie. The names of the main roads reflect the proud moment in 1941, when the Emperor was replaced on his throne by the British Army and Ethiopia became the first country to be liberated from the Axis powers.

The main avenue of the city, rising steeply up the hillside as a proud new dual carriageway from Haile Selassie I square to the new city hall, is called Churchill street. The roads that join it, flanking the hillside to left and right, are named after General Wavell and General Wingate. King George VI street joins the two most important squares to the north-east, whilst Eden street runs south-east from Menelik II square.

But there the resemblance ends. The thick-set African lumbers about the streets instead of the small-boned Indian. The busy business centres of De Gaulle square and the market are still known best by their Italian names of the Piazza and the Mercato, whilst away from the main avenues the little Fiat taxis rush along the narrow channel of road between the streams of pedestrians on either side, picking up and putting down passengers, who pay 25 cents for a seat in a vehicle that is going their way.

On the Sunday after my arrival I walked boldly out of the Ras Hotel, which lies in the lower part of the town near the railway station, and hailed one of these *seicento* taxis to take me up the hill towards the parliament building.

"Arat kilo," I said. It was the only way I knew to indicate the direction I wanted, for *Arat kilo* means "four kilometres" and is the name by which everybody knows Miazia 27th square and the day on which the Emperor rode back in triumph into Addis in 1941.

The gap between the lower and the upper town is still largely undeveloped and occupied by the mud and wattle huts that are the normal city dwelling places of the African poor, with outside standpipes for water and little sanitation. Even so, it is not far, and I might easily have walked, but I was still feeling the altitude of over 8,000 feet and panting and puffing at the slightest exertion.

The taxi puffed and panted too. It stopped to take on a thin, thick-lipped man in a city suit and a straw hat and a fat, round-eyed woman in a wide white dress with a scarf twisted tall on her head. Then it strained its way up the hill and turned the steep corner on to the level of Itegue Menen street, which skirts the wall of the old Imperial Palace.

Policemen in pale khaki tunics were in the broad avenue in unusual numbers, for this was an unusual day. It was the thirty-ninth anniversary of the coronation of the Emperor and the traditional day on which he proceeds in procession from worship in St. George's Cathedral, where he was crowned in 1930, to the opening of parliament.

I got out of the taxi just short of Arat Kilo and the column with the Lion of Judah on it, which was built in memory of the victory of 1941. Then I walked back downhill to take my place in the crowd at the entrance to the parliament building.

We were a mixed lot, some in modern trousers and shirts and other in the white jodhpurs of the country folk with the large, white shawl of coarse cloth called the shamma thrown across their shoulders. Some were hatless and others either sported a variety of straw hats of all shapes and sizes or the white sun helmets I knew as Bombay bowlers, which are still commonly seen in Ethiopia as the headgear of a man of some consequence.

B

Topis were also the most conspicuous feature of a line of soldiers of the Imperial Guard that faced the avenue with their backs to us. The men wore khaki Wolseley helmets. I had one once. It was issued to me at Aldershot for the voyage to India the same year that the Emperor returned to Africa from his exile in Bath. When I got to India I threw it away, to be issued with another, lighter pith helmet that also went the way of the first, when the Indian Army found that the boy-scout-style bush-hat was the only practicable sun hat in which to wage war.

But the Ethiopian guardsmen conservatively preserve their solar topis. The men in Wolseley helmets, and epaulettes adorned with furbishings from lions' manes, moved forward to block the traffic. A row of armed policemen kept us back. Some of them faced us with automatics tucked into their tunics, and I was reminded of the time when, though not in danger of his life, the Emperor nearly lost his throne in the bloody fighting in 1960.

A brass band, dressed in white topis and red jackets, came marching down the avenue from Arat Kilo. The crowd leaned forward. Pensioners, stationed under the trees, kept them back, making occasional threatening gestures with their large sticks. They were wearing their medals pinned to their chests, and many of them had the British Army Africa Star from the Second World War as well as the United Nations medal for service either in Korea or the Congo.

Then the cars began to arrive. The senators in their frock coats and the ambassadors flying their flags converged on the building. The latter seemed almost as numerous as the former, for the Emperor, in his subtle way, has very largely succeeded in making Addis Ababa the diplomatic capital of Africa. As the location of the Headquarters of the Organization for African Unity and the United Nations Economic Commission for Africa it is a natural focal point. Besides, the climate is good, and the diplomats have the advantage of setting up house in a hill-station instead of sweating in the plains. So they all converge on Addis—the majority of European nations and the new nations of Africa, the most important nations of Asia and America, and a few unimportant ones, such as Haiti, which have nothing in common with Ethiopia but the colour of their people. A thoughtful Emperor provides the means of access in his own Ethiopian

Airlines, for to get to the country by road is a lengthy adventure, not without danger and only practicable in the dry season, whilst, with the Suez Canal closed, the journey by sea is trebled for anyone coming from the direction of Europe or North Africa. So the national airline, with Alitalia and East African Airways the only real competitors, prospers as few airlines run by developing countries do.

After the last of the parliamentarians and ambassadors had passed through the gates, the guardsmen and police were ordered to attention. There was a shuffling of feet, a rapping out of commands in words that were just recognisable as English, and a straightening of shoulders under the heavy topis, as the noise of approaching cavalry grew louder. Then the first troop of lancers appeared, mounted on frisky greys, with their lances flying the royal pennant above their white Wolseley helmets.

The lancers were followed by the imperial car, a large maroon Rolls Royce, with the little Emperor sitting on the back seat in his military uniform, occasionally turning his face slightly from side to side, but in the main gazing straight ahead. Though his eyes were still sharp, he looked solemn and small and frail. He was an old man of 77, with all but two of his six children gone before him. Was he going to open yet another parliament, that had small mandate from the people and less power to carry it out?

The civilian cheer leaders waved their paper flags and a small shout went up. The Emperor passed by and entered the parliament building. The second troop of lancers followed, with horses rearing and backing nervously. The crowd surged across the avenue, carrying me with it, until I was extracted from it by a policeman and directed over to the open field in front of parliament which normally has cows and sheep grazing on it, but was now thronged with people waiting with statuesque immobility for the speech from the throne.

I waited too, looking at the two golden lions of Judah on the pillars of the gate, and beyond them at the three murals on the facade of the building—St. George slaying the dragon in the centre, and again that overworked heraldic beast, the lion, holding up an Ethiopian standard on either side. His Majesty's speech was relayed to the crowd by loudspeaker. He spoke of many things, reviewing the nation's progress in the previous year, but education was the subject to which he awarded priority.

"As we have repeatedly said," the Emperor declared, "education is the key to the development of our country, and it should therefore be given priority. Our people, realizing the importance of education, have for the last few years participated with the government in the expansion and development of educational facilities through self-help schemes. This co-operation between government and the people has resulted in the expansion of educational facilities to accomodate the ever-increasing number of school-age children."

This was an important comment on the educational explosion, which is taking place in Ethiopia today. But I had to wait for the afternoon edition of the *Ethiopian Herald* to read it, since the imperial speech was delivered in Amharic, which is the official national language of the country.

As the, to me, unintelligible and lengthy speech proceeded, I walked away from the crowd up the hill towards the square, grey building on the highest point of the city. I had not gone far before a small barefoot boy in a blue shirt and shorts attached himself to me, walking alongside me without speaking.

There was a beggar at the gate, holding out her hands and saying, *"Felege Christos!"*—For the love of Christ. This was the second phrase of Amharic that I learned. The small boy was still with me as I dropped a coin into her palms and entered.

The building stood foursquare above me at the top of the hill, with a dome in the centre like that of Les Invalides in Paris, and a pair of Trafalgar Square lions on each of the four sides. It was the mausoleum of Emperor Menelik II, who transferred his capital from Ankober to Addis Ababa in 1886, whilst he was still only King of Shoa and ten years before he defeated the Italians at Adowa with arms bought largely from French traders and from the Italians themselves.

The inscription beside the front doors to the mausoleum at the top of the steps reads as follows:

In commemoration of H.I.M. Menelik II
this mausoleum, the foundation
stone being laid in 1910 (e.c.)
inaugurated in 1920 (e.c.)

during the reign of H.I.M. Zewditu,
H.R.H. Ras Teferi Makonnen
the Crown Prince.

Ras Teferi Makonnen was the present Emperor's name before
he was crowned 'Power of the Trinity', whilst "e.c." refers to the
Ethiopian calendar, which is nearly eight years behind the
Gregorian calendar of the western world.

The doors were locked. I walked down the steps again and
watched two more visitors appear. They kissed the steps, the door,
the threshold of the door and the doorposts in solemn devotion,
but they, too, could not enter.

The small boy beckoned me round the side, and a man dressed
in khaki and white appeared from a hut on the far side. He was
the custodian, the *zebegna*, and he opened the doors at the back
to let us in.

From the external corridor we entered the circle under the
dome with its golden crown. A large mural adorns each of the four
walls. On the north wall Ras Makonnen, father of the present
Emperor, is shown describing to Menelik the victory at Adowa;
on the south wall the same Ras receives the keys of the city of
Harar, which was captured in 1887, and is appointed governor-
general; on the west wall Menelik's coronation is depicted, whilst
on the east wall there is a picture of the Queen of Sheba's famous
visit to King Solomon in Jerusalem, as a result of which, the story
goes, she bore a son who was crowned Menelik I and founded the
Solomonic line.

Thus I saw the key points in the life of the first emperor to try
to turn Ethiopia into a modern state, though he did not live to
see the railway from the coast at Djibouti completed. But we were
not finished. Begging me to mind my head on the edge of the
trapdoor, the zebegna took me down the marble steps to the actual
tombs in the vault below. The largest was that of the emperor,
himself, whilst those of his consort, Empress Taitu, and his daughter, Empress Zewditu, who ruled in her own right for fourteen
years, lay on either side.

The place was musty and silent, with a sad touch added by the
tomb of Princess Tsehai, daughter of the present Emperor, who
died tragically young in 1942. I was not sorry to get out of it again

and follow my diminutive guide through a small gateway into the outskirts of the Old Ghibbi, the wooden palace that Menelik had built, which is still used for imperial audiences.

The church of Kidane Meret, to which we made our way on the eastern edge of the Ghibbi, was the first of the round churches of Ethiopia that I saw. Shaped like a larger version of the ordinary circular tukul of mud, wattle and thatch, it was made of wood with a corrugated-iron roof. But this time, though there are interesting souvenirs of Menelik's reign inside, we could not enter. The priest who emerged from a house in the corner of the compound had not got the key. He offered his cross to a young man to kiss, walked with us a little way and watched us go.

Back up the hill I sat on the steps of the mausoleum and gazed at the crowds on the field in front of the parliament building below, and across at the upper part of Addis with the green hills behind. At that distance all the eyesores disappeared, and it was a place of beauty, with the domes of churches rising above the buildings and the countryside rolling away to the right in peace and plenty.

As I rested I gave the boy a coin. He kissed my knee in thanks. But he had not finished with me. Leaving another group of visitors kissing the threshold of the mausoleum, we went down again and skirted the crowd to visit another relatively old building in this modern city—the original Trinity Church.

Like the Kidane Meret, this church is tukul shaped, and, with its blue and white walls, its green foliage painted on the beams of the eaves and its fretted metal skirting to the roof, it looked rather like a Turkish kiosk. Again we could not enter, and I had to be content with looking at the tombs outside, with their photographs of the deceased, before going on to the new Trinity Cathedral, which was built in 1941 in thanks for the recovery of the country's independence.

This cathedral looks heavy and ponderous beside the lighter traditional buildings. It is rather Russian in appearance, with four ponderous statues of solemn dignitaries outside it sculpted by one, Georgakis, a Greek. But the surroundings are quiet and peaceful, for no one would dare to disturb the place where the ruling Emperor's consort and sons lie buried. We left a party of schoolgirls kissing everything they could touch, and returned past the back of the parliament building to the bustle of the main road, where the crowds were dispersing after the Emperor's departure for the Jubilee Palace.

I climbed into a *seicento* taxi to return to the Ras hotel. The small boy put his hand to his mouth as if he were Oliver Twist begging for more.

"*Felege Christos,*" the eyes seemed to say, though he did not speak.

3

Beer for Breakfast

It was a week or so after my arrival in Addis. The Lion of Judah had appeared to the public and returned to the palace. I was standing at an office window in my Ministry, facing the victory pillar in Miazia 27th Square, on which the clock stands for ever at twenty-five past two, the time at which the Emperor entered the city on his return in 1941. I was looking up King George VI avenue towards Yekatit 12th Square, which commemorates the attempted assassination of General Graziani in 1937 and the subsequent massacre of the Ethiopian martyrs.

All was not entirely sweetness and light. I had, as yet, no office of my own and was temporarily accommodated in a room containing two tables, two chairs, two electric typewriters and no secretary.

I had been to Addis parties, where they swopped horror stories of foreigners, or *ferenj*, as they are called, being beaten up by toughs, of blind beggars suddenly jumping up and running to catch the bus, of men lying supposedly injured in the road waiting for some soft-hearted person to get out of their car to help, whilst their accomplices waited to pounce, of women being jostled and molested in the shopping streets, of *shiftas* and footpads, vagabonds and thieves, and policemen standing idly by. I was tired of the pestiferous shoeshine boys and the ubiquitous sellers of chewing-gum and crosses and wooden stools and *Time* magazine. I was sick of the indigent students who tried to touch me for an unredeemable loan and of the bureaucratic manoeuvres needed to get my goods out of Customs.

I was, in fact, still in a state of culture shock, from which many *ferenj* unfortunately never emerge. So I welcomed the opportunity when an old hand suggested I should go out of town for a week in a Land-Rover that was going north-west into Gojjam as far as the shores of Lake Tana on a fact-finding visit to the schools.

The mere mention of that fabulous lake in the highlands, from which the Blue Nile starts on its long course into the Sudan, was enough to spark off my enthusiasm. And when the Land-Rover arrived outside the Ras hotel on the appointed morning with a charming lady aboard I felt I was well out of the dusty office.

As we headed into the hills north-west of Addis, I thought of the Emperor's words in his parliament speech, allotting priority to education. That the Ministry hardly knew what was going on in its own schools at the beginning of the school year was perhaps as much a reflection on the poor communications in the countryside and the insistence by local communities on pushing their children into the schools, come what may, as on its own shaky administration. Although only 5 per cent of the children were in school, a torch had been lit that was already in danger of becoming a bonfire.

It was a bright, cloudless fresh morning, as all the mornings had been since my arrival in Addis. The Italians compared the weather to early summer in Tuscany, and, looking round the wild, ill-kept hills and the fertile, wasted valleys, they must have often sighed about the kind of fruitful farms and gardens that were waiting to be created if only the natives would co-operate.

We passed through the forest of eucalyptus trees I had seen from the plane, planted in recent times on the Entoto hills to repair the ravages of reckless deforestation, and came down the other side into the wide open spaces of a tawny, fenceless land. It was a broad savannah, dotted with rough acacia trees spreading at the top in mushroom shapes. Herds of thin, long-horned cattle, tended by ragged little smiling boys, shuffled off the road as we approached. Horsemen in white jodhpurs and shammas passed by. Down in a valley to the left a splash of colour caught the eye. Two groups of people dressed in white were coming together, with their horses brightly caparisoned in scarlet, green and yellow.

"A funeral," our driver, Ato Kebret, said. And Woizero Yeshareg, with her jet black arm lying across the back of the seat next to my white hand, translated for me.

It was just beyond the funeral that we passed the turning to Mulu, to the one place in the hills of Shoa where a *ferenj* has proved how productive this land can be when fenced in and tended with careful husbandry. But he is not an Italian. He is an English brigadier, now aged 87, and already a legend in Ethiopia, for it was Brigadier Sandford and Major Wingate, the latter later to become a general, who marched back through Gojjam with the Emperor to restore him to his throne in 1941.

Ato Kebret, sitting at the wheel in his khaki slacks and tweed jacket, with the square back of his grizzled head facing me, knew the story. He had been imprisoned at Mogadishu in Italian Somaliland for his patriotic activities and had subsequently been a driver for the British forces.

As we passed some of the debris of modern life—a Volkswagen upside down beside the road and another with its side bashed in; a lorry blocking a low bridge, half over the parapet—we moved into more upland country, with splashes of yellow oilseed across it, the beige of ripe millet and the dark green of the copses hiding the villages. There was practically no traffic. Men walked past in white Bombay bowlers, held down by their shammas, others in an infinite variety of straw hats, whilst others, with their long staves held horizontally across their shoulders, looked like groups of people out of the Stone Age. Their horses were hobbled by tying the leading rein to the rear leg, but they themselves did not look as though they would ever want to be fenced in.

Ato Kebret began to tell the story of the Emperor's march. To him it was the most important thing to know about Gojjam, which is considered to be a backward province, but full of warriors and patriots. In 1940 the Emperor left England with Winston Churchill's support and went to Khartoum where General Platt, the Kaid of the Sudan, gave him a house on the banks of the Nile. There he met the chiefs, who had escaped from the Italians to come and pledge their support and raise patriot forces to fight.

In January 1941 the Emperor crossed the border into Gojjam and raised the Ethiopian flag on Ethiopian soil once again after five years of exile. Heading from the plains of the Sudan for Belaya, high up in the mountains, his party came to the end of the motorable track. The Emperor rode with Wingate the remaining fifty miles to Belaya, where he was welcomed by the people. The patriot army then went ahead to Debre Markos, the capital of the province. When the Emperor drove in, the old governor, Ras Hailu Tekle Haymanot, who had served the Italians, bowed in surrender to him. The end of the story, with Orde Wingate leading the procession into Addis Ababa on a white horse, is well known.

So the story came out bit by bit as we went northwards over the open hills, drinking in the fresh air and feeling as free as the galloping horses. A little over forty miles north of Addis we passed an unusually large patch of trees on our right, from which rose the three domes of a modern church, Russian-looking like the Trinity Cathedral in Addis.

"That is Lena Mariam," Woizero Yeshareg said. "It was built there at Debre Tsighe because that is the village the Abuna Basileos came from. He is the real head of the church, and he was the one appointed when they stopped sending the Abunas up from Alexandria in Egypt in 1950. But he is old, and Teophilos is the one who does the work. He comes from Gojjam."

"You can see his village from the road," Ato Kebret added.

Talking of churchmen, it seemed appropriate to turn to the right a few miles further on to visit the site of both one of the oldest and one of the newest churches in Ethiopia. The narrow road led us almost to the edge of a deep, broken canyon, which contains a tributary of the Blue Nile, and then descended somewhat from the upper rim of the gorge along a wooded shelf for two or three miles.

At the end of the road, hidden in this way from the marauders of ancient times, lay the monastery of Debre Libanos, which was founded in the thirteenth century by the saint of the Ethiopian church, Tekle Haymanot. He was in the austere ascetic tradition of the Egyptian Copts. He prayed for seven years, we are told, standing on one leg, so that the other leg withered away and fell off. This is the storklike attitude in which he is usually painted, with the lost limb standing like an old boot at his side. As a reward for his services in restoring the Solomonic line of kings, the monastery was given one-third of the empire by Yekuno Amlak, King of Shoa, and became so powerful in the land that the Ichege, as the prior was called, was often the real ruler of the Ethiopian church under its Alexandrian Abuna.

The original church was destroyed long ago in the sixteenth

century by Ahmed Gragn's Moslem terrorists, and the wooden church, in which the Emperor prayed on his triumphant return to Addis in 1941, has now been outdated by a new, large edifice in stone, built in 1961. It has a silver-coloured dome, cross and flagpole, and three panels on the facade—the coronation in the centre, St. George slaying the dragon on the left and an angel rising from the flames on the right.

It was 6.15 by the church clock, but 12.15 our time, for the Ethiopian day starts at six o'clock in the morning instead of at midnight. The iron gates were closed for the three-hour church service, so the Woizero had to be content with placing her palms together and kissing the iron bars. We went half way down the chasm to the sacred spring, where pious people wash away their ills, and we walked about amongst the family vaults that lay round about, for if you can afford it, it is considered a good and pious thing to be buried at Debre Libanos.

The commonest motif on the sides of the gravestones was of two cherubs holding a garland surmounted by a heart, whilst a photograph of the deceased usually adorned the headstone. Some of the bigger family vaults were built like miniature Greek temples and one was still being built.

"It's for Ras Mesfin, the Governor of the Province," Woizero Yeshareg said. "He's not dead yet, but he will be soon."

"So will I," I said.

She stopped short at another vault containing a mother and daughter. "I didn't know that girl was here," she said. "She was at school with me. Then she went to St. Godric's Secretarial College in London."

"And now she's here."

"Yes. She was too young."

Touched by this sadness, the Woizero went up to a passing priest, who was wearing a priestly version of a straw hat, which looked like an upturned wicker wastepaper basket. He put his hand into the folds of his robe above his heart, pulled out a large iron cross, dropped it on the ground, picked it up again and held it out to her to kiss. Then he slapped both her cheeks and her head with it.

Ato Kebret came forward for the same treatment. Then we set off again, with just a glimpse of the old Portuguese bridge on the edge of the ravine, which is the only visible remains of the mission which came to Ethiopia in 1520 and tried to convert King Lebna Dengel to Catholicism. They did not succeed in this, but their priest, Alvarez, has left us an absorbing account of the country as it was at that time.

Our road took a sharp turn to the left to run alongside the canyon, and we passed a family of baboons running over the brow of the hill in their ungainly way. It was the signal for Ato Kebret to mention Ras Hailu again for although the chief co-operated with the Italians in return for being left in power in his feudal fief of Gojjam, where his father had been king, and went out to offer his homage to the Emperor in an Italian general's uniform and an Alfa Romeo car, he is thought of in Ethiopia more as an amusing, witty figure than as a traitor.

"You know, Ras Hailu was once invited by an Italian count," said Kebret. "And after they had eaten, the count took him into the garden to show him his pet baboon. The count looked at Ras Hailu and then at the black face of the baboon. He wanted to show Ras Hailu who was master, so this is what he said:

" 'Ras Hailu, it is a strange thing that, whenever I look at this monkey of mine, I am reminded of your face. I wonder what was in God's mind when he made you so alike.'

" 'Indeed, sir,' Ras Hailu replied in a most polite way. 'That is most true. And the ways of the good God are certainly inscrutable. Why, for instance, does your face resemble so exactly that baboon's red backside'."

After we had finished laughing, Woizero Yeshareg capped Kebret's joke with another one.

"Ras Hailu went to Europe," she said. "And in those days very few Ethiopians travelled that far. One of the big chiefs of Europe asked him one day whether he spoke English or French or Arabic and so on. Each time, he said 'No.' Of course, he had to make use of an interpreter. When he said 'No' to each of the languages mentioned, one by one, they thought he must be a very ignorant man. Then Ras Hailu said, 'And what about you, Sir? Do you speak Amharic?' 'No,' said the chief. 'Gallinya?' 'No.' 'Tigrinya?' 'No.' 'Gurage?' 'No.' 'Then,' said Ras Hailu, 'you and I are obviously equally ignorant'."

We laughed again, and it was Ato Kebret's turn once again.

"Ras Hailu was a very rich man." he said. "After all, he was Chief of Gojjam, and what is the use of being chief if you cannot be rich? One day he went into a big shop in England and he saw some things he liked in one department of the shop. So he asked them how much he would have to pay for everything in the department. They thought he was joking, so they just thought of a sum of money, a few thousand dollars, something like that, and told him.

" 'All right,' said Ras Hailu. 'I'll pay.' And there was a lot of argument before it was properly straightened out. 'You people are very strange,' Ras Hailu said. 'In Gojjam, when we make a bargain, we keep to it'."

So, swapping Ras Hailu stories, we came late to Fiche, visited the new school, built with help from the Swedes, and carried on without stopping for lunch. A few minutes for a coffee in the next straggling village, brought out to the Land-Rover from a small restaurant at the roadside, was all we allowed ourselves before going on to the next school fifty miles down the road from Fiche.

It was at a place called Gohatsion; and here the local parents had been so keen to get their children into school, that they had built six new classrooms out of the mud and wattle and chaff called *chika*. They had added corrugated-iron roofs and completed the job in six weeks. Of course there was no equipment, and the teachers were overstretched. The little children sat on logs on the bare, earth floor of the classrooms, and rows of little black faces goggled at us as we went in. The principle seemed to be to somehow get the children physically into the classrooms, and after that the Government would have to do something to them called 'education'.

In this school, as at Fiche, two members of the United States Peace Corps were struggling on with English instruction to the older pupils. Not unnaturally perhaps, it was the coloured young man at Fiche who seemed to fit in best, and was happiest working in what he found to be peaceful and rewarding surroundings far from the acute racial tensions of his home state in the U.S.A.

After an hour or so we left the flagpole of the Gohatsion school behind us and started the long plunge down into the deep gorge of the Blue Nile. This is one of the great sights of Ethiopia, deeper than the Grand Canyon of the Colorado. As one spirals down, the heat grows more intense and the vegetation changes where the cliffs are not too steep to be cultivated. Maize replaces millet and bananas take the place of mulberries. At one particularly difficult point the road leans out into space on a viaduct, and at another a cross marks the spot below which one of the secret churches of Ethiopia is cut into the rock face.

As we got closer to the bed of the gorge, we could see that the Blue Nile, which is called the Abbai in Ethiopia, is not at all blue. It is more of a muddy brown colour, full of the silt from above, which lies uselessly in Lake Tana but goes to make Egypt fertile in the yearly inundations of the river.

Before the fine modern bridge was built, it was a difficult crossing on rafts, with the beasts swimming. At one point we saw the old mule track going off to the left. But crossing into Gojjam was nothing for us, though it was a long climb up the other side to the village of Dejen.

It was our last call before the provincial capital, Debre Markos. The school was built on the edge of a tributary canyon to the Abbai gorge, which the school director proudly showed us. As the lowering sun threw deep shadows from the descending shelves of rock, it looked as though a giant cleaver had been hacked into the earth's crust.

The same sun glared straight into our eyes as we headed west for another fifty miles. By the time we reached Debre Markos it was dark, and the first impression was of a long avenue of eucalyptus trees, with little bungalows and huts below them. It was dim and unlit, and even the stony main square was shadowy and dark as we crossed it to reach a lowly building called the Tana hotel. Nevertheless this was clearly the best that the town could offer. Woizero Yeshareg went off to stay with her father, who was provincial treasurer, taking our driver with her. I was left alone.

Where did the great Chief of Gojjam, Ras Hailu, stay? I wondered, as I walked into the hotel to face three women and an Italian expresso machine behind the bar.

We had no common language. I had, as yet, got no further than *eshe*, meaning *yes* and *yellem*, meaning *no* in my Amharic studies. But presumably my bag indicated that I wanted to stay the night. Eventually one of the women detached herself from the trio, and led me behind a curtain and through a doorway into an interior quadrangle with the rooms ranged on three sides.

I was given one of them and left to my own devices. Though bare, it was clean and tidy, and so was the bed. I could have fared much worse. But then came the problem of ordering a meal, for no one in the establishment appeared to speak English. This time, after I had made eating signs with my hand to my mouth, the cook came to the rescue from his shack at the back beside the lavatories and the disused water-heater. He was an Italian speaker, and he soon had me enthusiastic about spaghetti and spezzetini.

Whilst the cooking was under way, I returned to the bar into a frightful din of wailing folk music from a tape-recorder. I faced the ranks of bottles containing Italian-style drinks manufactured in Addis and Asmara—grappa and anis, vermouth and cognac, and a strange concoction called artichoke wine. Two police officers and a sergeant came and went. I drank a fruity cognac and went behind the curtain for my meal.

After that there seemed to be nothing else to do. I went to the doorway, and a diminutive shoeshine boy got up from his squatting position against the wall of the porch and pointed at my shoes. Finding no response, he squatted down again and picked up a tattered book. I looked over the top of it and saw that it was full of arithmetic sums—school homework done in difficult circumstances.

I turned to go in again, but at that moment Ato Kebret appeared from an even humbler establishment across the road—a refugee from the noise, he said, now that they had got tired of replaying the taped music in the Tana hotel.

I soon discovered that Mr Kebret spoke a sort of Italian jargon, and there had consequently been no need for the Woizero to interpret for us throughout the day. "A nice old man," she had called him, though I had begun to doubt it, when he treated the Land-Rover like a battering-ram, crashing into ditches and forcing a way through gateways and almost through the doorways of the school directors' offices that we had visited, and when with the supreme self-confidence of the stupid, he took blind corners firmly on the wrong side of the road.

But he had driven her around as a schoolgirl, so there was a special relationship. And now, chatting on the verandah of the

Addis Ababa: listening to the Emperor's speech at the Opening of Parliament

The contrasting styles of Addis Ababa: (*above*) the old palace church, (*below*) Africa Hall, home of the Organisation of African Unity

Tana hotel, I was inclined to agree with her. His mind went back
to the coversation of earlier on.

"Wingate," he said. "He came here to Debre Markos before the
Emperor. He was a great man. The British lost a great man when
he was killed in Burma. They should have let him stay here to
work with the Emperor for our country. The Italians were all
running away, and Ras Hailu sent the best Italian car there was
in Debre Markos down the road to fetch the Emperor. Some
people didn't like the Italians. For me, they were all right. In
some ways they did good. They showed us many things we were
too stupid to see. Good mechanics, good brains, good with hands.
But always shouting and getting excited too. Why get exited?
Death comes to everyone. The English, they weren't like that.
Always straight. The Englishman, he decides what he wants to do
and goes straight forward to it, not turning right of left. We should
have had the English here to teach us, like Brigadier Sandford and
Wingate. No Italians. It was the wrong place for them, and some
of them got too excited. But the Duke of Aosta, he was a great
gentleman. He tried to do what God gave him to do."

So Kebret rambled on, passing judgement on his peers with the
full perception of the illiterate mind. Wartime reminiscences
fascinate men the world over, and he was no exception. To him
it was as if the Emperor had driven into Debre Markos that very
day.

Next morning I was up early, drinking tea and eating rolls at
the expresso bar, served by a girl with a cross tattooed on her forehead and rings tattooed round her neck. It was too early. Waiting
for Kebret, I watched an old woman come in for her kettle of hot
water; then two men in dark glasses walking down the rough
road, accompanied by a ragged boy carrying a suitcase; then a man
with a topi on his head, a shamma round his body and a fly-whisk
in his hand; then a goat-like sheep; a trio of schoolboys, the first
of the daily flood; a fat man with collar and tie, raincoat and hat;
two barefoot girls picking their way delicately over the stones on
their way to school; a long-horned cow and a small boy with a stick;
a man with a canary-yellow peaked cap and green jeans; more
schoolchildren with exercise books in their hands; a girl in a lacy
white communion-style dress; a little boy in big Wellington boots.

They all passed; the fit, the halt and the lame; the ragged, the

c

smart, the laughing and the grim. A man in black trousers, a dark shirt and jacket and a huge pineapple picker's straw hat, came in for a glass of milk. A youth in much-patched short pants and a tee-shirt brought in some bottles of Ambo mineral water in a cardboard carton. A tiny curly-topped girl in a psychedelic red and green flower dress ran past, trying to catch up the rest.

Then Ato Kebret arrived to take me across the square in the Land-Rover to Woizero Yeshareg's father's house. He sounded the horn, and the zebegna came running up to open the gate of metal sheeting. The Woizero walked out as far as the banana tree in the garden and called us inside up the steps into a small wooden bungalow with photographs on the wall and a big Pan American Airways poster of the Statue of Liberty.

They were in the middle of a substantial breakfast of *injera* and *wat*, and the Woizero's father offered me his forearm to shake as his right hand was messy with food. Kebret and I sat down and ate a little of the dunlopillo bread and curry-like savoury meat. Amongst the photographs I saw the Woizero's wedding group and the Woizero as a girl guide being presented to the Emperor. Between the photographs and the Panam poster, round injera dish covers of woven basketry were stuck to the wall, looking like large coloured hats. The floor was bare boards, but through the open doorway of the treasurer's bedroom I could see the carpet pinned up against the side of the house.

Coffee and cognac were produced, then beer, to stoke up the boilers for the exertions of the day. I accepted the cognac, but refused the beer, though the custom of drinking beer for breakfast, which has died out in England, is still very much alive in Ethiopia, where plain water is always to be avoided except when it comes direct from mineral springs.

So we set out, well fortified to visit the schools of Debre Markos, where Indian teachers were working away at getting the English language into the high-school children of Gojjam. The Indian vegetarians found the food supply problem tricky in this land where not much besides bread and meat is eaten, unless it is a few sweet beans plucked from the pod and eaten raw, or an occasional egg.

We spent all day in the town, and had time to visit the so-called citadel, on which, behind a flagpole and a small archway, the

modest provincial offices are raised a few feet above the surrounding tracks on the highest point of the hill, on which Debre Markos
has grown up. At the far end of the single-storey office block a
well-appointed but by no means luxurious villa serves as the
governor's residence. Altogether it is a very small set-up with
which to administer a tract of land 250 miles across, containing
all that territory enclosed in the great loop of the Blue Nile
between its source and the border of the Sudan.

Behind the governor's residence stands the round church of
Markos, or St. Mark, which gives the place its name. It was sunset
as we passed it, and people stopped in their tracks for the lowering
of the flag in a way I had not seen since my army days in military
camps, Perhaps it was hardly surprising, for the outlying provinces
are run largely on military principles. Orders are given from above
and are expected to be obeyed.

Next day I and Kebret went back to the Woizero's father's
house for a breakfast of bread, tea and cognac.

"His name is the same as mine," the Woizero said, when I
enquired. "You see, some people think we Ethiopian women are
most emancipated, because we don't lose our names when we get
married. We keep them just the same."

She took a fond farewell of him, and we set out on our journey
once more. Visiting schools on the way, we gradually approached
the Woizero's home town, which was a place called Bure, 70 miles
from Debre Markos. It lay a little off the main road up a hill to
the left, and in the fork of the turning there was a small public
house at which we stopped for a midday break.

Woizero Yeshareg went off to visit her aunt, leaving Kebret and
me seated in the *tej beit*, which was run by her great aunt, a large
woman as fat as her cat was thin. She pressed *injera* and *wat* on us,
lifting up the cover of the *injera* basket to show it to us. I took a
coffee without milk, called *buna*, which was very good. Then a
sergeant came in to eat, together with a noisy young man in
civilian clothes. They ate hunks of raw red meat, gripping them in
their teeth and slicing off manageable chunks with a steak knife a
hair's breadth from their noses. When they had finished eating,
they picked up bunches of the green grass stalks that were
scattered over the floor, to wipe their hands.

Presently the Woizero returned, loaded up by her aunt with

country produce, which a lad put into the Land-Rover. There were lengths of sugar-cane, cobs of maize, homemade beer, bottled in old cognac bottles, a cardboard box full of little eggs and bottles of oil from the yellow sesame seed that splashes the fields with colour.

With these goods safely stacked away, we went on up the rough and stony side road that led to the village, stopping on the way to drink from the mineral spring that provides it with a pure water supply. It was a rough, straggling place, reminding me of some of the poorer villages in the foothills of Nepal. Even the village square was pitted with trenches eaten into it by water runnels during the rains.

The Woizero was disappointed, since the place where she had spent her childhood looked as if it was going to the dogs. The school where she had learnt her Amharic ABC, was full of flies. Yet it had its redeeming feature. A magnificent view was framed in the archway of the main block, looking across a broad valley to the mountains beyond in a wide sweep of open land.

As soon as we left Bure, we found that the view from the school had not been deceptive. We entered a strikingly beautiful country-side of horses grazing on short turf and green fields of *teff*, the cereal that looks no more substantial than grass but provides the flour for the *injera* bread. Here and there, both near and far, rose up those vertical crags with flat or rounded tops, that are called *ambas* when they provide the protection for a cluster of *tukuls* or a fortified place.

We were entering the country of the Agau people, who seemed to be both happy and respectful. Men and boys in sheepskins doffed their hats, if they had them, or waved their hands as we passed by. Tiny children, tending horses, sheep, cattle and donkeys jousted with their staves. One felt a little like royalty riding through a loyal and well-loved region. Every few miles a large ring of trees hid a circular church from view, whilst in the villages the houses looked neater and better kept than the ones we had passed before.

Injabara was typical of these upland Amhara and Agau places. Its striking setting between two great rocks made it the key point of the area, and the school was built on the side of a hill that had once been fortified by the Italians. In response to pressure from the people, the school was expanding, but I could not help wondering what book-learning was going to do to these Arcadian herdsmen and shepherds.

Coming down off the hills again, we crossed a small river in a gully that is called the Watet Abbai, or the Little Blue Nile. This river is not the only stream that flows into Lake Tana, but it is the biggest and it has always been known by Ethiopians as the young Blue Nile, which they identify with the Gihon of the Bible, one of the four rivers that flowed out of the Garden of Eden:

"And the name of the second river is Gihon: the same is it that compasseth the whole land of Ethiopia."

Gihon means source or spring in Amharic, and the source of the Blue Nile in a spring near Injabara has been regarded as sacred since ancient times. The place is well described by Father Lobo in his *Voyage to Abyssinia*, which was translated into English by Dr. Johnson and published in 1735. "On the top of this mountain", he says, "is a little hill which the idolatrous Agaus have in great veneration. Their priest calls them together at this place once a year, and having sacrificed a cow, throws the head into one of the springs of the Nile; after which ceremony, everyone sacrifices a cow or more, according to their different degrees of wealth or devotion. The bones of these cows have already formed two mountains of considerable height, which afford a sufficient proof that these nations have always paid their adorations to this famous river."

We descended still further from the upland Agau country to reach Dangila, which is at the westernmost point of the long loop the road makes to skirt the Choke mountains and was for a considerable time the residence of a British consul, who used to take up his post from the Sudan. By now we were in the lowlands. But they were only low in relation to the lake, which lies at 6,000 feet above sea level. It was another 50 miles to Bahar Dar, 'The Gateway of the Waters', across a red and rocky countryside.

Bahar Dar is laid out alongside the lake in long, straight dual carriageways, which we found still only partly paved. They were still happily free of traffic too, and a high proportion of the pedestrians who wandered about them seemed to be students, many of them no doubt from the Russian-sponsored polytechnic as well as the other government schools. As we drove along, we could see the flat waters of the lake through the trees, and Ato Kebret pointed out some of the marshy banks which, he said, had been creeks and inlets not long ago. We ended up at the Abbai Minch, the Blue Nile Source hotel, situated close to where the broad River Nile flows south-east out of the lake.

Our driver was tired, and Woizero Yeshareg was careful to speak to him politely. "Gash Kebret," she said. "You must take me back to the school now. I have some work to do there."

Kebret muttered something about woman's place being in the home, but did as he was bidden. I walked down to the lakeside alone, through a lush garden of flame trees and pink and white oleanders. It looked tranquil and peaceful, but empty—a fine sheet of water where no one swims because of the dreaded bilharzia, which is the scourge of Africa's lakes; one of the noble sources of the Nile, yet with a rich harvest of fish hardly touched. It is an unused, almost virgin sheet of water, its surface broken only by the islands dotted around its shores, many of which have churches and small monasteries on them.

A cloud of insects, swarming up from the lake after the sun had gone down, drove me into my room, which was fitted up with fine-mesh wire netting to keep them out. This was another of the drawbacks of romantic Lake Tana. After sunset the patio above the shore, which I had been shown on my arrival and which had looked so attractive with its white tablecloths and arbour of bougainvillea, was firmly sealed off. One ate one's dinner in the shut-in heat of the main dining-room, provided with indifferent food by a tired old Italian chef.

Next morning I awoke to the sound of birdsong and walked into the garden which, like the brigadier's farm, was a living proof of what can be done with this bare land by means of a little thought, determination and work. The cheeps and chatters and twitters were a welcome change from the insect hum of the night before. And like a constant motif in symphonic variations, one unchanging sequence on the oboe rang out time and again, as if the player were tapping out a message in morse code.

After breakfast Woizero Yeshareg suggested a visit to the Emperor's country house, which was only a few miles away. So we set out down the first furlong of the road to Gondar, to cross the bridge below which the famous river rushes out of the lake.

The volume of water is so considerable and the feeder streams to the lake are so few that one would have thought the river would have emptied out Lake Tana long ago. But apparently the summer rains on the wide sheet of water, nearly 50 miles across, are so heavy that they restore the level.

We turned right at the other end of the bridge, and followed the left bank of the Nile for a short distance, being now in the neighbouring province of Begemder. The road took us up a low hill, from which we gained a magnificent view of the lake. The water was divided into two parts by a clear line. The part nearest to us was muddy brown, containing the silt that gives life to Egypt, whilst the further part was a clear grey-blue, receding into the distance of the further shore, which was faintly visible.

In the other direction we faced the gates of the imperial residence. It was an ultra-modern villa of one storey, built on pillars above garage and storage space in a series of curves one stage removed from the circular *tukul* of tradition. The Emperor was not there. Even so, I was rather surprised when the Woizero asked the sentry if we could go into the grounds. He ran up to the house to ask the major-domo, then ran back to open one of the gates.

We pottered about the imperial grounds, where a garden was beginning to take root. Then we went back to the Land-Rover and skirted round the edge of the estate to the far side of the low hill, which at that point was much higher, as the ground fell away steeply to the muddy river and a valley planted out with coffee bushes. In the copse where we stopped there was one of the bee-hives made of bamboo, wattle and dung that the people put up into the branches of the trees to get the honey from which they make their mead. The bees are lured into these hives by a sugar bait, not realising that they are going to be robbed of their life's work as soon as it is complete.

So we left Begemder and returned to Gojjam heading back for the capital city. As we passed through the Agau country they were harvesting the *teff* with tiny sickles, and further on the peasants in their white *shammas*, tramping behind their wooden ploughshares, looked like figures out of a Bible picture book. At Bure we drank some of auntie's beer, which looked and tasted like a particularly fruity Guinness, and collected more farm produce, including bunches of chick peas still in the pod and on the stalk, which we shelled and ate raw, as the country people do to keep up their strength as they walk along.

By midday the next day we had been down into the great canyon and up out of it again and were bowling along the smooth asphalted road of the plateau. We passed a posse of armed men riding towards Addis, and I wondered if there had been a revolution I hadn't heard about. Goats, sheep and cattle were hurrying in the same direction and veered off the road at the last moment as we descended on them.

As we got closer to the capital, the people were more indifferent, and we no longer felt like royalty passing through. They were more sophisticated too, without that desperate desire to run across the road in front of us that we had noticed in the more primitive parts.

I was in two minds about returning to the city. But there was no mistaking the Woizero's pleasure when we breasted the ridge of the Entoto hills and looked down on that fantastic result of fifty years of hectic growth, the capital of the Empire of Ethiopia.

"Home," she said.

"You like it there?"

"Of course. Everyone loves their home."

"Your children will be looking out for you."

"Yes, they will."

"One day I shall go home too."

So we parted, she to her home, Ato Kebret to his family, and me to the Ras Hotel.

4

Some Native Customs

Back in Addis Ababa I went up the hill a little further from my
office at Arat Kilo to the next square, Yekatit 12th, which everyone calls Siddist Kilo, or 'Six Kilometres'. In fact the distance
between Four Kilometres and Six Kilometeres is only just over
one kilometre, but perhaps the track that wound up the hillside
before the straight road was cut through was twice the length.

The Prime Minister's office is there, and next to it the office
without which he can do nothing, the Ministry of Finance. And
across the road there are some rather unhappy lions, locked away
in cages for people to gape at. But it was for none of these things
that I went up to Siddist Kilo. I had to visit the Haile Selassie I
University, which was founded in 1961 to complete the top tier of
Ethiopia's educational system.

I left my *seicento* taxi at the gate and walked into the grounds
past the splendid Arts Faculty building on my left, which was
completed in 1965, and the brand new Kennedy Memorial
Library on my right, which was opened in 1969. The road led
straight to an older building, the original palace in the university
grounds, which now houses the offices of the President and the
Vice-Presidents and the Institute of Ethiopian Studies. Now
called the Ras Makonnen Hall, it was known as the Prince's
Paradise before it became the nucleus of the university in peculiar
circumstances. On the opposite side of the avenue from the fine
stone gateway, by which I entered, and as if to remind the students
of what could befall them if they should become too unruly, stands

the headquarters of the Imperial Bodyguard—the secular arm of an emperor who claims for himself, like James I of England, the divine right of kings.

The peculiar circumstances were these. In 1960 the brigadier commanding the Imperial Bodyguard, together with his brother, who was a graduate of Columbia University, New York, and a provincial governor, staged a *coup d'état*, in the course of which the Crown Prince was detained in the Prince's Paradise together with important ministers.

The coup was triggered off when the Emperor was out of the country on a series of state visits in West Africa and South America. Nevertheless the regular army and air force fought the revolutionaries in the streets of Addis in a battle in which there were probably about 2,000 casualties, and in a few days overcame them. But before the brothers faced certain defeat, in their despair and in their determination that Ethiopia would never again be ruled by the same men, they fired on the great men of the realm in the room in which they had imprisoned them and slaughtered more than a dozen, wounding more. Rases and dejazmatches, generals and ministers were sprayed with machine-gun fire and fell to the floor.

As I walked into Ras Makonnen hall and turned right into the Green Salon to meet the gently cultured Vice-President and his secretary, it was difficult to believe that the airy room with the lofty ceiling had been a scene of carnage not ten years before. But it was easy to see why the royal family no longer fancied living there.

The interview with the American Vice-President proceeded with academic calm and dignity. So did the conference in the Arts Faculty lecture hall, which followed it. But when the question of the national language was raised, the temperature of the discussion went up, for Amharic is the mother tongue of only about a third of the population of the Ethiopian empire, and English, through the medium of which all secondary and higher education is conducted, is the mother tongue of practically none. Therefore the people of the north in Tigre and Eritrea, and the Galla people of the south and the other minorities, who have to learn the difficult language of the dominant tribe in order to take part in national affairs, feel themselves to be at a disadvantage.

But this was not the reason why the students marched with the revolutionaries in 1960 and why they sang songs calling on their countrymen to wake up. In the new awareness of the world that their education had brought them they were indignant that, in spite of a tradition of independence going back for 3,000 years, Ethiopia was still a backward country compared with many others in Africa. And in their more recent strikes the same dissatisfaction with the rate of progress, and frustration with what they felt to be lack of opportunities for those who have worked their way to the top of the educational tree, was apparent.

The debate on the language problem was over, and the discussion returned to the calm academic level with a discourse on the differing forms of address in the Amharic language, depending on whether one is talking to one's mother-in-law or the district governor and so on. Laughs and smiles returned. It was a pleasant note on which to leave and anticipate the evening activity of the language conference, which was a dinner at the Addis Ababa restaurant.

When I arrived at the restaurant in my hotel taxi, most of the people were already there. Servants bowed on the steps of the big old house at the back of the restaurant, as I walked up to the door. They were dressed in white jodhpurs, with coarse white shirts and shammas thrown across their chests, which made them look very like the country gentlemen of Nepal. The house had once belonged to the Empress Taitu, who took the Emperor Menelik II as her eighth husband, and the salon which I entered was decorated with large mirrors in heavy gilt frames, dusty chandeliers and suits of colourful ceremonial clothing, which were almost falling apart with age. A garish red and brown lavatory linoleum covered the floor.

The guests were seated on wooden stools such as the street vendors pester one to buy every time one stops to look in a shop window. Perched on these hard Jimma stools, they were arranged in circles round what looked like large circular linen baskets, waiting for something to begin.

The beginning was the tej, the honey-coloured mead which the Ethiopians love to such an extent that the colloquial name for their drinking houses is *tej beits*. It was brought in by the serving wenches in individual flasks, shaped like the common beakers of chemistry laboratories, and one drank it straight from the neck of the receptacle, placing the flask on the floor when one had, for the moment, had enough.

I found myself in a mixed circle, between the president of the university on my right hand and two teachers from the Ras Makonnen high school on my left hand, whilst on the other side of the basket a middle-aged American professor and his wife sat on their stools. A younger American lady, wearing a short white Ethiopian dress with black fish-net stockings, sitting in a rather exposed position on her stool, completed the party.

This was the situation when, with a flourish, the serving wench whipped off the patterned lid of the basket to reveal, not a pile of dirty linen but a large tin tray, covered from rim to rim with a whitish-grey layer of injera. Next she brought water, soap and towels to wash and dry the right hand. Then she slopped the first kind of wat into the injera out of a large bowl. It was a reddish brown oily, spicy, mincy mess. After that she slopped down some floppy, extra white sheets of injera, that looked like latex out of a rubber tree, and bade us set to. In spite of trying to get the wat up in the injera, our hands were well oiled up by the time the next kind of wat came—a dark chicken wat that looked like a curry, with a yellow cake of injera to go with it that had not got quite such a beery, fermented flavour as the ordinary basic grey type. This was followed by more latex and a light brown mutton wat and finally a spinach-like vegetable.

Each of these courses was dumped down on the previous one, which itself had been well and truly churned up by the twenty-eight fingers and seven thumbs of seven hands. Well cooked and politely served though the food was, looking at the stirred up mess as the spinach was dolloped down on it, I could not help thinking of poor Arthur Rimbaud's plaintive cry to his mother from Harar in 1888: "Obliged to chatter their gibberish, to eat their filthy messes. . . ."

Of course it was unfair. The food was quite palatable, the company polite. And then came the *pièce de résistance* of politeness. It was a happy, jolly, companionable thing to do to feed one's neighbour. This the President, who was born a simple villager, knew well. It was the thing to do to take a gob of wat, roll it in a flap of injera and stuff it into one's friend's mouth. He did it most dexterously. I did not care for it, but the gob was mercifully small, and I felt that not everyone can say that they have been stuffed by the president of a university.

My neighbour on the other side was not so fortunate. For it is an even more jolly and companionable thing to do to make the gob of wat as big as possible and laugh at one's victim's struggles to get it down. And in order to avoid spilling the mess down his shirt front or spluttering it out all over the assembled company, the victim will turn his head upside down, and risk choking himself out of his wits in order to get it all in.

The young American lady, dressed Ethiopian style, an expert in the habits of the people she was studying, knew this well. She rolled a huge gob for one of the two teachers from the Ras Makonnen high school. The teacher twisted his head upside down and opened his mouth wide. The gob went in, his cheeks swelled, his eyes popped out and his throat gurgled. I expected the whole thing to be spattered out of his mouth at any moment in an uncontrollable explosion. But the crisis passed. Bit by bit he gulped it down and breathed again.

"Well done," I said to the lady. "But it's a pity you cheated. Rolling up that injera and wat, you used *both* hands."

All this time our tej flasks were being continually refilled, and we had music to amuse us. It came from a group of rustic drummers and fiddlers, which has been preserved and held together by an American Peace Corps Volunteer, Charles Sutton. Wearing the white national costume, playing their primitive instruments and singing their plaintive peasant songs, they reminded me, like the men at the door, of the hillmen of Nepal, though they were much darker in complexion, and in the main coarser featured.

The instruments were all made of genuine materials. The mesenko was a kind of fiddle, with a diamond-shaped soundbox, made of goatskin stretched over a wooden frame, and a single horsehair string. The deeper tones in the strings were provided by the begena, which is a primitive wooden harp, whilst the lead in the woodwind was the shepherd's washint, a reed pipe made out of bamboo. The native fife was the imbilta, made of bamboo like the washint, but a more dignified instrument, often used on ceremonial occasions in the past.

These plaintive instruments of strings and wind combined with the drums of the Blue Nile group to transport us out of Addis into the country villages. Songs of seedtime and harvest, love and war, filled the salon, some sung by the tall, lean American himself. To a resounding roll of drums a dancer leaped out of the other room, through which the servants came and went, and performed his ritual, beginning calmly, then shaking his whole body with shuddering limbs and contorted, ugly face, then stamping the ground in symbolic communication with the Earth Mother. A little woman did the same. The three kinds of drums—kebero, negareet and atamo—beat out their tom-tom rhythm.

Thus we ate, drank and listened until it was time to go. People got off their stools and left their circles to mix with other circles. There were brief felicitations and partings. Then we went out into the cool night of Addis to make our various ways home.

Three weeks later Dejazmatch Takele Wolde Hawariat, sometime Afe Negus (Lord Chief Justice) and anti-Italian patriot, was served with a summons accusing him of plotting "against public security". The police stated that conspirators already under arrest had revealed his complicity. Rather than submit to interrogation by the Criminal Investigation Department the old marshal, according to the official report, shot and wounded the policeman bearing the summons, then shot himself dead.

In Addis, where there are no newspapers that print real news, rumour was about again. Might this have been another 1960? Was Takele planning another *coup d'état*, that might have led to more street fighting and carnage in another Green Salon? The *Ethiopian Herald*, loaded, as ever, with fullsome praise of the Emperor, gave no clue. The general public gossiped in abysmal ignorance as before.

5

The Historic Route

In its travel pamphlets the Ethiopian Tourist Organization adopts the motto "Thirteen Months of Sunshine". It is slightly misleading, as there are annually several months of rain in the Ethiopian heartlands. But there are certainly thirteen months in the year, twelve of them being thirty days long and the thirteenth lasting only five days.

Another phrase that has been coined in recent years is the 'Historic Route', and this is substantially more accurate, for the route which goes from Addis Ababa through Dessie and Makale to Asmara, and returns by the more westerly road via Axum and Gondar, either passes through or runs reasonably close to most of the places that have made Ethiopian history. In the middle of Hedar 1962, or in other words at the end of November 1969, I set out on the 'Historic Route' with my friends from Addis and Haile Michael, the Ethiopian driver of our Land-Rover.

The first 80 miles of the 668 miles to Asmara run fairly smoothly over a tarmac surface, and one wonders why heavily laden goods lorries go lumbering past with cars perched precariously on top, loaded by cranes in Asmara to be off-loaded in Addis. The countryside rolls steadily past. Only here and there a slight gap in the hills reveals a great gash in the plateau, like a crevasse in a glacier, that hints at things to come.

But at Debre Berhan, where only a year before troops had been pitted against students in one of the frequent clashes between the heady wine of new ideas and the old beer of feudal dictatorship, the tarmac suddenly stops. The Land-Rover crunched down on to the flinty gravel surface, which continued right up to the border of Eritrea. Nor was it simply a harmless gravel surface. During the five years of the Italian East African Empire—the five years in which they laboured so long and hard for so little return—the road was tarred all the way. Now the tarmac is broken up and disintegrated, and one rattles and shudders over the stone foundation as if one were driving for hours over cobbles.

As we had stopped to visit people in Debre Berhan, it was already afternoon when we began to climb on to the high ridge that we would have to cross before reaching Debre Sina, the next small town. Still known by many as the Mussolini pass, which is the name it got when Italian engineers tunnelled through the mountain to complete the motor road, the 10,000-foot pass is the highest point on the route.

It is truly awe-inspiring. As the road climbs, the plateau seems to break and crumble away on either side. On the left a vast dun-coloured gorge appears. On the right there are glimpses of a vast empty space blurring into the flat brown desert of the Danakils. A few of the hardy highland cowboys stand by the road offering woollen hats for sale. Their fathers, in the past, would have been swift to answer their chief's call to arms. For this is the edge of Menz, the heartland of the Amhara country, close to the old capital of Ankober, cold by African standards, with the people lean and dour in their dirty white or brown togas, suspicious and quick to take offence.

The countryside grew wilder and more precipitous. Strange mountains, shaped like great pillars, came into view. Then we plunged into the chilly tunnel at the top, peering through the deisel fumes left by the big Italian lorries. Emerging the other side, we seemed to be almost on the edge of the world, for now, instead of overlooking the river gorge to the left, we were hair-pinning down a sheer escarpment. The pillars and giant thumbs of the mountains stood to the right, with the hills dropping down to the desert to the left. At one point the only way the engineers had found to get the road past the cliffs was by building up a hairpin bend artificially over the void.

As we looked down on Debre Sina, named after Mount Sinai, spreading along a hill far below, I felt that this huge rampart must

Axum: (*above*) the fallen
pillar, (*right*) the Imperial
Crowns

Gondar: Debre Berhan Selassie Church

Angels on the ceiling of Debre Berhan Selassie Church

have been the natural border of the ancient Amharic lands. After the tidal wave of the Galla invasions had spent itself, these home-lands, surrounded by cliffs and precipices, were never conquered until the Italians marched up the escarpment in 1935. And they might have held out longer even then, if the Emperor had not decided for political reasons to send his generals forward to give battle at Maichew.

Yet they are the lands of a people who make little of their heritage and still, after their vaunted 3,000 years of civilisation, live in primitive huts of mud and wattle. A large proportion of them, denied the ownership of the land, have little incentive to improve it, whilst the men of substance, inclined to the laziness that is typical of warrior races, get what they can out of the empire that their honoured emperor has gathered in for them and accept indifferently the dislike of their subject peoples.

Debre Sina, like most of the Amhara towns and villages, stands in its grove of eucalyptus trees with the sign of the pink elephant, donated by the Wonji sugar company, spelling out the name in English and Amharic and reassuring us of our position on the map. We had already gone down 4,000 feet when we passed through the straggling town, but we were by no means at the bottom of the descent. The Amharas build their homes in high places, and although we had already lost a lot of height, there was another drop of 1,600 feet to spiral down before reaching the bottom of the escarpment—the plain of Robi, which is not much above the level of the rift valley to the east, through which the Awash river flows.

We could see the curves of the road for miles ahead, and on them the big oil-tankers toiling infinitely slowly up the long ascent. Shell, Total, Agip, they were all carrying the same petrol to Addis from the refinery at Assab, set up by Russian technicians with Russian equipment. With two men in the cab, the journey would take three or four days at their snail's pace, though a car could do it in two.

It was hot in the plain of Robi, and the dry wheat-brown sorghum was ripe for harvesting. We saw two brave attempts at making the wilderness fruitful—the farms of the government tobacco monopoly, from whose factory Silver Star and Gisella cigarettes emerge; and the cotton plantations not far from them.

D

For the rest, apart from the bridge over the Robi river and the watchtowers of the prison, the plain was as primitive as the hills, though it was a relief to drive along a few miles of straight road.

A tribe of people of Semitic appearance was on the move in the opposite direction to us. They were small people with lighter skins than the Amharas and Gallas have. The women wore their hair in braids hanging to the shoulders, and this fashion, together with their finely chiselled features, made them look very like the people one sees in ancient Egyptian paintings. One imagines that the folk responsible for the ancient Sabaean civilization in the northern part of Ethiopia might have been of a similar kind. And now these remnants of a once-noble race were trekking through the plain with their horses and camels, donkeys, goods and chattels, as nomads in search of new pastures. Their own armed men ensured that they did not go unprotected.

In fact they looked like a remnant of the old Semitic stock, which is now mainly absorbed into the large ethnic division of the Cushitic peoples. This is a broad umbrella, which covers such diverse groups as the Amhara and Tigre people of the Abyssinian highlands, who often like to refer to themselves as black Arabs, the Gallas, the Agaus, and the lowland Danakils and Somalis.

The Cushitic division, which accounts for by far the greater proportion of the population of modern Ethiopia, is distinguished from the Nilotic division, the tall black 'people of the Nile', who are represented in the western marches of the country on the borders of the Sudan. The Bantu, widespread over vast areas of Central and Southern Africa, are only found in Ethiopia in the extreme south near the frontier of Kenya.

At the other end of the plain of Robi we started climbing back up the escarpment. In all the 100 miles since leaving Debre Berhan we had not passed a single private car, although this is the most direct main road between the two principal cities of Ethiopia—Addis Ababa and Asmara. But now, climbing up to Karakore at the head of the next pass, we came upon a little red van bravely battling its way over the jagged gravel surface with a picture of a gurgling infant painted on it and the name of a baby food. Nothing could have been more incongruous in this Amhara and Galla country, where babies are fed on mother's milk until the supply runs dry and then put straight on to injera and wat or the poor pulp of the false banana plant.

As we passed the cliffs of Karakore, which had been rent and burst asunder by the earthquake of 1961, the sun started to go down. Yet we still had nearly sixty miles to go to the road junction at Kombolcha, where we had decided to spend the night. There was another plain to cross, with the Borkenna river swinging over it, and another steep ascent. It grew dark, and we watched out for the Total petrol sign to tell us we were five kilometres from our destination. But the first "Total 5 kms" sign led us not to Kombolcha, but to Fontanina. After considering whether to stop there at the small hotel, we decided to press on.

There was another long stretch of winding, dusty road before we reached the next "Total 5 kms" sign. It heralded the welcome sight of street lights, shops lit by electricity and the Agip Hotel. We pulled in below the hotel terrace, got out of the Land-Rover, shook ourselves and staggered up the steps to book our rooms. A short, middle-aged Italian woman got up from her cash register to greet us.

"I am very sorry. *Mi dispiace*. All the rooms are full. But there is another hotel in Kombolcha. Clean and tidy. I will send someone to show you. Of course you may come here to eat, if you wish."

Disappointed in our hopes of *ferenj* standards of comfort in Kombolcha, which was the reason why we had originally decided to stop there instead of going on to Dessie, the capital of Wollo province, we went up the road and across it to the Paradise Hotel. It faced an obelisk, surmounted by the three-pointed imperial cypher, which looks very like the trademark of Mercedes cars.

The obelisk was in the centre of a roundabout, which stands at the point where the road forks left for Dessie and right for Assab. The road junction is the reason for Kombolcha's two hotels and numerous lodging houses, for travellers stop there both as a staging point on the road north and as a stopping place in which to gather strength and check their gear for the long haul of 300 miles across the desert to the Red Sea. The place is one big lorry drivers' pull-in, and half a dozen lorries were already there, parked along the street.

The Paradise Hotel was clean and tidy, as the *Signora* had prophesied. The shower worked, the bed was comfortable, and three or four people came forward to look at us and see whether we were all right. The reading matter in my room included a Polish magazine and *Soviet Reality*, which contained a long article in both English and Amharic about Dejazmatch Takele, who had just lost his life when faced with police interrogation. There were photographs of him in Russian uniform in 1909 and as an old man in 1969.

Back at the Agip Hotel for dinner we found the *Signora* at table with five or six other Italians, attacking their pasta with the relish that most Italians bring to the process of eating. Even here in this remote little place there seemed to be a community of half a dozen or more. They would be managing the hotel, the garage and possibly the petrol stations, and perhaps the electricity plant, for behind almost every enterprise in the Empire that demands organizational or technical skill there is to be found a *ferenj*. And there would also be Italian truck drivers passing through, for wages are high for a reliable man driving, say, £10,000 worth of goods over 700 or 800 miles of some of the roughest roads in the world. For one or two Italians, at least, truck driving has been the foundation of their Ethiopian fortunes.

The *insabbiati*, they are called in Italy, the ones that never went home after the Second World War, either because they had nothing to go to or because they had too much to leave. Literally 'caught in the sand,' or more colloquially 'washed up on the beach', they carry on with their jobs in East Africa, mostly based on Asmara, but not a few living in Addis Ababa as well.

As we sat down to eat, the *insabbiati* were filling their mouths with pasta, whilst the manageress sat at the head of the table like a kind of mother to them. Only one of them sat apart, his cloth cap still on his head, his leathery face blue with the day's growth of beard, gazing moodily over a plate of minestrone. Impossible to say what he was thinking about—the noisy streets of Rome, a flat calm in the Bay of Naples with the sun going down and Vesuvius in the background, or a white house and a crowd of children in rugged Calabria, or perhaps only the day's frustrations in the workshop. He bent his head down to his soup and sucked it in off his spoon with a noise like water in a wastepipe, and his expression did not alter in the slightest degree.

After dinner we walked the three ways of Kombolcha from the

obelisk at the centre of the road junction. One led uphill to start the ascent to the pass that one has to cross before going down into the Danakil desert on the road to Assab, the second led downhill into the valley before the climb to Dessie, and the third was on the level the way we had come. But all three were similar. Little shops were mixed in with rows of *talla beits*—small bars for the traveller to drink in. And if he wanted to make an arrangement with the woman behind the bar, he could usually do so.

We turned in early, and I awoke early too, listening to the roar of heavy engines as the lorries warmed up in the chill of dawn to get away as soon as it was light. Fat pigeons were stamping about on the nearby roof and, judging by the noise on the corrugated iron, on our own roof too. If we had not had business in Dessie, which could not be done before nine o'clock, we would have set out early too. But Kombolcha to Dessie is only fourteen miles, and although most of it is a steep, winding climb back into the Amhara high-lands, it was not more than half an hour's ride. So we let the lorries roar away and sat over our breakfast till half-past eight before going across the valley and into the hills and the eucalyptus trees that screen the town.

Dessie is the third largest town in Ethiopia, with a population of about 80,000, but you would not think so either passing the houses hidden in the trees or looking at the market-place and the shops in the main street. Like Addis it reminds one at first of an Indian hill-station, though a much smaller one. The name means 'My Joy' and some have claimed to get to like the place. I, myself, was not there long enough for that. It looked too much like a typical drab Amhara settlement, though it started life as a pro-vincial town of Tigre, when King Yohannes of Tigre, the Emperor John IV, appointed his son, Ras Michael, to be Governor of Wollo.

But after the death of Menelik II, Ras Michael sided with Lij Yasu, Menelik's grandson, who, though the legitimate heir, was deposed in 1916. Ten years later the present Emperor, then Ras Teferi Makonnen, captured Dessie and built it up as an Amhara stronghold. His son, the present Crown Prince Asfa Wossen, was subsequently appointed governor. He still retains the appointment as a sinecure, and so in Wollo it is the deputy governor who deals with the affairs of this buffer province between Amharic Shoa and Tigrinya Tigre.

After paying our calls we filled up with petrol in the main street of Dessie, watched by four lean and wizened beak-faced beggar women, who looked like four fates silently warning us of the perils on the road before us. Then we set out for Makale, another 235 miles, at about ten o'clock.

Only 235 miles, but in that distance there are three major passes to cross, the Lomata, the Maichew and Amba Alagi, as well as many others, which have not even got names. So there was a hard drive ahead of us.

Just on the edge of town we saw a signpost pointing up to the left to Debre Zebit and Debre Tabor. Now only passable for horsemen and mules, during the Italian time one could drive along this road, over the mountains and through the gorges, right up to Gondar, which they made the capital of their province of Amhara. The road has crumbled away, and the signpost does not tell you how far you can get. But I would have dearly liked to see for myself since the route passes quite close to the great rock of Magdala, which Lord Napier's troops stormed in the heyday of the Victorian era to make Emperor Theodore release the British and other European people he was holding captive.

Haile Michael drove straight past, saying simply that the road was gone, and we went on over the hills to Haik, where we had a glimpse between them of the lake down to the right with its ancient island monastery. After that there were many more ups and downs through Wichale and Woldiya until, passing through a narrow gorge that was like a fissure in the rock, we came down to a broad plain.

This was the wide plain of Alamata, where cattle is king and man is his servant. It stretches for thirty or forty miles, and crossing it on the long straights, one begins to feel that one has left the mountains behind, though they are still there on all sides as a backcloth to the scene. The plain was yellow with ripe sorghum, and we passed herd after herd of cattle with long, curving horns converging on the village of Kobbo, from which a rough track leads 85 miles into the mountains to Lalibela and its churches.

The cattle drovers, wielding their long sticks, and the herds passing each other, trampled up great clouds of dust along the road, through which we had to drive slowly and carefully. The herds seemed to be endless, though each animal knew to which one it belonged. They are the wealth of the Galla people of the plain, who have never heard of banks and own no property. Rarely is an animal killed, and then usually only when it is so old that the meat is tough and the hide coarse and worn. In the meantime they take up the people's whole time in tending them, whilst most of the plain is given over to the sorghum which is their fodder. In India it is the holy cow that survives whilst humans go hungry. In Africa the cattle overgraze and eat the pasture dry, turning good land into parched and cracked earth, whilst the men that look after them live, like the Gallas of Alamata, in little straw wigwams that cannot even offer the comfort of a tukul.

The plain lacks water. When we crossed the river that runs through the middle of it, we could see people in the river bed filling up 40-gallon drums. Some were being loaded into trucks, but most of them were equipped with two rubber rings and were being rolled along the road to their destinations by one-man power.

Just short of the pink elephant announcing the village of Alamata we stopped for a midday break, We sought the shelter of an acacia tree to shade us from the heat, and there we sat, listening to the chatter of birds and the rustle of the breeze in the sorghum. Presently the rattle of the sorghum stalks grew louder. We looked up to see a whirlwind of dust approaching from the direction in which we had come. The brown twister came nearer. We debated whether to pack up our things and get back into the Land-Rover. Then it veered away to the west, towards the mountains, and we were left in peace.

From Alamata the road climbs out of the plain in the steepest and narrowest ascent of the whole journey to Asmara. It is the Lomata pass to Maichew, rising 3,000 feet back up into the highlands. The heavy lorries inch their way slowly down, with their trailers behind them, whilst on the return journey empty to Asmara they carry their trailers on their backs to make their way more easily round the hairpin bends.

From high up on the pass we looked back to see the road stretching as straight as a ruler across the plain. Then we looked forward again, facing into the cool highland breeze. As on many of these passes, the road did not descend again immediately on the other side, but wound its way through a plateau containing the village of Korem and then round the side of an upland lake, the waters of Achangi, with its broad lakeside pastures and cowboys in brown and white woollen caps.

Another pass brought us across the next ridge into the valley of Maichew. It was here that the Emperor, after his forces had marched north gathering the clans together on the way, gave battle to the Italians in 1936. Air power proved decisive. The Ethiopians were defeated and pursued as far as Lake Achangi, from where they dispersed, each clan to its own homeland. As we came down the side of the mountain, we saw the place of the battle, singled out by the rows of whitewashed tukuls of the army camp there.

Apart from that there was nothing to see. We stopped for petrol in this, the first town in the province of Tigre, and saw the same crowds of lean men and boys in unwashed white robes, grey with dirt, that we had grown used to in the Amhara places.

But from Maichew onwards the countryside changed significantly. The next pass led to Amba Alagi, a great flat-topped mountain that is remembered as the place where the Italians were defeated in their turn—this time by the British forces coming down from the north in the Second World War. It was the last stronghold of Fascist resistance, and the Italian troops had been told by their Blackshirt advisers that they would certainly be slaughtered by the Indian soldiers if they were captured. Many of them were very surprised to be offered cigarettes instead and told by the British officers how lucky they were to be knocked out of the war. The winding mountain road went round on a hairpin bend built up out of cement-filled oil drums, and passed a ruined Italian block-house with the words *Duce*, 'Leader', and *Imperatore*, 'Emperor', still scrawled on it.

Then at last we came down off the escarpment on to the dry plains of Tigre, the 'Wild West' country of stony slopes and of sandstone rock sculptured into fantastic shapes by wind and weather. Here the houses were made of dry stone instead of wood, continuing a building tradition of 2,000 years and making the villages look rather like Mexican pueblos. They glowed golden in the lowering sun as we roared along, making up for time lost on the mountain tracts. The commonest vegetation was the euphorbia, a tree-sized candelabra-shaped cactus pointing its many fingers to the high, blue sky.

It was dark by the time we reached Quiha, and we could have spent the night there at the Touring Hotel. But we had business next morning in Makale, so we turned off to the left from the main road to continue across the arid plateau until the land fell away down an escarpment. There at the bottom, on another, lower plain, shone the lights of Makale, capital of Tigre.

We drove straight through the quiet little town up to a hillock at the other end, surmounted by a castle built of stone. The castle was built by a dejazmatch, literally a marshal of provincial head-quarters, but now simply a nobleman's title equivalent to a count. The dejazmatch was named Abraha Aria, and it was the end of the nineteenth century, when, after the death in battle with the Dervishes at Metemma of Emperor John, who ruled Ethiopia from Makale, King Menelik of Shoa fought John's son, Ras Mangesha for the imperial crown and won through with the arms he had bought from the French and Italian traders. But he allowed Ras Mangesha to remain at Makale as governor of Tigre. The governorate has remained hereditary, and John's great grandson, also Ras Mangesha, is governor today, The Ras Mangesha of our times founded Tigre Agricultural and Development Ltd, a company which, amongst other things, rebuilt the castle and turned it into the Abraha Castle hotel.

A strong wind was blowing as we walked through the castle archway and up the long flight of stone steps to the exposed terrace, on which the dark grey castle stands. To tell the truth it looked rather forbidding in the dark. But inside all was comfort and light. We were surprised to be greeted by an Indian lady, who told us in a faultless Kensington accent that she had to apologise for not being able to give us too much attention, but the whole place was being taken over that evening for a wedding feast. Of course she was certain we would be very welcome to join in.

So it was that at the invitation of the Begum and her husband, a leading doctor of Makale, who no doubt see something of the old feudal way of life of Rajasthan lingering on in Tigre province, we joined the company of the wedding guests, eighty strong, including all the official dignitaries of the town. We ate their food, including the hot ziggany of Tigre, drank their champagne and whisky as well as the less successful wine of Asmara, and took part in their celebrations.

I found myself seated at the head of a table with a missionary from Ulster at the other end and two Bulgarian doctors and their wives between us. The bride and bridegroom, well-connected people who had come back to their native land from Addis for the entertainment, sat opposite the governor, Ras Mangesha, and his lady, Aida, the Emperor's granddaughter, an Ethiopian princess just like the heroine of Verdi's opera.

There were no toasts or speeches, but after the food and drink the tables were pushed back and the few ladies who had been brought withdrew, the only ones remaining being the Princess, the bride, the wife of the master of ceremonies, our hostess, the Begum, and some *ferenj* women. A musician appeared with a one-stringed diamond-shaped fiddle and began to sing, extempore, a sort of calypso in high pitched raucous Tigrinya. It was the signal for the men to dance. The portly bourgeois of Makale came forward one by one to seek the muslin shamma from the shoulders of the M.C.'s wife, wrap it round their waists and throw it over one shoulder of their city suits. They then circled the room in a kind of shuffle, vaguely keeping time with the screeching fiddle, until the moment when the music rose to a crisis point and they exerted themselves to stamp out a sort of shoulder-shaking finale like a little orgy going off at half-cock.

The Tigre people got at the Amhara visitors from Addis to take part. The Amharas, stiff and self-conscious, took a good deal of persuading to go through the token motions of joining in the dance. Then, quietly, without a word either to right or left, the good-looking governor got up and walked out with his wife. It was the end. If I had expected real jollity, with the drums beating and the fiddles and pipes playing and everybody joining in the merry-making, as in India and Nepal, I was disappointed.

With a two-year-old copy of *Playboy* for bedside reading, I went to bed. A white bearded patriarchal angel, with the good book in his left hand and a cross in his right hand, looked down on me from a large painting on unframed canvas stuck to the wall. There were also copies of the *Quotidiano Eritreo*, the Italian newspaper from Asmara, and English and Amharic versions of the Bible presented by the Middle East General Mission, in case I got tired of *Playboy*. Not caring for any of them, or for the full moon outside, I went to sleep.

Next morning I was awoken early by crows cawing and pigeons cooing. I went down to find that I was first at breakfast. But I was not sorry. After looking at the two-pronged barbed swords, the shields and the daggers that made a suitable decor for the hall of the castle, I had time to study the paintings on the walls of the dining room. They were a series of pictures of the Tigre rock churches, done in 1968 by Elizabeth Otto.

Tucked away in inaccessible places, chiselled into the living rock and hidden by boulders or in fissures in precipices or on almost unscalable mountain mesas, these churches kept the religious traditions of Tigre alive when outside the mountain fastnesses all seemed lost against the onslaught of Moslem invaders. These traditions, with the ritual inherited from the Coptic church of Egypt and the art ultimately from the Byzantine age, still survive. Tigre, with the holy city of Axum, where the emperors are crowned, and its old stone churches and monasteries far more venerable than the wooden buildings and modern constructions of Shoa, can well lay claim to being the heartland of the Ethiopian faith and people.

Indeed, when John was emperor, it was the heartland. But the rivalry between Tigre and Shoa grew up in the middle of the nineteenth century, when Lord Napier left Ethiopia after Emperor Theodore's suicide, leaving no emperor in his place. Eventually Menelik agreed to serve as a king under John, the Negusa Negast, the King of Kings. And in the tradition of feudal societies the pact was sealed by a marriage between John's son, Arya Selassie, and Menelik's daughter, Zewditu. But Arya Selassie never inherited the throne. It went to Menelik and after that to his daughter, who was empress from 1916 to 1930.

Rivalry between Shoa and Tigre is still significant, though at the top level dynastic marriages have blurred the division. In the nineteenth century Italy supported Menelik against Tigre in the Machiavellian tradition that the king on one's own border is the enemy. Tigre was on the border of their new colony on the Red Sea coast.

So the Italians thought that they had achieved their objective when, on the death of John, the seat of Ethiopian power shifted south to Ankober and then even further south to Addis Ababa. With the treaty of Wichale, the little town between Dessie and the plain of Alamata that we had passed through the day before, the Italians thought that they had put the seal on Menelik's subjection.

The place is called Ucciali in Italian, and the *Trattato di amicizia e commercio tra il Regno d'Italia e l'Impero Etiopico*, the "treaty of friendship and commerce between the Kingdom of Italy and the Empire of Ethiopia", states in Article 17 that *S.M. il Re dei Re d'Etiopia consente di servirsi del Governo di S.M. il Re d'Italia per tutte le trattazioni di affari che avesse con altre Potenze o Governi*. (His Majesty, the King of Kings of Ethiopia, agrees to make use of the government of His Majesty, the King of Italy, for all dealings with other Powers or Governments.) The treaty was signed in 1889, the year Menelik came to the throne.

But the Amharic version of the text did not say the same thing. It simply stated that the King of Kings *might* make use of the government of the King of Italy. When the Italians claimed that Ethiopia was now an Italian protectorate, Menelik naturally objected. How could a king of kings be a vassal of a mere king? He wrote to the king of Italy, and these were his words: "When I made the treaty . . . I said that because of our friendship, our affairs in Europe might be carried on by the sovereign of Italy, but I have not made any treaty which obliges me to do so." Less than a year after signing the treaty he also wrote to the other European powers, saying, "Ethiopia has need of no one; she stretches out her hands to God."

Five years later the Italians, outnumbered and outgunned, were defeated at Adowa, close to the holy city, largely by the weapons they themselves had supplied in helping Menelik to the throne. It was the custom of the Ethiopians to castrate their prisoners, but Menelik was magnanimous. That fate was reserved for the tribesmen who had sided with the Italians. After long negotiations the Italian prisoners were returned to the coast with their manhood unimpaired, except for those who had suffered in the heat of battle.

The Italians were to have to wait nearly forty years to wipe out the shame of that defeat in the battle of Maichew. This time they had aeroplanes, armoured cars and even poison gas on their side. In the eyes of the rest of the world the later victory was as shameful as the previous defeat. It was an invasion based on a border dispute over a tiny oasis in the Somali Desert. The Italians had joined the ranks of the colonial powers too late.

After paying our calls in Makale we left the town by the new road that leads north, thus avoiding the necessity of retracing the route to Quiha. The plain was quite treeless, with a stark escarpment ahead, up which we had to climb to get back to the higher plateau and the main road. This plateau was equally treeless, encroached upon by the gorges that join up in the west with the grand canyon of the Takazze river. Villages were oases in a stony desert, over which one could see the road sweeping for miles ahead.

Not far from the point where we rejoined the main road we came to the village of Wukro, with its advertisements for tangerina, the local orange drink, and its Italian style *bar ristorante*. Passing through it we found the ancient church, cut into a sandstone boulder, that the local people claim to have been founded as early as the year 336—that is actually a little before King Ezana made Christianity the state religion. It lay to the right of the road on the left bank of the stony river that passes through the village.

Almost as soon as we had stopped, a priest emerged from the church. He stood above the river with his staff in his right hand, looking like Moses about to strike the rock, and gestured to us to go back across the bridge and round through the village to reach him and see the church.

And indeed there was much to see. For it is claimed that Wukro escaped the attentions of Ahmed Gragn, the left-handed hammer of the Christians, and the depredations of his iconoclastic Muslims in the sixteenth century. The priests attribute the damage that there is to the pagan Queen Judith, who wreaked havoc in Tigre in the tenth century, as is related in *The History of the Patriarchs of Alexandria*.

In the first chamber of the church three of the twelve very old paintings of the apostles have survived, and by the door the martyred patron saint of the church, St. Cherkos, stands, being consumed by the flames, with his mother beside him. On the ceiling the four gospellers, Matthew, Mark, Luke and John, are represented symbolically by animals. The main chamber of the church is in the shape of a cross with cruciform columns on either side of the aisle. There are many friezes carved on the walls of this part of the church, and many questions regarding their origin and interpretation still remain unanswered.

But we had no time to linger and went on northwards into country, in which the marks of the Italian era became more and more noticeable. Fantastic rock formations—boulders perched one on another, peaks jutting perpendicularly to the sky, cliffs cut off sheer as if with a giant knife—followed us as far as Adigrat, where a pink building in the severely functional style of Fascist architecture still stands in the main square. Here the road to Adowa cuts into the mountains on the left, passing the crag on which Debre Damo stands, to which visitors have to be hauled up on ropes as in the Greek monastic settlement of Meteora in Thessaly.

At Adigrat, with its large Catholic church, the tarmac that we had left at Debre Berhan started again. It took us swiftly to the border of Eritrea, with the fang-shaped peaks of Adowa rising behind the great canyon of the Mareb river on our left.

Eritrea was an Italian colony from 1889 to 1935. It was then incorporated into the Italian East African Empire, which collapsed in 1941. After eleven years of British administration it was handed over to Ethiopia in 1952. In theory it was to be an autonomous unit, federated with Ethiopia under the Ethiopian crown. In practice it has become regarded by the central government as just another province, and considerable resentment is felt there when, under the system of government patronage in Addis Ababa, more and more appointments go to the Amhara people.

But the effects of colonial administration could be seen, even before we reached the border, in the shady avenue of eucalyptus and juniper trees that lined the road from Adigrat and in the carefully tended farms that made the desert produce vegetables and greenstuffs wherever there was water to be had. Unfortunately water is as scarce as whisky for most of the way, and the only thing that grows to any purpose apart from the camel thorn is the prickly pear. Only when one approaches Decamere does one reach the shady trees again, and the bright green of market gardens where the water runs.

Yet, though the people there wear brighter clothes than the drab peasants of Tigre and Shoa in their eternal dirty white, Decamere itself is a ghost town. The vast barracks that the

Italians built there to turn the place into their East African Aldershot, stand nine-tenths empty and mostly ruinously gutted. The garrison cinema is boarded up, the Italian equivalent of the N.A.A.F.I. windowless and bare. The signs of small shops—the grocer, the barber and the hardware store—still stand above broken doors and empty premises. Of the 6,000 Italians who used to live in Decamere, not counting the troops passing through, scarcely even an old *insabbiato* remains.

It was an eerie feeling driving through the empty town and past inscriptions on the roadside boulders. A monument that had never been knocked down commemorated, Roman style, *la gloria di Colonia*—the glory of an empire that has gone.

From here I had thought it would be an easy run of 25 miles to Asmara. But again the road twisted and turned, looping up into a pass and down again into a defile. Following the eternal bends, carefully graded by the colonial engineers, and looking at the parched and pitted landscape, one wondered what madness had ever possessed the Italians to advance into that moonstruck land. If, by advancing into the highlands, they had hoped to settle there, like the white settlers in Kenya and their own colonisers in Libya, they were doomed to disappointment. The Ethiopians never gave them a chance to settle, and all they got out of the country was hard work, frustration and despair.

Then, at last, we reached the plain, with Asmara at the far end of it on the edge of the escarpment which goes down to the sea. Driving down Addis Ababa avenue and into the Viale Haile Selassie was almost like entering a European town, a Mediterranean town with palms lining the main street, shops under arcades and a Catholic cathedral ringing out the chimes.

6

The Red Sea Land

Alfredo Menghetti's Albergo Italia opened in 1899, only ten years after the Italians took over the little Tigrean fort close to the rim of the plateau and began building their colonial city of Asmara beside it. The stuccoed ceiling in the dining-room and the clusters of plaster grapes hanging over the windows belong to the plush *fin de siècle* age, and when I entered my bedroom and found a vast bed there as broad as it was long, I felt that it, too, belonged to the same period. There was none of the atmosphere of modern international hotels, in which it is hard enough to find a double bed at all.

Menghetti, himself, the son of the founder, presided over affairs. The menu, with its *pasta* and *zuppa pavese*, its kid cutlets, its asparagus Roman style, and its chops prepared from lambs that could hardly have been much larger than puppies, was as Italian as one could find anywhere from Turin to Taormina. We were thankful, for we stayed several days in Asmara and appreciated gastronomic comfort.

Of course the town has changed. The old opera house is now a cinema, and the Italian population has shrunk, though there are still business men from Italy as well as the *insabbiati*. Conversely the American population has increased with Kagnew, the United States base on the edge of town. But with its Viale Winston Churchill and its Viale William Platt, named after the Kaid of the Sudan, Asmara, like Addis, still commemorates the liberators of 1941. However, its civilised streets sit uneasily in the midst of a rocky, dry country where to talk of going out to Keren, Agordat or Massawa is inevitably to talk of *shiftas*.

The word *shifta* has, of course, become debased and generalised. It used to mean an outlaw, who has turned to robbery as a means of livelihood, like the highwayman in eighteenth-century England. Now it means anyone who holds up a vehicle on the road for whatever purpose. In Eritrea a *shifta* is considered to be a member of the Eritrean Liberation Front, Moslem and Arab backed, which is committed to prising Eritrea away again from Christian Ethiopia.

The road to Keren, where the Indian Army stormed the heights in 1941 in one of their first engagements of the Second World War, is regarded as being particularly vulnerable. Not long ago the British consul was seized on this road and subsequently released. And beyond Keren civilian traffic is frequently not permitted to travel along the one motor road that leads to the Sudan. Since Ethiopia also sees fit to keep the frontier at Metemma, to the west of Gondar, closed, there is often no road traffic at all between the two countries.

The reason is that the whole of western Eritrea is affected by the liberation movement, and the Imperial Ethiopian Army is unable to guarantee the safety of travellers. The movement has cogent arguments in support of its cause, but, like the Arab terrorists who train in Jordan and Syria, it has lost a great deal of international sympathy by its attempts at piracy in the air and hijacking Ethiopian planes. Such movements seem to forget that, since the aeroplane is the usual vehicle for diplomats and men concerned with international affairs, the best way to antagonise them is to threaten their safety in the air.

Our safety seemed assured, however, in the streets of Asmara. They are more orderly than those of Addis, where an increase in beatings up and attempts at robbery seemed to be giving the city the reputation of trying to emulate New York. We walked out and dined out in perfect tranquility, though in the chill of the winter evenings, with the *signoras* sporting their fur coats, we walked fast to keep warm.

And one of the most fascinating places where we dined was the *pizzeria* at the top end of Viale Haile Selassie, close to the railway station from which the trains run down to Massawa. We passed through the outer restaurant into an inner room, and there we

E

found an ancient *insabbiato*, reputedly over 80 years old, presiding with the aplomb born of half a century's experience over an enormous oven.

Standing out from the back of the room like a miniature blast furnace, the oven was kept hot by means of charcoal fed into one corner. The food to be cooked, whether bread for toasting or fish or meat for grilling, was inserted into the remaining space on a steel platter at the end of a 6-foot-long rod. This rod was wielded by the ancient's wife, a tall, thin, flat-chested Somali woman, who slapped the steaks on to the iron after they had been marinated with sauces, spices and unguents by the skilled hands of the *insabbiato*.

Though we were charged plenty for the size of the portions, the resultant dishes were delicious. The old man darted about with the agility of someone half his age. He sized us up and reckoned what we ought to pay. Fresh prawns, tender cuts of beef in a land of tough, wiry meat, and even lobsters were his to provide. His age permitted him to be familiar with his patrons. An animated mixed party entered and ordered their dishes, but one of the women became impatient for her fish. The aged *insabbiato* was not put out. "Why are you in such a hurry for *pesce*?" he shouted out for all to hear. "You've got your husband with you, haven't you?"

Only those who know the double meaning of the word *pesce* will appreciate the joke.

From the *pizzeria* we walked smartly back the way we had come, along the tree-lined avenue past the Catholic cathedral. The shops were full of Christmas displays, and most people were wearing overcoats. But we, not expecting such cold in tropical Africa, had to be content with hunching our shoulders. There was a slight drizzle, which would have pleased the local people if it had been heavier. For Asmara, like many another town that has outgrown its site, suffers from a severe water shortage.

Past the Piccadilly Nightclub and the Adulis Bar, named after the ancient Sabaean ruins thirty-five miles down the coast from Massawa, past other drinking dens less classically minded and a pimp who told me I must be the British consul, we returned to the *albergo*.

Early next morning, though it still seemed to be the middle of the night, I was awoken by a deafening noise of chanting. It was as though a band of monks had gathered in the very street below my room to serenade me with their sacred song. At first I thought it must be a midnight funeral, or perhaps an early morning wedding. But both ideas seemed ridiculous and I remained mystified.

Then the chanting was joined by another penetrating noise. This time it was the wail of the *muezzin* on the Grand Mosque near the Piazza Hamel and the Arab market. And as if this addition to the religious concert were not enough, the two opposing noises, each magnified by its own loudspeaker, were joined shortly afterwards by the clanging bells of the Catholic cathedral warming up for the Angelus.

The cacophony had all the makings of a nightmare, and though I had identified two of the ingredients with some certainty, I was still mystified by the third. It was not until later in the morning, when I discovered that it was the feast of St. Mary, that the mystery was solved. When we passed St. Mary's Coptic church next morning, we saw the slopes round the white building thronged with people, and there was a busy coming and going past the Ethiopian saints painted on the edifice of neo-Axumite style that stands to the right of the main gate.

By this time we were on our way out of town to take the plunge down to the Red Sea. It was only two or three miles to the edge of the escarpment, passing through woods of eucalyptus and juniper, which are protected by the forestry police. Amongst the trees on the right lies the well-kept cemetery for the Commonwealth dead of the Second World War, including a fair number of Indian troops.

The descent is more than 6,000 feet, but, awe-inspiring though many parts of it are, it does not take place in one fell swoop. The road first goes down a steep ridge to Nefasit, with the narrow gauge, single-track railway looping and sweeping round the contours of the steep hillsides first on one side and then on the other. Crosses beside the road mark the spots where people have gone over the edge. Near the villages the stony hills are speckled with prickly pear, with beaver-tail cactus leaves and purple flowers.

Nefasit is a junction, where the direct road from Decamere comes down the escarpment by another route. It must have been an important military post for detraining, embussing and convoy halts in the days when Italy had a quarter of a million men in East Africa. Barred-off side turnings mark the tracks to abandoned ammunition and stores dumps, and an empty flattened area is all that remains of a deserted parade ground or vehicle park.

The second plunge, from Nefasit to Ghinda, was not as steep as the first. But, except for some brave attempts at terracing for sisal, the hills were as bare as before. However, Ghinda itself was surrounded by green farmland, for a lake formed by damming up the river above the settlement had been made to irrigate the whole valley.

It was like the relic of a colonial cantonment, with the pink-coloured police-station on one side of the road, and on the other the hotel with its restaurant downstairs and rooms above. Ancient Fiat cars, that would have fetched high prices as vintage models in Europe, were parked beside the hotel, and inside, past the beggar boys lying in wait at the door and the espresso bar, sat the smartest *insabbiato* I had yet seen. An ageing gentleman with grizzled hair, he was dressed from top to toe in Sunday white—shirt, shorts, long stockings and shoes. He looked like the last remaining member of some once august colonial club, forced by the bitter wind of change to share its premises with the lesser breeds.

The third plunge, from Ghinda through the coastal range to the plain, was comparatively gentle. Just over thirty miles further on we came to the village of Dongollo, where the mineral water from the hot spring is bottled. With tap water unfit for drinking, Dongollo water is consumed as widely in the north as Ambo is in the south, even for cleaning one's teeth. In fact Dongollo is better known today than nearby Dogali, where the Italians suffered their first defeat from the Ethiopian warriors, led by Ras Alula, in 1887. But the temporary setback was soon retrieved, and the Ponte di Dogali, with its commemorative plaque to an Italian general still standing on the bridge, marks the crossing of the river from which the European troops eventually pressed on up on to the plateau.

Down at sea level again after over a month in the heights, I breathed freely once more. The road led straight across the coastal plain through arid scrubland that looked more like Egypt and the Middle East than the regions from which we had come. Camels and mosques, women half veiled, and donkeys carrying water bags from wells proclaimed the presence of Islam and the desert.

Massawa was originally built on the outermost of two islands. It therefore had maximum security from the mainland during the Turkish time. Even after the two causeways had been built connecting Massawa with Taulud island and Taulud with the mainland, it was secure enough during the Italian period. The remains of the three hundred years of Turkish occupation are still visible on the old houses with their fretted lattice work and wooden arcades, tucked away in the squares of the old town, which are gathered round the mosque. But of course the Italian influence is far more prominent. The first building you come to, as you reach the other end of the second causeway, is the Albergo di Savoia, the Savoy Hotel.

Massawa was briefly occupied by the British long before British troops took over the place in 1941. The Egyptians, newly independent from the ailing Turkish empire, occupied Massawa in 1865, and the British moved in after they had taken control of Egypt in 1882. They had some sort of an arrangement with Emperor John that when they left he could succeed them. But the arrangement was never fulfilled. As a counterbalance to the growing French strength in the southern part of the Red Sea, it was decided to let the newly united nation of Italy take it on. So the sign of full nationhood in the Europe of the nineteenth century—a nation state with overseas colonies—was conferred on Italy by Great Britain. Massawa was the capital of Italy's new colony of Eritrea from 1885 until the seat of government was moved to Asmara in 1897.

The white hotel on Taulud island, with its cavernous arches and air-conditioned interior, was a fit place to occupy on such a hot sea coast. Yet it was a dry heat, not too sultry, and it would not have been too uncomfortable sitting outside in Red Sea rig, as prescribed by the Royal Navy, even in the heat of the day.

Of course the Red Sea is no redder than any other. Nor are those of its coasts that I have seen red either. No one knows where it got its Greek name of the Erythrean Sea, from which the Italians named their colony Eritrea—literally 'the red land.'

Without waiting for the cool of the evening, we set out for Green island across the placid lagoon in front of the hotel. Our much-painted, dazzling white, hired dinghy was rowed by a wizened little

man in a haji's cap, with veins standing out on his stick-like legs
and a skin so black it was almost blue.

The island was only a quarter of an hour away, and no distance
at all compared with the Dahlaks, which are scattered far out into
the middle of the Red Sea, the home of brilliant and weird tropical
fish. But although it was close to the shore, it had its attractions
too. As we approached the shore, we were greeted with the sight of
a swarm of half-naked chocolate-coloured nymphs gambolling
about at the water's edge. What was more, as soon as they saw us
they leaped towards us, seized our bathing gear and led us by the
hands to the seaward side of the island.

I am not an unduly modest man, but I could not help thinking
that they might have mistaken us for some other people. There
were six of them and only three of us. That was all wrong for a
start. And furthermore, in obedience to *ferenj* prudery, they had
put on the tops of their swimsuits before approaching us. Shortly
afterwards my suspicions were proved correct. We had hardly had
time to exchange Christian names and find out which cabaret they
inhabited in Massawa, before the real object of their desires came
chugging across the bay from the region of the Yacht Club—a
motorboat full of American servicemen.

With promises of future dates and farewell embraces, the
nymphs deserted us for the other fish that they had in their net,
and left us to ourselves. We pottered about amongst the coral,
looked at the whitened shells for sale near the ruinous building by
the tomb of Sheik Said, and returned to the mainland.

Later, in the early evening, I walked out of the hotel to look
more closely at the first building that one sees as one crosses the
causeway on to Taulud island. Dead centre at the end of the
causeway, the white square towers and white dome of the new
Coptic church rise above the dark-green tamarisk trees like a
symbol of the take-over by the Christian Empire.

One would have expected the people to be proud that I should
wish to take home a souvenir of such a noble sight. But as soon as
I got my camera out of its case a gang of ragged children came
running from some huts behind the church and started to attack
me with shouts and gestures. They were determined that I should
not take a picture and the ringleaders were a little girl about 4
feet high and a little boy about $3\frac{1}{2}$ feet high. The little boy picked

up a stone off the roadside and threatened to throw it. The little girl drew her finger across her throat in a gesture of slitting it.

A young man who was standing by remonstrated with them telling them not to be so ridiculous. Perhaps he was a Muslim. But anyway it was to no avail. As for me, what interested me in the violent behaviour of these little Christian people was firstly the fact that none of their elders wanted to call them to heel, and secondly the fact that such behaviour could not have come from their own heads but must have been the result of indoctrination, in all probability by the priest in the little church school at which, no doubt, most of them were students. I was reminded of a certain missionary when I asked him how he set about converting Christian Ethiopians to Christianity. "We lay stress on different things," he said.

Not wanting to provoke an international incident so early in my stay in the land of the Lion of Judah, I beat a prudent retreat. I had no wish to be stoned by the ancient Christians as a martyr for the new, so I went back into the garden of the hotel and took my photograph as a side view instead of from the front. All I desired was friendship and cordiality, just as it was expressed on the plaque beside which I was standing. It declared itself to be a "permanent memorial of the happy day on which His Majesty Haile Selassie I, Emperor of Ethiopia laid the first stone of the Red Sea Hotel, an enterprise of the Ethio-Italian Hotel Share Company, symbol of an ever closer collaboration between Italy and Ethiopia".

Perhaps these violent Christian children had some tradition handed down to them of the time when Christianity was banned from the land of Massawa, when the Christians had to build their church out over the water at a point now marked by a cross behind the petrol station at the Taulud end of the causeway. Their current liberty was a new, heady thing, and somehow the camera seemed to threaten it.

Fanciful ideas! We left the Land-Rover behind to walk the quarter of a mile to the second causeway, past the barred gates of the Imperial Palace, which a Swiss adventurer built for himself, having got himself made governor by the Egyptians. We crossed the causeway, sat down at one of the round tables outside the Savoy Hotel, and ordered drinks. I took the local *zibib*, which is the *ouzo* of the Greeks and the *absinthe* of the French. In front of us was the end of the little railway line, which started high up in Asmara, disappearing through the dock gates.

Beyond the railway tracks lay the harbour, with one or two cargo vessels against the wharf and some native craft at anchor. There was no great activity, for now, with the Suez canal closed for so long, the Red Sea is a backwater. There is no through traffic, and the most fruitful trade is with Israel through Eilat on the Gulf of Aqaba. For Ethiopia, with its long Solomonic tradition, is one of the few friends Israel has in a world region of vicious, implacable Arab hatred.

To our right, surrounded by four Trafalgar Square lions like those round Menelik's mausoleum in Addis, stood the new statue of the Emperor, wearing an admiral's fore-and-aft hat and pointing out across the harbour in a gesture of urging the nation to make use of the sea coast that it acquired in 1952. In fact the finger on the statue points more or less in the direction of the Naval Academy across the bay, where British officers are in charge of training.

We left the Savoy to walk round Massawa island, which is really quite small, with only two short main streets, and those mostly occupied by bars. As we walked, a young man came up to me and asked for a cigarette. But he was not begging. What he really wanted was a job. Mistaking me for a sailor, he went on to tell me what voyages he had made and to ask me if I had a place for him on my ship.

I could not help him. Nor could the Emperor with his finger pointing out to sea. Nor could the Ethiopian patriots commemorated on the plaque at the entrance to the port cantonment. Trade was in the doldrums. The bar girls fought for our attentions with an almost savage venom in their voices.

Having done the circuit, we sat down again at the same table as before outside the Savoy, and ordered another round of drinks. As I watched the water cloud the *zibib* in my glass and wondered what unboiled, unfiltered source it came from, the pedlars approached. One was selling postcards, another chewing-gum, another flip-flop rubber sandals. Then came a fourth, a little boy with a dirty wicker basket containing peanuts, and a fifth, a girl, who was simply begging. The boy was the one who had been prepared to cast the first stone outside the Coptic church, and the girl was the one who had warned me I would have my throat cut if I took a photograph.

I did not feel inclined to give alms to people who had threatened my life. But the girl was most put out. I offered her a postcard I had bought, trying to show her that the church had suffered no ill effects from previous photography. But I fear the analogy was lost on her.

Later that evening we looked in on the cabaret that the nymphs on Green Island had described to us. It was in the open air, with tables grouped round a circular dance floor, and furthermore its card in the reception office of our hotel called it the place "for the happiest evenings in town".

We entered full of hope. But the first person we saw sitting there, facing a rather superior and mature nymph who was possibly Madame, was a United States Army Military Police corporal in full white tropical parade uniform. It was enough to dampen anybody's ardour, especially that of a man who has spent many years in the army himself, and mine did not recover. The ultimate result was that we all went chastely back to the Red Sea Hotel to bed, pursued by rude signs in the Italian style, not two fingers but the whole arm, from the viragos of the waterfront bars, which have deceptive names like Nazareth and Paradise.

7

The Holy City

After a couple of days we went back up the hill to Asmara. But before leaving Massawa I had the privilege of being shown something that remained in my mind with far greater intensity than the nymphs of Green Island or the Coptic church or the Emperor's finger pointing out to sea.

Luciano Perino looks like a young Adonis. His slim, bronzed body reminds one of the Hermes of Praxiteles, and his sun-bleached blond hair and classic features would stir the heart of any Venus with blood in her veins. Yet it was not the image of Luciano that stuck so forcibly in my mind, but the impression of his fish. For Luciano, as Director of the Ethiopian Live Fish Export Company, spends half his time in the Dahlak Islands and the other half at his house on Taulud Island with the marine creatures he brings back alive.

The hundreds of Dahlak islands, about thirty miles out to sea from Massawa, vary in character. The largest, Dahlak Kebir, is thirty-five miles long and has five villages on it. Now that pearling has declined, many of the villagers live by smuggling. The rest are mostly rocky, waterless, uninhabited coral islands. But they are only waterless and uninhabited above sea level. Below the water-line there is a teeming, vivid life of brilliant and odd tropical fish that, together with the strange animals of the larger islands—the dugongs, the dorcas and the green turtles—and the birds of the air, will attract far more visitors in the future, when the Ethiopian

Tourist Organisation has developed communications and facilities for accommodation.

When I met Luciano, it was before the British Army expedition from the Royal Military College of Science had set out on its five weeks' investigation to study the islands' potential. Luciano would probably have been able to give them as much detail as the Tourist Organization needed to know. But the handsome Italian prefers to work on his own, and some of the results of his labours can be seen in the polystyrene baths in the shed in the compound of his house.

The dull-coloured puff fish, which blow up like balloons when disturbed, contrast with the brilliant yellow and black stripes of the butterfly fish. Most of the species have to be handled with care. The ballista looks like a plastic toy, with its enamel blue design and its bright yellow painted mouth. But that innocent looking mouth, which is capable of eating living coral, can also tear a chunk of flesh out of a finger. The sluggish, reddish creature, that looks like a sea anemone, can kill a man with the scorpion-like poison it injects through its spines. So these brilliant and sometimes lethal fish flit about in the baths, waiting to be flown in plastic bags to Europe and America to spend the rest of their lives in aquaria.

I left Luciano deep in lengthy negotiations with some Arab suppliers of tropical shells. And when I think of Massawa now, it is of the Dahlak islands and his vivid harvest of the sea.

Our journey back to Asmara was uneventful except that at one point we came upon one of the overladen grain lorries toppled over on its side a few feet from the precipice. Bags of grain were scattered over the road and down the mountainside. But it would not be surprising if more of these dangerously top-heavy vehicles did the same. The drivers might then have second thoughts about the high pay they receive to carry these enormous loads.

The next day we set out at a quarter to eight on the western loop of the 'Historic Route', which was to take us through the holy city of Axum and the old capital of Gondar. About an hour and a half later we reached the border of Eritrea and crossed over into Tigre again. The crossing was marked by a monument at one end of an iron bridge over the Mareb river, and by the ending of the asphalt and the beginning again of the rough, dusty trail.

Coming up out of the gorge of this small river, we had our first really good view of the fangs of Adowa. Those fantastically shaped peaks, which stood as a background to the famous battle of 1896, are as striking, in their way, as the Dolomites. From the crossroads at Adi Abun up the *cul-de-sac* into the valley of Adowa was a distance of only a mile or two, but it brought us even closer to those tooth-shaped sentinel peaks amongst which the battle was fought.

General Baratieri, who had been mauled on the plains of Makale by Ras Makonnen's forces, was in retreat, approaching Adowa from the east. Knowing that Menelik had rallied his forces near Axum, Baratieri hoped to knock them out with a master stroke on Sunday, 1st March, the eve of the fifty-six-day Lenten fast, expecting them to be celebrating at the Holy of Holies.

But Baratieri underestimated both their numbers and their sense of priorities. Menelik's scouts soon saw the three columns of Italians advancing on 29th February. The southernmost column, misled by an inaccurate map, lost its way and was attacked separately from all sides. The other two columns were also attacked separately and defeated, the odds being four to one, since Menelik had managed to muster 80,000 well-armed men. Amongst the peaks of Guna and Dirian, of Magdalawit and Abba Afranghi death and destruction came to the *soldati*. The terror and shame of their defeat by these supposedly savage men with their furbishings of lions' manes and their strange black emperor, with his broad-brimmed hat above the tight white bandana bound round his head and his claims of descent from King Solomon himself, lay heavy on the minds of Italian military men for a generation.

We stopped in Adowa for a few hours. The town's reputation was still suffering from a nasty incident in which two United States Peace Corps volunteer teachers had been badly beaten up by boys of the secondary school after attempting to impose a certain amount of discipline on the students. The battered men had been flown to Asmara, and the Queen of Sheba school had returned to work with new teachers from Ceylon to take the place of those the students had stoned. For, ranging far and wide in their desperate attempts to fill the teacher gaps, the Ethiopians had sent their envoy to Ceylon and even as far as the Philippine islands to recruit unsuspecting reinforcements.

As for filling the gaps from their own people, the production of educated and qualified men is slow, and of those who qualify few wish to teach. Teaching is generally regarded as beastly work, only to be undertaken as a last resort, when all else fails. So we have the familiar situation in African developing countries. Everybody wants to study, but no one wants to teach.

From Adowa to Axum it was only fifteen miles through rolling country, and we were there before midday. This did not help us to get into the Touring Hotel, however, since it was booked for a package tour. So we went down into the town to the King Ezana Hotel, a public house of no pretensions, with a host who welcomed us with no sort of cordiality in spite of the portrait of Queen Elizabeth II next to that of Emperor Haile Selassie I on the wall behind the coffee machine.

The King Ezana Hotel was our headquarters for exploring Axum. I have called it a holy city, for city it undoubtedly was in olden times. In the third century A.D. a historian, named Mani, put the Axumite kingdom on a par with Babylon, Rome and Egypt as the four greatest empires within his ken. The source of Axum's vitality in those days was the trade between the Red Sea and the interior of Africa. Ivory, gold and slaves went down to the coast at Adulis, and cotton cloth, glassware, metals and manufactured weapons came up. In a way the goods were not very different from those that Menelik II traded in during the nineteenth century.

But now Axum, though still the religious and mystical centre of a very extensive empire, is scarcely even a town. It has shrunk to the size of a large village. The Italians—who with immense labour removed the largest of the great pillars, called stelae, that remained unbroken and erected it in the Piazza di Porta Capena in Rome—cannot be blamed for this decline. It had happened before they came, starting long ago, shortly after the conversion to Christianity.

In order to see the evidence of Axum's former might we had to walk a short distance from the King Ezana hotel back the way we had come to the point where the road from Asmara divides into two. Within the triangle of the road fork a garden has been planted out with cypress trees, and in the garden various stelae, capitals and monuments have been erected more or less at random after recovery from nearby sites in amongst the houses of the town.

The Stele of King Ezana, which stands near the main entrance to the Persian-looking garden, is a slab of stone about 8 feet high and 3 feet wide. It is the Rosetta stone of Ethiopia, for the inscription is in three languages—Greek, Sabaean and Ge'ez. Sabaean was the language of the land of Sheba in South Arabia to which the Axumite empire probably owed its origin, and Ge'ez was the early language of Ethiopia, which became the classical language of church liturgy and ceremonial and is still so used today.

The stone gives us the nominal extant of King Ezana's realm. "Ezana, King of Axum and of Himyar, and of Raidan and of Ethiopia, and of Saba and of Salhen, and of Siyanio and of Bega, and of Kasu, the King of Kings, the son of the invincible god Ares."

But there is another thing, for which King Ezana is famous, besides the size of his kingdom, and that is the conversion of Ethiopia to Christianity. The legend of Frumentius, set in the early fourth century, tells us how it occurred. A Syrian trader was sailing down the Red Sea with two young boys on board his boat, named Frumentius and Aedisius. They were set upon by pirates, and the trader, Meropius, was killed. The boys escaped, however, and were later discovered sitting under a tree, studying their books.

The two boys were taken to the Emperor of Axum, Ella Amida, who made the clever one, Frumentius, his treasurer and secretary, whilst Aedisius became his cupbearer. After Ella Amida's death the widowed Queen Sofia begged Frumentius to educate her young son, who was crowned King Ezana when he came of age. This Frumentius did, but Ezana was not immediately converted to Christianity. In the early years of his reign he retained the symbols of the sun and moon on his coinage. Only later did he replace them with the Christian cross.

As for Frumentius, he was sent to Alexandria in Egypt to request the Patriarch Athanasius to appoint a bishop to Axum. He replied that there was none better than Frumentius himself for the task. Thus, with the appointment of St. Frumentius as first Abuna of Ethiopia by St. Athanasius, began a tradition that lasted until 1951, when the first Ethiopian archbishop was elected and the link with Alexandria was broken after a period of over 1,600 years.

We do not know what the religion of Axum was before the conversion. But the symbols of the sun and moon, and the connections with South Arabia, would point to some kind of ritual based on stargazing and astrology. It is also possible that Judaic monotheism was known, for the legend of Solomon and Sheba, on which the Emperors of Ethiopia base their claim to the Solomonic succession and the blood of the ancient Hebrews, must have arisen out of some real connection between Axum and Israel, of which the Falasha Jews, who now live in the Gondar area, may be a vestige.

One can read the story of King Solomon and the Queen of Sheba any day on the big sheets of shamma, painted like strip cartoons, which pedlars hold up in the streets of Addis for your inspection. As everybody knows from the Bible, the Queen of Sheba went to visit King Solomon and was royally entertained: "And when the Queen of Sheba heard of the fame of Solomon, she came to prove Solomon with hard questions at Jerusalem, with a very great company, and camels that bare spices, and gold in abundance, and precious stones: and when she was come to Solomon, she communed with him all that was in her heart."

But what everybody does not know is that the Queen of Sheba, in other words the Queen of the Sabaeans, came from Axum, and whilst she was in Jerusalem she lay with King Solomon. It happened in this way.

Once upon a time the people of Tigre used to bow down before a mighty serpent. They had been sacrificing goats to this great python for four hundred years, when a young man came along and promised to rid them of the monstrous snake if they would make him king. To this they agreed. Whereupon the young man prepared a poison and fed it to the next goat that was to be sacrificed to the python. The snake ate the poisoned goat and died.

The *Kebra Negast*, the Chronicle of Kings, goes on to say that, after the hero had been crowned king, he produced a daughter named Makeda. She was the Queen of Sheba. As is related in the Bible, she went to visit King Solomon to "prove him with hard

questions" and judge for herself of his wisdom. Before the Queen
and her servants left, Solomon gave "all her desires, whatsoever
she asked".

According to the Ethiopian legend, which is said to have been
found in manuscript amongst the treasures of Haghia Sofia in
Constantinople, they had a feast. When the time came to go to
bed after the feast, King Solomon told the Queen of Sheba that
she could sleep alone only on condition that she took nothing
belonging to him. She agreed and went to bed. A short while
later the highly spiced food that the King of the Jews had given
her had its premeditated effect, and she got up to have a drink of
water. King Solomon, who had only been pretending to be asleep,
quickly reminded her of her promise. She acquiesced and got into
bed with him. When she returned to Axum, she was pregnant, and
in the fullness of time she gave birth to a child, who became
Menelik I.

One sees little of the glories of the Queen of Sheba and King
Ezana in Axum today, as one walks around the rough roads,
pursued by beggars and flies. After pottering about amongst some
old tombs on the hillside to the right of the road, we went on from
the garden of cypresses to the main centre of interest, which is
the Park of the Stelae.

Here, thanks to the efforts of the Governor, Ras Mangesha, the
houses, built higgledy piggledy amongst the great stone monuments, have been cleared away from the principal antiquities.
Consequently they can now be seen in the open, standing on a
grass lawn, and one gains some idea of the strength of a community
that could erect memorial stones of such magnitude.

The whole site is dominated by the largest of the standing stelae,
which is 70 feet high, carved out of a single block of stone. It has
been calculated to weigh 130 tons. The tall monolith is further
carved in relief in the form of a many-storeyed house, with a door
at the bottom and floors containing false windows. The top is
curved, and there is evidence to suggest that there may have been
a metal plaque attached in the space within the curve.

It is not certain what the purpose of these huge stelae was but
it is likely that they were funeral monuments. Of the six tall sky-
scrapers only one remains standing. Apart from the one removed
to Italy, the other three lie shattered on the ground, including the

tallest of all, which is 110 feet long, whilst a fourth appears to have been still under construction when the work was left. Of course I was able to examine the fallen stelae more closely than the one still standing, but if any inscriptions were ever carved on them, they have long since worn away.

Recent discoveries have, however, established the manner in which these huge blocks of stone, larger than Cleopatra's needle and other Egyptian obelisks, were prized out of the cliffs. In 1969 a French group of archaeologists discovered evidence of quarrying a short distance away. One giant monster lay supine on the ground, not yet quite cut out of its matrix, and in another place a line of wedge shaped cuts had been made into the cliff face. These cavities would be filled with wedges of wood, which would then be soaked in water. The swelling timber would then split the rock and free it from the main block.

But in this case the laborious quarrying never came to fruition. Some twist of history caused the work to be left unfinished—left to lie there as mute evidence to this day, after 2,000 years or more of silence.

Standing amongst the broken remnants of former grandeur in the Park of the Stelae, it was natural to wonder why there were no relics of former buildings as well. The next site that we visited was another graveyard. Past a restored reservoir known, like the water cisterns of Aden, as the Queen of Sheba's bath, we went up a little track to a flat place on a hillside, which the men of old excavated to make tombs for King Kaleb and his son, Gabre Maskal.

King Kaleb lived two centuries after King Ezana. By this time the links with South Arabia were not at all what they had been earlier, and Kaleb spent a lot of time fighting the pagans who were persecuting the Christians of the Yemen. This is what has led to the tradition that at one time there was a passage, which led from the king's underground tomb to the coast of the Yemen, passing under the Red Sea. Ato Kidane Mariam Gebre Michael, who was our guide, told me in all seriousness that the passage, which must have been at least 300 miles long, existed, and did not think it beyond the capability of the great civilization of Axum to construct it.

King Kaleb was helped in his task of protecting the Christians by

F

the hermit, Abba Pantaleon, who spent forty-five years in a hole in the ground about three miles away on the road to Adowa, praying for his success. The church in this place now claims King Kaleb's bones, for after his victories in battle, the king also became a hermit and spent twelve years there in prayer before he died.

Of course, as in most of the royal tombs of antiquity, the stone coffins are open and empty, so the church is wise to claim that the bones of their saintly king are really in another place. Down the hill again, back by the Park of the Stelae, we were able to observe more closely the power of the church in Axum. For across the open space from the shattered monoliths, which still lie as they may have been left after the Falasha Queen Judith sacked Axum in the tenth century and reduced it to a shadow of its former glory, another stele has been built, even taller than the one that still dominates the park.

This new monument stands in front of the new St. Mary's of Zion cathedral, which was still being completed in 1969, although it had been ceremonially dedicated by the Emperor on the occasion of Queen Elizabeth's flying visit to Axum in February 1965. The new house of God, with its silvery flat dome and carven doors, is the pride of the Greek firm of Doxiades but the despair of archaeologists, since it has been built precisely in the spot where they would have liked to dig for Axumite remains. To hidebound churchmen, however, this is sacred soil, cheek by jowl with the old St. Mary's of Zion, and their way of preventing the unedifying sight of foreign busybodies hacking away at the ground was to build on it.

We walked over the dusty open space past the new stele towards the stone gateway of the old St. Mary's church. There was a crowd of peasant people gathered under the trees near the approach, some of them sitting on the stones called the Thrones of the Judges and others standing near the larger platform called the Throne of David, which is said to have been used in the coronation ceremonies in the Middle Ages.

I was somewhat apprehensive. These people were pilgrims, still there after the feast of St. Mary, which had taken place at the weekend. It was possible that, in their simple way, they might object to foreigners going into their holy place. But the worst that we got was a number of curious and rather suspicious looks as we crossed the threshold of the arched gateway, that penetrates the high wall not unlike a sally port in a mediaeval castle. The guns in the porch—with "Ishmael" inscribed on them in Arabic, captured by Emperor John in battle with the Khedive of Egypt's forces at Gura in 1876—preserved the warlike image, for after the battle John sent his Egyptian prisoners back to the coast with the following message: "Here are your soldiers, Ishmael. If you want any more eunuchs for your hareems, send me the rest of your army."

The discomfited Khedive accepted British protection in the end, as a consequence of which a similar pair of his light cannon is to be found in the porch of Eltham Palace in South-east London, though far better preserved, with shining brasses and clean black muzzles and wheels.

Once we were through the gateway, the church of St. Mary faced us at the top of a terrace of steps. But it, too, looked more like a small castle than a house of worship, and the crenellated inner wall that surrounds it only emphasised the impression. The reason is that it was the castle builders of Gondar, who built the present church in the seventeenth century. The second church, or cathedral to give it its correct title, which was seen by the Portuguese priest, Alvarez, in the sixteenth century, was destroyed during the Moslem invasion. The first church suffered the same fate in Queen Judith's rampage.

The existing church is not an imposing building. Standing at the point where we entered the compound, we faced three arches filled with lattice screens, and the crenellated parapet of a flat roof with a small belfry in the middle. It was one side of a rectangle, flanked on the left and right by bell towers, one for ringing out good news and the other for the bad. Age and a certain amount of decay mingled with the flies and the smell of excrement. As in the holy shrine of the Nepalese at Gorkha or by the sacred outflow of the Ganges at Hardwar, hygiene rarely goes hand in hand with traditional sanctity.

Even so, it was difficult to believe that somewhere in that little old building lay, not a copy or an imitation, but that very Ark of the Covenant, containing the actual tablets of the law, that Moses brought down from Mount Sinai—the Debre Sina of the Ethiopian tale. This is what some of the priests maintain, but if it is true, they should show it to the learned, for a sight of the Ten Commandments of the Mosaic law as they were actually written would be of supreme interest to the whole of the Jewish and Christian worlds.

According to the old story it was the Queen of Sheba's son, Menelik, who brought the Tablets of the Law to Ethiopia. He went to Jerusalem to meet his father, who honoured him exceedingly, and he returned with a large escort of Jewish noblemen and clergy and the 'Holy Zion'. The Ark was first taken to Cherkos island in Lake Tana, and from there it was brought to Axum. But nobody is able to say exactly what it was like.

We went round to the left to the back of the church, and there a priest in white vestments and a round black hat opened up the treasury for us to show us the crowns donated by the emperors. He brought them out one by one, and eventually there were five, set out on a table in a row, with a church drum beside them and a large and elaborately worked processional cross between them. Fasildas and Michael, John and Menelik, the Emperor Haile Selassie—the crowns look brassy and theatrical to the modern eye, yet they are the genuine stuff of the Middle Ages. It was for such a crown that York and Lancaster fought to the death in the Wars of the Roses, with its mystic aura and power that no one has described better than Shakespeare.

The square base, embossed with figures, and the round cap surmounted by an orb and a cross of Fasil's crown look Byzantine in inspiration. So does the wholly square crown of John. They are pastiche, and their only value is in their workmanship, for copper gilt and coloured glass do duty for gold and precious stones. But these are the crowns for which the Rases and their feudal levies fought.

We got back to the King Ezana Hotel in time to see the Governor, whom we had previously met at the wedding feast in Makale, driving off in his Mercedes. Then we went a little way out of town on the Gondar road, past the airstrip, which is hardly used except for tourist flights, to try to find what had seemed to be lacking amongst the other antiquities—the remains of buildings and habitations instead of tombs and graveyards.

In fact the biggest of these remains lies right astride the Gondar road, stretching on both sides to a distance of 120 yards. Excavations that have taken place there have revealed the hypothesis of a central castle or palace of four square towers, connected together, standing in a large compound flanked by a solid wall of buildings on all four sides of an oblong. But it is no good going there and expecting to be able to picure the scene from the outline of the walls that the archaeologists have left. To get a real idea of what the large complex of buildings, now called the Taeca Mariam, may have been like it is necessary to study Littmann's reconstructions in his account of the German Axum expedition, which was published in 1913, seven years after the first excavations were started.

As I scrambled over the piles of stones and the coarse grass between them, a small pock-marked boy came up to me, rummaged in his pocket and produced a small, black idol for my inspection. Cut to fit against a vertical surface, the image showed the squared, armless torso of a man sitting on a low chair. A branching spray, like a plant rising from his loins, was cut up the flat chest, and only the round head, with long, flat nose and thick, protruding lips stood free. I had seen other, similar figures in the shop by the tourist office, some said to be genuine antiques and others copies. But there was no reason why the small boy's offering should not be an original.

The same applied to a strange figure of one head mounted above another, done in a lighter coloured stone, which must have been a corner piece of some item of furniture, and to another flat piece of stone with round-eyed faces cut into it, the top one surmounted by a cross and the lower one with paws in the place of hands, representing, perhaps, the holy one's beast of burden. I bought them all for a few cents, and we were both well pleased.

Back at the King Ezana Hotel at the end of the day, we sat out on the flat roof. Modern Axum lay around us, bounded by Mount Libanos and Mount Zohodo. In the backyards with their rubbish dump appearance, cluttered up with old bits of wood and iron and stone, women were drawing water or tending cooking fires or pounding grain. Children were jumping about, playing or fighting or looking up at us and calling, *"Ferenj!"* In the street itself the older boys slouched about like dogs on a purposeless prowl, and the beggars did their evening rounds of the shops before closing time.

Not one of them, I would guess, knew or cared that he was standing on land that would almost certainly produce a rich haul of relics from the past, if only the graceless modern shacks could be cleared away, as the French cleared away the Vlach village from Delphi, and serious archaeological investigation could begin.

8

Gondar and the Smoke of Fire

Next morning we set out before seven from Axum after drinking tea in the Leul Ras Mangesha Seyoum Hotel. The moaning of a beggar, hunched up in his shamma against the cold in an angle of the houses, was still in my ears. But even so we were later than the bus, whose efforts to get started had woken me up before six o'clock.

The first part of the road as far as Enda Selassie, which is a distance of about forty miles, crosses a fairly level plain, dotted with the cactus candelabra of the euphorbia trees, though it has to make a wide detour to avoid a river gorge, that has eaten its way up into the plateau. Before entering the small town we stopped for breakfast at the H.I.H. The Crown Prince Mered Azmatch Asfa Wossen Hotel, and, sitting on the verandah, we watched the children walking to the new junior secondary school close by on our left.

After Enda Selassie the road finds it impossible to avoid the gorges any longer, for it has to cross the Takazze river, which flows right along the southern border of Tigre with its source in the Lalibela region far to the east. Though not as deep as the grand canyon of the Blue Nile, it is a mighty ravine. As we descended, the air got hotter and more sultry. The trees and bushes looked tinder dry, as if they might burst into flame at any moment. At the bottom we crossed the river on an iron bridge with a Fascist block-house on it. Then we chugged and roared up the other side, a long ascent to the village of Adi Arkai, where we stopped for a coffee in the local *buna beit*.

From there it was possible to see the weird peaks of the Simien mountains to our left. The basalt plugs, left standing like giant monuments, whilst the softer ground around them was being washed away by the rains of millions of years, stab the sky like the Fangs of Adowa. They contain Ras Dashan, over 15,000 feet, which is the highest mountain in Ethiopia, and *ambas*, which in the past were used for solemn purposes. These flat-topped mountains with almost sheer sides were the prisons of the royal princes, who were incarcerated there lest their fighting for the succession should upset the realm.

After the Takazze river, gorge followed gorge, until we came to the final massive ascent to the plateau of Begemder. It is called the Wolkefit pass, and in less than 15 miles there is a rise of over 5,000 feet. But it is not a true pass, as after reaching the top there is no descent ȯn the other side. It is, in fact, a long precipitous climb up an escarpment, and at times, as the road claws its way up a practically vertical crag, one feels like a fly clinging to a wall. It seems incredible that there is no easier way up, no river valley that rises into the plateau by gentler degrees. But there is not. Every approach to this mighty natural wall ends up in a sheer cliff.

Amongst these heights, which drip with streams and waterfalls, the vegetation was green and luxuriant, and a welcome relief from the dry and dusty north. Then, up on the cool plateau, we were back in the open grasslands of the herdsmen and horsemen, similar to the country I had been through previously in Gojjam.

From Debarek, which has become the jumping-off point for treks into the Simiens, through Dabat and the country of the Falasha Jews and as far as the final descent into Gondar, the plateau held its own. There were no more fatiguing descents into the ravines—but only just. Close to Gondar the plateau narrows to a ridge. To the left the land falls away into the basin of Lake Tana, and to the right a vast vista opens up. An escarpment drops down into the deep canyons of the Angareb river, with beyond them the long blue-grey line of the Eto mountains, which are still largely unmapped and unexplored.

This was the last we saw of the canyons and gorges for some days. The Gondar countryside is on the whole gentle and undulating. It is generally more pleasant and fertile than the steep slopes of the Entoto hills, on which Addis Ababa stands, and it has a milder climate. Gondar was the capital of Ethiopia for over two hundred years from the mid-seventeenth to the mid-nineteenth centuries, and the Italians, during their period of occupation, attempted to build it up again by making it the capital of their enlarged province of Amhara. In many ways it is a pity that Gondar is not still the capital today, though of course Addis is much more central for the Empire as a whole. It is still the cleanest, pleasantest and tidiest of the small towns of Ethiopia.

We went straight to the Itegue Menen Hotel, which is well situated on a low hill overlooking the valley to the south of the town. It also overlooks the main centre of interest in Gondar, which is the compound containing the royal castles of the seventeenth and eighteenth centuries. As I stood in the carefully tended garden of the hotel, amongst the papaya trees and the geraniums, and looked over the back gate at a mellow reddish-grey stone wall, with the castle buildings and towers rising up amongst the trees above them, I suddenly felt a stab of homesickness. It reminded me of something English more than anything else I had seen on my travels in Ethiopia. It recalled the ruins of medieval castles in countless towns and villages in the English shires.

As I walked down to the nearest of the twelve gates that penetrate the wall, the impression grew. Crows were cawing and pigeons were cooing in the trees above. It only needed a man in a blue uniform and cap to sell me a ticket at the gate to complete the illusion.

But there was nobody at the gate, so I went on in, and so doing, broke the spell. I found myself in a small, grassy yard, which contained a square church. It looked as though at one time the church had been surrounded by an open cloister. But most of this had gone, and what was left was screened off to form an extra room for the church, giving it a lopsided, dilapidated appearance.

From there a gap in the wall led to another yard, this time with a round church in it, built of the same reddish basalt, held together by crumbling mortar. Both of the churches were surmounted by crosses, encircled by the white globes of ostrich eggs and by cut-out representations of black and white crows. In each of the stuffy, malodorous yards the lepers came forth to collect their dues.

There was no other exit from the second yard, and in any case the light was failing and it was too late to go further. But next day I was back at the perimeter wall, walking alongside it, under the two stone arches, to the main gate on the southern side. It was afternoon. Little children were going back to school. They called out *"Come sta?"* and *"Va bene!"* as they passed, and some wanted to touch hands.

I felt it was strange how the Italian has persisted even into the new generation, for whom the official second language is English. For even now, a generation after the end of the Italian occupation, which in any case lasted for only five years, Italian is still more useful than English as a means of communication in many provincial regions.

That morning I had been to the government offices, which are housed in office blocks that were once efficient, with their phallic sentry boxes shaped by mere coincidence like the Gondar castle towers, which the Italians erected for their *Quartiere Generale*, the headquarters of the province. Now little money is spent on repairs or maintenance, so they are becoming tattered and decayed. But the little children still insist on saying, *"Come sta?"* and *"Va bene!"*

Entering the Royal Compound, with its phallic watchtowers, from the southern end, I came immediately upon the earliest and largest of the castle buildings. It is the castle that King Fasildas built, when he moved the capital from Gorgora on Lake Tana, whither his father, King Susenyos, had retreated in the face of the Galla invasion from the south. Though Fasil reigned for thirty-five years, he did not live to see the building completed, and the work was finished in the reigns of his successors, King John and King Joshua the Great.

The castle towers and parapets, with their crennelated walls, the domed turrets and the arched windows look unexpectedly European in the context of tropical Africa. This, and the fact that King Susenyos' castle at Gorgora was designed by the Jesuit Father, Pedro Paez, has led many to attribute the style of the Gondar castles to the Jesuit 'advisers'.

But after a religious battle, in which there were 8,000 dead,

Susenyos abdicated in favour of his son, who expelled the Jesuits from the realm. The evidence is that King Fasil had an Indian architect, and it is true that the general appearance of the Gondarene castles recalls similar constructions in India and is very different from the Spanish padre's ornate work in Gorgora.

I climbed up into the castle, which instead of a moat, has its main entrance 10 feet up the wall, connected with the ground by a steep staircase. Then I walked from floor to floor in the wake of an Ethiopian general, who had half a dozen armed soldiers with him, combining an educational visit for them with personal protection for himself.

From the top of King Fasil's residence there was a good view of the other castles and buildings that were subsequently added to the precincts of the Gondar royal court. Nearby, but smaller and lower, stood a similar castle built by Joshua the Great. On the far side, against the northern wall, stood the long single-storeyed building, with a funnel-shaped interior courtyard, put up by King Bakaffa. And next to it, last of all, when already Gondar's days were numbered, was the two-storeyed castle of the Dowager Queen Mentuab, built in the shape of a broken square.

Between these castles lie other half-ruined and ruined buildings—a library, a House of Song, the castle of King Joshua II, which contemporary accounts describe as being by far the most luxurious. But little of these remains. Gondar was stripped by Emperor Theodore, great patriot or madman according to one's point of view. The buildings were also bombed by British aircraft in the Second World War, since the Italians were still holding out in the west after the surrender in Addis.

I left King Fasil's castle and walked amongst these ruins, visiting a cage of lions similar to those in the sad little zoo in Addis. Then I went over to the western side to visit the church of Ghimjabet Mariam and the tomb of Walter Plowden. To get to the 'Treasurehouse of St. Mary' I had to go out of the Royal Compound by one of the twelve gates, for the entrance to the churchyard is from the road.

It is only a small church, although it was originally Fasil's royal chapel. Since no one may enter the *Keddusa Keddusan*, the Holy of Holies, which is said to contain a picture painted with the tears of King John I, it would hardly have been worth a visit but for the tomb. The stones of the sarcophagus have somehow got out of order, but it is still possible to read, "Plowden, first British Consul to Abyssinia" in the inscription that runs round it.

Plowden persuaded Lord Palmerston, the British Foreign Secretary of the day, to appoint him consul in 1848, and he became a close friend of Emperor Theodore II after the latter's coronation in 1855. It was the end of Gondar's period of prosperity, for Theodore was continually on the move, setting up his head-quarters wherever his camp happened to be, and favouring Debre Tabor and Magdala as his fortresses rather than the more vulnerable Gondar.

Walter Plowden gave a very complete picture of Theodore's character and ability in his reports to the British government. If these and his posthumous work, *Travels in Abyssinia and the Galla Country*, had been published earlier, the events leading up to the Napier expedition of 1868 and to Theodore's suicide might have taken a very different course. Plowden was killed by *shiftas* in 1860, and such was the Emperor's regard for him that he not only buried him at Gondar with full ceremony, but also had executed 500 people who were alleged to have been implicated in the assassination.

The consul may, perhaps, be fairly called the second of the British 'advisers', the Portuguese being in eclipse for religious reasons. The first was, of course, James Bruce, who spent nearly two years in Gondar between 1769 and 1771, about the length of time a modern adviser spends on his initial two-year contract. This is how Bruce describes the court ritual at the time.

Formerly his face was never seen, nor any part of him, ex-cepting sometimes his foot. He sits in a kind of balcony, with lattice-windows and curtains before him. Even yet he covers his face on audiences or public occasions, and when in judge-ment. On cases of treason, he sits within his balcony, and speaks through a hole in the side of it, to an officer called Kal-Hatzé, the 'voice or word of the king,' by whom he sends his questions, or anything else that occurs, to the judges who are seated at the council-table.

The king goes to church regularly, his guards taking pos-session of every avenue and door through which he is to pass, and nobody is allowed to enter with him, because he is then on foot, excepting two officers of his bed-chamber who support him. He kisses the threshold and side posts of the church-door, the steps before the altar, and then returns home: sometimes there is service in the church, sometimes there is not; but he takes no notice of the difference. He rides up stairs into the presence-chamber on a mule, and lights immediately on the carpet before his throne; and I have sometimes seen great indecencies committed by the said mule in the presence-chamber, upon a Persian carpet.

Looking back from St. Mary's at the castle of Fasil and the rickety wooden balconies on the first and second floors, which I had not cared to step on, I wondered which of them the king had used for his public audiences in Bruce's time. But I need not have bothered to look, for Bruce is not describing an emperor at all, he is writing about Ras Michael Seul of Tigre, who caused the ruling emperor to be strangled and seized the power. His residence was outside the Royal Compound to the west of the town, and it is still the palace of the Emperor whenever he visits Gondar.

Meanwhile in the Royal Compound no new buildings of any note had been erected for thirty years or more, since the great days of King Bakaffa and Queen Mentuab. The imperial family had become mere puppets in the hands of the Rases. For an account of Gondar in its prime we have to turn to Charles Poncet, who went from Cairo to treat the Emperor Joshua the Great and became at the same time ambassador for Louis XIV. This is how he describes the Emperor seventy years before Bruce came on the scene.

After having conducted me through more than twenty apartments, I entered into a hall, where the Emperor was seated upon his throne. It was a sort of couch, covered with a carpet of red damask flowered with gold. There were round about great cushions wrought with gold. This throne, of which the feet were of massy silver, was placed at the bottom of a hall, in an alcove covered with a dome all shining with gold and azure. The Emperor was clothed with a vest of silk, embroidered with gold and with very long sleeves. The scarf with which he was girt was embroidered after the same manner. He was bareheaded and his hair braided very neatly. A great emerald glittered on his forehead and added majesty to him. He was alone in the alcove I mentioned, seated upon his couch, with his legs across, after the manner of the Orientals. The great lords were on each side of him, standing in their ranks, having their hands crossed one upon the other, and observing an awful silence.

Like Bruce, Poncet was not believed in Europe. The Jesuits had never mentioned Gondar, which is scarcely surprising, as the city did not exist in their day. But because of this, the so-called experts could not credit that the place really existed.

The talented and cultured Queen Mentuab was the last flaring of the imperial flame until Theodore, in his violent way, tried to restore the strength of the Solomonic line. It was to her final abode that we next went, driving up a short distance into the hills that flank the Gondar vale. But first we stopped on the way to look at a charming square building in the early Gondar style, which stands in a tank in the middle of a shady copse of old baobab trees.

The tank, which is filled once a year at Timkat, the celebration of Christ's baptism, is called Fasil's bath, and on that day the priests bring their arks from their churches and consecrate the water, which is then sprinkled over the people. Since it is a pleasant, shady place the guide tells you it is where Fasil kept his mistress. Nearby a small mausoleum stands over the tomb of his favourite horse. A mistress and a horse, both pleasant things, fit for a king, you may say.

On the side of the wooded hill behind the bath lie the ruins of Kusquam castle, built for Queen Mentuab when she was regent during the youth of her son. The first thing one comes to, inside a high wall, is the large circular church of Debre Tsehai, the 'Mount of the Sun', in a churchyard that is darkened both by the juniper trees and the wall in spite of the name.

On the far side of the churchyard we passed through a narrow opening in the wall into the sunnier area of the Queen's castle. The best preserved of the ruins that we saw, now undergoing partial restoration, was the oblong reception hall, In appearance not unlike the dining-hall of some small college at a university, it still had on its honey-coloured walls a few decorative motifs that could be distinguished. Coptic crosses, a lion, an elephant, a bishop, and a saint riding a lion, carved in red tufa, still survive. Kitchens and storerooms would have been in the deep basement, and a sentry would have been posted in the tower at the far end, with a superb view as far as the waters of Lake Tana, gleaming between the intervening hills.

Here the Queen resided, whilst her confessor, the Bishop of Debre Tsehai, counselled her on affairs of state through a thin wooden partition dividing the tower, built into the wall, in which he lived, from the Queen's own grounds. Sometimes she may have looked back down her long life to the days when she was a farmer's daughter and nursed the king back to health, not knowing it was him. For the story goes that King Bakaffa was travelling incognito, when one day he fell ill. After Mentuab had restored his strength by her careful attentions, he left still unrecognised. But later on he sent for the beautiful girl and married her.

I, myself, had already grown quite used to her, for she was featuring on the 60-cent stamps I was putting on my air letters home. For some reason or other Afework Tekle, one of Ethiopia's best known artists, who was trained at the Slade School in London, had given her pale lemon-coloured features, unknown amongst Ethiopian farmers' daughters. What strange conceit persuaded him not to portray her dark?

In Kusquam now they show you three open coffins in a crypt, each one with a collection of bones in it. One is said to contain the remains of the Queen, one those of her son, Iyoas, and the third those of her grandson.

After looking at these mementoes of mortality, we left Kusquam for the other side of the town, where the most famous of the forty-four churches of Gondar stands. It is the Debre Berhan Selassie, which means the 'Mount of the Light of the Trinity'. When this church was built in the reign of Joshua the Great it was reckoned to be one of the richest of its day, with a golden roof and brilliantly painted interior. Much of this is gone, but the church is well worth a visit for the sake of the pictures that still cover the walls and ceiling and the impression they give of the Ethiopian vision of Christianity.

We entered the churchyard, which is surrounded by juniper and olive trees, through a gateway in a defensive tower, and came upon a rectangular building, with a gently sloping roof, flanked by the stepped-down roof of an ambulatory. It looked small and unpretentious, on the same scale as the other old churches I had seen, and to start with it appeared that we would not be able to get in.

I walked round the church on the sweet-smelling hay that had been spread on the floor of the ambulatory, tentatively trying a bolted door here and there. But presently the small boy who is always on the spot in such places returned with the custodian, who opened up for us and also switched on the electric light.

The light revealed the bright stories in paint that we had come to see—on the eastern wall, under the rising sun, the Trinity, the Annunciation, the Nativity and the Crucifixion; opposite them, on the western wall, St. Mary, Queen of Heaven, King David, Mahommed led before the Virgin, and pious kings and commoners. On the southern wall the story of Jesus is unfolded, with the Agony and the martyrdom of the Apostles, whilst on the northern wall we can see the Virgin Mary's life story and the Saints riding into battle for the faith.

The pictures, painted like strip cartoons on cloth which is glued to the walls, are still vivid with bright colours. No doubt they have been added to down the years since the first ones were done in the seventeenth century, though luckily the church escaped Mohammedan vandalism. The priests say that, when the Dervishes approached it bent on destruction, they were driven off by swarms of bees.

Certainly in the staring eyes and the colour schemes and haloes there is a strong affinity with Byzantine art, and yet a native Ethiopian creativeness shows through. The tight rings of black hair round the heads look like black haloes; the Saints go riding in, with lances at the ready and spotted and starred cloaks streaming out behind; the blood fountains out of John the Baptist's decapitated body, whilst the head looks up at a rather perturbed Herod like a headmaster warning the boy not to be so naughty.

And in addition, from every space and corner of the ceiling, in starry speckled frames of white spots on black, the heads look down. Painted full face in rows, some head to head and others chin to chin, the round heads with round black haloes of hair and big black eyes gazing out of reddish pink features, hang up there in disembodied suspension. They represent the angels of heaven, and on some of them you can see their bird-like wings.

(*Above*) Gondar: the empty bath of Fasildas

(*Below*) Lalibela: St. George's Church

Lalibela: at St Mary's Church

The church is actually divided into two and these striking paintings are in the front room which was originally reserved for the nobility. The retainers would have gone into the back room which contains a more haphazard collection of paintings not placed in any particular order.

It was the last we saw of the ecclesiastical art of Gondar, for, although to the devoted expert each church holds some treasure of interest and delight, to the ordinary visitor most of the paintings have a sameness of naïve inspiration about them that can pall as much as the works in an art gallery that has too many examples of a single school.

The churches of Ethiopia, however—many of them difficult to reach, many jealously guarded by their priesthood, still barely catalogued or enumerated—are now the challenge of the Western art historian. In the late nineteenth century it was Italy and its *trecento* triptychs and wealth of half neglected art in village churches that attracted the hunter-connoisseur. Then, in this century, it was Greece and Byzantium, still being revealed from under the whitewash of the Iconoclasts. Now, in the latter part of the twentieth century, the hunt is on in the Ethiopian highlands in order to observe and record vital works and to save them from neglect and decay.

We left Gondar at a leisurely hour for the short run round Lake Tana to Bahar Dar. The road does not follow the shore of the lake, however. After reaching Azezo, where the airport is situated, it turns sharp left to climb back into the hills, whilst another road goes straight on over the plain to the lakeside at Gorgora and a third, impassable to all but the hardiest Land-Rovers, though now being improved, goes over the mountains and down the escarpment to Metemma and the Sudanese border at Gallabat.

Our road, no doubt, followed the line of the historical route, which probably swept inland to avoid the numerous creeks and streams of the lakeside, the flooding in the rains and the unhealthy, mosquito-ridden air. On the other side of the range of hills we looked down on the rows of corrugated-iron roofs of Addis Zemen, the 'New Era'. As well as being a new settlement it is the point where the road goes up into the mountains to Debre Tabor. The name means the 'Mount of the Transfiguration', for the word *debre* has the double meaning: of a high place that is also, in some

G

sense, holy like the 'High Places' of Israel; and also the church that is on it.

From Addis Zemen onwards the route was over the flood plain of the lake, a straight road with birds striped pink and bright blue standing on the loose gravel until the last moment before taking off in front of our wheels. Large numbers of men and women, carrying bundles on their shaven heads and driving their laden asses, were heading towards Bahar Dar like ourselves. When we reached the bridge over the Blue Nile at Chera Chera, they were still with us, using the road as well as the footpaths on either side.

We went down the unsurfaced dual carriageway, which Bahar Dar has laid out for the future, and after buying a few supplies, we carried straight on out of town to visit the Blue Nile falls. Past the big market area, on which all the people we had seen on the road were converging, the dirt track led in long straights across a level savannah for 20 miles, first southwards and then south-east. Now the Agau peasants were coming towards us instead of going with us, and we had to scatter them off the road to get by. Birds were again much in evidence. There was the heavy ungainly Abyssinian ground hornbill, which only flies when absolutely compelled to do so, a black toucan, storks and egrets.

The power station lies at the end of the road, with a gateway through which one has to pass to get to the track that leads to the falls. I was reminded of the prophetic words of Major Cheesman, who visited the falls in 1927, when he was British Consul at Dangila: "The falls would provide an excellent site for a power station for electricity, but at present there is no demand for the current, and it would have to be conveyed 180 miles to reach Addis Ababa."

Now the demand is there, and the current is used principally by the cotton mill between the falls and the town, which is a splendid undertaking, giving employment to students from the polytechnic as well as saving on imports of manufactured cloth. It was a pity that at the time of our visit the mill was running at a substantial loss and the Indian managing director was facing trial in the High Court.

We could already hear the roar of the falls as we passed through the precincts of the power station, and the noise became louder when we bumped down the rough track into the gully below, through which the river rushes. The gully is neither deep nor wide, giving no hint of the vast canyon that lies downstream. In fact it is so narrow that a small stone bridge, with a single arch, has spanned it for centuries. The water rushes through the narrow funnel below at a tremendous rate.

As with so many other bridges in the Lake Tana area Europeans tend to call it Portuguese. But Father Lobo, who was in Ethiopia for ten years at the beginning of the seventeenth century, says that it was built after he and the other Jesuits had been expelled from the country, and that Indian masons were obtained for the purpose. I crossed it rather carefully, for although iron rails, supporting wooden beams, had been thrown across on top of the old bridge, they did not look much steadier than the crumbling 300-year-old masonry itself.

By this time we had collected a retainer. He was a dignified man, dressed in off-white jodhpurs, with bare feet and a cream-coloured plastic topi on his head. He carried a forked stick and a cream-coloured umbrella for additional shade. Though the others did not want his company, I thought of the rigid protocol Cheesman had had to face, first obtaining permission from the Ras of Begemder to cross over to his side of the bridge and then getting the Ras of Gojjam's permit to return to his own side. The cost of one innocent retainer seemed a small price to pay in comparison.

So we walked up the other side of the gully in single file. It was a hot day, and there was no hurry. The retainer's umbrella was a welcome accessory to my straw hat. Meanwhile the noise grew louder, as of some great monster roaring to eternity in some cavernous cage.

After we had walked uphill for a little over a quarter of an hour, the footpath reached the edge of a bluff and veered round to the right. There, suddenly revealed before us, not obliquely or sideways on in intermittent glimpses, but in a complete panoramic front view, were the Tisisat falls, the Falls of the Smoke of Fire. The whole glorious vision was only possible because, as soon as the cascades of water have plunged over the escarpment of lava rock, they take a right-angled turn to the right, being driven on their way by the Alata, a small tributary that comes in at right angles from the left. They then get squeezed together into the gully that we had already crossed. Furthermore the bluff that gave

us such a superb wide-angle view was a little higher than the top
of the falls, so that we could see the river water above the falls
slowly approaching the edge, then suddenly falling over and
plunging into the rocky depths below in a cloud of spray, which
drifted across to us like a cool mist.

There are three main falls. The first, next to the power station,
shoots over the edge and drops down 150 feet in one fell swoop of
white water. The second, divided from the first by an outcrop
covered with rank green vegetation, is a similar arch of spray-
filled water. The third stretches right across the centre of the
river and is divided into a number of cascades, which first hit a
shelf about a hundred feet below the top, and then drop the
remaining fifty feet into the gully in another, combined cascade.
When we were there, the cascades to the right were comparative
trickles. But then it was the dry season. When the lake is full
practically the whole of the width of over a third of a mile is covered
with falling water.

The incredible thing is how all this water gets forced into a
gully only twenty feet across. It seems to me that there is only one
solution to the mystery. Not only is the flow in the gully very fast,
but the water must also be very deep, and in all probability the
river has hollowed out a semi-underground channel so that the
width below is greater than the width at the surface.

The palm trees and the lush vegetation, growing in a hothouse
atmosphere of sunshine and eternal rain, an inaccessible swimming
pool on a purple-clad pinnacle of rock, the sluggish water above,
spreading round low islands and tree-clad promontories, suddenly
transformed into a rushing maelstrom, and the high bright sun
shining on the whole wide scene, creating rainbows, flashing on
churning white water and lighting up the patches of brown silt
being borne down to the cornfields of Egypt, give the Tisisat a
supremely exotic, majestic appearance that many of the other
great waterfalls of the world lack. For once one could say, even
having seen photographs and read and heard descriptions, that
one was not disappointed.

Our retainer sat at a discreet distance, whilst we ate our lunch,
walked down the bluff to get a closer view, took photographs and
discussed the scene. The two youngest members of our party
climbed down into the ravine of the Alata and went swimming

there. Then we returned to Bahar Dar and took up residence in the Ras Hotel, which stands on the lakeside close to the jetty and to the new St. George's Church. It was the second time I had been beside Lake Tana, but its quiet waters, ruffled in the daytime by a breeze that died as evening came on, still exerted a powerful charm.

Down on the shore of the lake there were some of the canoe-shaped boats called tangkwas that the Waitos make by binding bundles of dry papyrus reeds together. They looked frail and unstable, yet it is only recently that the Navigatana company has had its motorboats on the lake. Before that it was the tangkwas or nothing, and some of them were quite large. But they did not last. After a couple of weeks the papyrus became waterlogged and had to be dried out in the sun before the boat could be launched again.

Yet most of the islands on the lake have been inhabited since the Middle Ages. Of those that I could see in the bay of Bahar Dar, one contained a church built in the early fourteenth century and on another there used to be a nunnery. On Debre Mariam— Mount St. Mary—a fourteenth-century church possesses an illuminated manuscript of the gospels, which is one of the earliest found in Ethiopia.

And these islands within my view, as I stood on the spit of land behind the Ras hotel, were only a few of the many scattered round the shores. It was not for nothing that Lake Tana had no proper boats, for the islands were the receptacles of the precious heritage of religious culture when fire and the sword swept through the land. The rare manuscripts, the ikons and the price-less relics were ferried across to be hidden on the lake isles till peace returned.

Perhaps the most evocative of all the islands is the one that rises like a cone near the centre of the lake. It is higher out of the water than the others, and it is called Daga Istephanos, St. Stephen's Mount. Hither were brought several of the Ethiopian emperors to their final rest. Joshua and David, Constantine and Za Dengel, and Fasil the founder of Gondar, were brought across in the frail papyrus tangkwas to the place where the winds meet, after they had breathed their last. The bones of the first four and the mummified body of King Fasildas are still preserved there and can sometimes be seen.

It must have been a solemn sight when the shrouded bodies of these emperors were sent out from the shore and poled or paddled across in the funeral boats. If there was ever a setting for the Lake Isle of Avalon and the last journey of King Arthur, it was here, with the gentle slap of the water on the sides of the reed boats and the rustle of the sedges on the shore.

Next morning early we left Bahar Dar and returned in one long day's drive of 360 miles to the rush and bustle of the capital.

9

Getting Mobile

On my return to Addis Ababa for the second time I grew tired of
the taxis and diffident about cadging lifts from willing friends, so
I decided the time had come to buy a car. For this kind of business,
as for many another in Ethiopia, there are brokers who put the
seller in touch with the buyer, and it was not long before, having
made my intentions known, I had one on the phone.

Cars are expensive in Addis. Customs duty accounts for 60
per cent of the cost, and on the more expensive cars a kind of
surtax can go up to as much as 90 per cent. In addition, since the
closing of the Suez Canal freight charges can increase the price of a
new car by as much as £150.

My broker, Tadesse, explained all this when I muttered at the
high prices of the second-hand cars he wanted to offer me.

"Why don't you get duty free?" he said.

"I'm not entitled."

"Not Embassy? United Nations? U.S. Aid?"

"Unfortunately no."

"Better you buy 'duty paid'. Then there's no trouble when you
leave."

"All right."

"I have just the car for you. A Volkswagen Variant, like you
said."

"Where is it?"

"We have to go to the *mercato*. The owner has a shop there."

Tadesse, who was a serious businessman, wasted no time. We

took a taxi up the steep gradient of Churchill street, circled left into Tekle Haymanot square, and from there went on into the market area.

It is rather a drab part of the town, laid out in two sets of parallel streets at right angles to each other, with the shops, bus-stations, cattle-pens and market stalls in between. If one is prepared to spend time and temper bargaining, things are available there at half or a third the price in the European style shops elsewhere. But if not, one gets home with a hard-won purchase and finds it is not as good as one had originally thought.

Tadesse directed the taxi-driver off the asphalt on to a switchback of earth in front of a row of single-storey shops. We got out of the taxi and walked into one of them, where the main stock was bags of nails and boxes of screws, hooks and handles. A middle-aged man, with an Arab's thin face and piercing eyes, came out of the gloom. He took us to the car, which was standing outside the shop, and showed us round it without speaking. Then he told us to get in and we drove off.

"The price is 3,500 Ethiopian dollars," Tadesse said. "Very good price. I know this man."

"The top coat of paint is off on the front," I said. "And the back looks well worn."

"Perhaps a little," said Tadesse. "He uses it to carry goods."

"The price is high."

"Perhaps he will come down."

As we drove off towards Abuna Petros square, the Arab began to talk to Tadesse in his own language, which is still used in the Addis market-place.

"Somali woman," he said. "What is the price?"

"Somali women are much the best," said Tadesse. "They know their business well. Of course, you know that."

"I know that."

"You will have to pay $3,000. Then you will have to buy her clothes and things a woman needs."

"The price is high."

"But the goods are highly valued."

The Arab grunted and drove on until we reached the car-park of my ministry, where we again examined the vehicle, this time looking at the engine as well.

I was lukewarm. "Ask him if he'll take three thousand," I said.

Tadesse spoke to the Arab and then again to me.

"He says he has already received an offer of more."

"Then I'll leave it at that."

"I do not think he'll come down. He has many expenses," Tadesse said.

So we parted. Tadesse showed me several more cars, but none of them seemed to be a good buy, and in the end I made my own arrangements with a Jew, who occupied an office in Africa Hall. His wife had gone home to Israel, where his daughter had to commence her national service, so he was selling off one of their two cars.

I made an appointment, and entered the great hall, facing the vast, modernistic stained-glass windows, which take the place of a rear wall and show Africa struggling for freedom and progress in the conception of the Ethiopian artist, Afework Tekle. I found a lift, for the Jew's office was on the fifth floor, and I went into the bureaucratic regions where the work of the Economic Commission for Africa is done.

But for some time I could not find his office. I passed open doorways, through which I could see men and women sitting about in quiet inactivity or in leisurely conversation. I was reminded of a remark made by an Ethiopian official about a colleague who hadn't been seen for over a month. "He's not very active these days," he said.

I found the number below the Jew's office number and the number above it, but not the number I was looking for. After some time I plucked up enough courage to ask one of these leisurely well-groomed people for advice. He could not help me. A minute later I had better luck with a woman I waylaid in the corridor.

She told me to go right to the end of the corridor. But still the Jew's number was not to be seen, so I boldly broke into the office with the number below it and found an anteroom with three coloured gentlemen sitting quietly at desks in it, doing no harm to anybody. The mystery was solved. The Jew had an inner office, and so, like one of those people who keep their phone numbers out of the telephone directory, he was a man whose office number did not appear in the corridor at all.

"You didn't tell me how to get to your office," I said, after I had introduced myself. "I had a lot of trouble finding you."

The Jew was a nervous, jumpy man. He didn't seem sorry. Indeed, he didn't seem pleased, either, that I had come to buy his car. I took him for a harrassed, tense New Yorker before he told me he was an Israelite. We went back down the lift to the car-park of Africa Hall, and there the car stood shining in the sun—an Opel Kadett painted a very light cream. The Jew showed me the dents first, then the inside, then the engine.

"You can't help a few dents in this country," he said.

"No," I agreed.

"I want you to see the car just as it is."

We got in and drove around for a while. The Jew drove very slowly and cautiously, never getting out of third gear.

"Israel was responsible for those," he said, as we passed the traffic lights near Maskal square. "The traffic adviser is from my country."

"Is there anything they do of their own accord?" I said.

"They build churches."

We got back to Africa Hall, and for a few minutes we stood beside the car discussing it.

"All right, I'll buy it," I said.

The Jew still didn't seem particularly pleased. But anyway we made an arrangement for me to return to his office in two days' time, when he would have the bill of sale prepared and the registration book and I would have a cheque.

The second time, of course, I walked straight into the outer office, where the three coloured gentlemen were still sitting quietly doing nobody any harm. We dealt with our preliminary business in the Jew's office, exchanging cheque and bill of sale quite happily. Then we descended to the car to commence the various procedures necessary to effect a change of ownership.

"First it's the valuation," the Jew said. "Then it's the High Court to register the sale. After that, I'm through. You have to go on to the Municipality to register, but you can do that by yourself."

"Sounds cheerful."

"Of course the valuation's nothing to do with me. You'd be wise to try and get it as low as possible, because the High Court charges two per cent of the valuation."

"You don't come into this?"

"I just have to sign."

"You don't pay?"

"The buyer pays."

"Right. Let's go then."

We drove up Churchill street past the magnificent new Head Post Office, turned right and found the low yellow buildings of the Highways Authority behind it. But there was a chain across the entrance, with a guard attached. The Jew drove up to the chain.

"Estimations office?"

"Closed."

We looked at the notice. It said that the hours were from two-thirty to five.

"We'll have to come back this afternoon," the Jew said.

"Just a minute."

I saw a man in a blue beret standing near the estimations office and asked him what to do.

"First you must go to the office," he said.

"Isn't this the office?"

"No. The office is by Mexico Square. There you have to pay.

I turned to the Jew. "We may as well do that now," I said.

So off we went to the office of the Imperial Highways Authority off Mexico square, and I paid $15, whilst the Jew watched. Then we went to the offices of the Blue Nile Insurance Company to effect insurance, as the Jew had decided this must be done straight away, since he was unwilling to risk his no-claim bonus by letting me drive on his policy. The visit upset him somewhat, as he found that the wrong registration number had been put on the file copy of his policy. Every five minutes during our negotiations he leant across the desk at the insurance clerk.

"Look," he said. "Will you please alter that number on the file. I never wrote that number. It's not the right number. And it ought to be altered."

Finally, with the air of a man doing a great favour, the clerk agreed. The Jew, a little mollified now, asked me to drive him back to Africa Hall.

"When you've done with the estimations, come and pick me up here," he said, "and we'll go to the High Court. Then that's me finished."

I went back to the 'estimations' at two-thirty, but the office was closed. At two forty-five the man in the blue beret came back. I followed him into his office together with three other men. "I've paid my fifteen dollars," I said.

"He will come soon," the man in the blue beret said.

"You can't do it?"

"Just wait a little."

I waited. There was a great shuffling of pink registration books and white forms on his desk. The other men handed in their books to be shuffled about. After half an hour I spoke again.

"Is the man coming now?" I said.

"He will be."

"Perhaps you can do it."

The man in the blue beret looked up as if the same thought had suddenly struck him.

"You have your car here?"

"Yes."

"Come with me."

We went outside to the car, which was parked in the street as I had not been allowed to drive it across the chain. The man in the blue beret walked around it, noted the dents and scratches, told me to get in and start up, switch the lights on and off, sound the horn.

"All right," he said.

"What's your estimation?" I said.

"Three three."

"Thank you."

Back in the office the form was filled in, and after a total of an hour and a half of wasted time I felt that I had achieved a small victory in the contest with bureaucracy. Clutching the registration book and the vital form, I returned to Africa Hall to pick up the Jew and take him to the High Court. As before, the three coloured gentlemen were sitting quietly in the outer office doing nobody any harm.

"I just have to sign," the Jew said, as we drove down the Jimma road to the High Court. At some stage I have to sign, and then I'm through."

Perhaps it was because he actually was a Jew that I did not tell him the 'estimation' was $500 less than his sale price, as we went in through the iron gates and parked outside the portals of justice. Once in the entrance hall we looked around for help, and it came, strangely enough, from a bookstall in the corner.

"Motor-car registration?" said the Jew.

A smart young man leaped forward. "Estimation?" he said.

"Here it is," I answered eagerly.

"You need two photostat copies. One dollar please."

I willingly parted with a dollar. He disappeared with the precious estimation paper, whilst we waited, moodily gazing at the copies of the Ethiopian Penal Code on sale at the bookstall and wondering what mysteries it contained. In five minutes he returned.

"This way please."

We followed him along a corridor and into a bare and comfortless office, occupied by clerks.

"Sit there please." He pointed at a row of stools against the wall.

"Four dollars for the stamp."

I handed over another four dollars.

"Follow me please."

We went upstairs to another, slightly superior office, with slightly superior men in it. I signed and the Jew signed.

"You have to pay seventy dollars," our mentor said.

"Why?"

"Two per cent."

"But that's sixty-six."

"They only go in tens."

"Very well."

I paid $70. Something was written across the two stamps and a chop was applied. We went two doors down the corridor, this time to a definitely superior office with a definitely superior man in it, who glanced at the papers, ripped one off, initialled another and handed the remains back.

"You'll have to pay the fixer something," the Jew said.

"O.K. Here's three."

"That's me through then," the Jew said. "Will you drop me by Fiat's to pick up the *seicento*. Then all you have to do now is register at the municipality."

"All right," I said.

I took the Jew to Fiat's, but his *seicento* was not ready, so I had to drop him back at Africa Hall. Never mind, I thought, I've still got time to get to the municipality.

"I really hope you really *enjoy* that car like I and my wife did," the Jew said as we parted. I drove carefully out into the traffic and made my way up Menelik II Street past the new Hilton hotel, and along the hillside roads to the superb new city hall, that stands at the top of Churchill street, floodlit at night, watching over the city like a fond mother cherishing her only child. I found the window marked for motor-car registration and handed in my sheaf of documents—registration book, estimation and stamped-up registration of sale, together with the receipts for 15 and 70 dollars.

The clerk glanced at them. "Inspection?" he said.

"Here," I answered.

"That is estimation. You must have inspection. First go to the Ministry of Communications."

I backed away, almost losing heart. If the weather had not been so consistently beautiful and a constant mockery of man's inept turpitude, I might have gone straight back to the Ras Hotel and flung myself on to my bed in despair. But there was still time. I plunged down the hill again, back to Mexico square. Somehow I already knew where the Ministry of Communications was located. I bumped on to the rough between the two lanes of the avenue to park and strode up the steps. In the doorway to the left two clerks sat at the counter.

"Motor-car registration?" I called enthusiastically.

One of the clerks took my documents.

"Inspection?"

"Yes."

"I think it is too late now. And you must have two more copies."

"Photostats?"

"Yes please."

I rushed back to the only place I knew to get photostats quickly—the High Court. Providentially the fixer was still there to help me. Then, overtaken by closing time, I went back to the Ras to recover my strength for the next battle with bureaucracy the following day.

As night fell a terrible ululation and wailing arose from amongst the humble homes the other side of the wall of the hotel compound. In the dusk I could see men and women moving about and men carrying poles and bundles. Next morning the wailing continued. A marquee had been set up for a funeral, and the reason, I discovered, was that a schoolboy had been killed in a road accident. It was a bad omen. I thought of all the stories I had heard from the *ferenj* about the shocking standard of driving of the local people in Addis.

Of course, it was no use starting early. But I did aim to reach the Ministry of Communications by nine o'clock. I drove cautiously out into Haile Selassie I square. A Peugeot suddenly shot across in front of me. I looked at the driver and saw that it was a white man. I drove on towards Mexico square. A Volkswagen suddenly popped out of a side turning, causing me to swerve suddenly into the oncoming traffic. It was a white woman at the wheel, with a schoolchild at her side. I began to wonder which were really the bad drivers.

Back at the ministry all was much as before.

"Go down to the inspector's office," the clerk said. "It is down by Fiat."

I drove towards the Fiat workshop. I drove up and down, looking on both sides of the road, but I could not find the inspector's office. I was about to give up the search and return to the ministry, when I saw a little hut in the middle of the road and stopped opposite it. A youth came running up.

"Give me please."

I showed him the papers. "Inspection," I said.

"Yes, I do it."

The youth got two forms, written in Amharic, and together we filled in the particulars of myself and my car. Then the inspector himself arrived and told me to switch on lights, indicators and windscreen wipers and to sound the horn. Then there was a brake test, completion of forms, a visit to the little hut to have the particulars entered in a large ledger, and a dollar for the fixer. After that back I went to the ministry. I had not got out of my car before another fixer came up to me. He spoke Italian.

"*Documenti*," he said.

"Wait a minute."

"I'll do everything for you," he said. "That is my job. Come with me."

I followed him back to the counter with the clerks.

"Fourteen dollars," he said.

"What for?"

"Inspection."

I handed over the money.

"And a ten cents stamp."

A clerk took the money; a rather superior clerk, with his desk on a raised dias, looked at the documents and wrote on them; another man in an inner room, who was so definitely superior that I did not see him, did something else to them. My fixer returned to the outer room where I was waiting, sitting on a stool. He only had one document with him. I was alarmed.

"What about all the papers?" I said. "There were six or seven of them. Now there's only one."

"It's all right," he said. "This is the procedure. Trust me. It is my job to help you. *E mio mestiere.*"

"Well, if you say so."

I went back to my car. I got in.

"Well, thank you," I said.

But the fixer's hand was already on the handle of the other door. "Now we have to go to the Municipality," he said.

"I can go," I said. "I know the place."

"*We* go," he said firmly. "It is my job to help you."

"Very well."

We drove together up the steep hill of Churchill street, and now I became alarmed about the car. It seemed to be abysmally short of power. I had forgotten about the effect of high altitude on cars of modest capacity, and the use of special carburettor jets. Back at the Municipality I felt bereft, for I was left without a single one of the documents for which I had fought so hard for nearly a day and a half. The only one that remained was in the hand of the fixer.

We went to the window that I had approached the day before, and the solitary document was handed in together with the registration book. After some time the fixer turned to me.

"You must pay thirty dollars," he said.

I did so willingly. I was coming to regard him as my friend, as detainees sometimes regard their jailers after subjection to suitable treatment. I did not even dare to ask what the money was for. We made a trip to the cashier, obtained a pink receipt, handed it over

Lalibela: the Tabot coming from Libanos Church

Lalibela: boys with genet sticks

Harar: the reputed house of Arthur Rimbaud

for inspection, and then at last the pink registration book came back to me, admittedly without a single document, but with the magic circle of the road tax card, with 1962 written on it, the equivalent of 1969 to 1970 in the Gregorian calendar.

As we emerged from the municipality, the warm friendliness between the fixer and myself suddenly evaporated. He wanted $20 for his hour's work. There was an unseemly argument, at the end of which I gave him $5. It was worth it to come out of the other end of the tunnel of bureaucracy and emerge, a free man, in the streets of Addis with all my papers in order.

H

10
Christmas Eve in the Bishoftu Road

A few weeks later I was sitting peacefully in the apartment I had rented near Maskal Square, watching the antics of five wattled ibis on a big branch of one of the eucalyptus trees that screened me from the road, when the bearded Angus came in. It was Christmas Eve for the second time in a fortnight, for the Ethiopian Christmas, called Genna after the Greek word for 'birth', was on the following day. After some weighty deliberations the Ethiopian Orthodox church had declared that, although it fell on a Wednesday, it would not be a fast day, and people would therefore be able to enjoy their meat.

Angus was restless, as we listened to Radio Voice of the Gospel playing over its recordings of Christmas carols for the second time. He wanted to eat out, and as for me, I did not cook at home, so I had to eat out anyway. Thus it was that after nightfall, and a good while after the big brown and white ibises had gone to roost, we set out. Leaving Maskal square, and the new St. Stephen's church, where the Emperor was to worship that night, on our left, we drove off southwards over the railway tracks.

The turning we took is still known as the Bishoftu Road, although the Gallinya name of the town to which it leads was changed some time ago to the Amharic Debre Zeit, the 'Mount of Olives'. For the first 5 kilometres it is a dual carriageway, passing through the industrial area of the big oil-storage depots and the factories.

We bumped happily along this road in Angus' Volkswagen, driving rather carefully, for in spite of the fact that the two opposing flows of traffic are kept apart by a central kerb, it has a bad reputation for accidents. Furthermore, dark people in dark suits or jerseys were difficult to see in the dim street lighting. The blue, red and purple neon strips outside the bars shone much more brightly. Ben Hur, Apollo 11, the High Life, the Moon Club—their shining signs beckoned one inside. Some had Christmas decorations round their doors—branches of juniper and coloured lights—and some had red lighting inside as well as out.

The poorer places, however, just had open doors and bare electric light bulbs within. Outside, a stick with an upturned tin on it gave the message, as it were, "brewing tonight." For these were the *talla beits*, the beer houses of the ordinary people. It was not surprising to see them there, for they are scattered all down the length of countless of the lesser streets of Addis, far more numerous, even, than public houses in Portsmouth.

We were just approaching the first of the big oil-storage tanks, when we reached the sign that we were looking for—the Villa Verde—this time in green, and turned off to the left up a rough track. After bumping over a branch line of the railway, we turned left again along the front of another series of bars, and then turned into a yard in front of the restaurant that we had come to visit.

Il padrone of the Villa Verde was a bustling fair-haired Italian, long resident in Addis, who produced homely Italian dishes at moderate prices, perhaps the best value for money in the whole of the city. He called out his welcome.

"*Buona sera, Signori!* Sit down here, please. What you having? *Carbonara?* Yes? *E dopo?*"

I preferred to order *lasagne* rather than the spaghetti and ham called *carbonara*. But we both had *gamberi* to follow—prawns flown up from the Red Sea specially for the tables of Addis. They were fresh and tasty.

There were not as many people in the restaurant as we had expected, and after we had eaten, our *padrone* had time to talk to us. First he offered us cognac, and then the fiery yellow liqueur, with a twig of a tree coated with sugar standing in the bottle, called *Fiore Alpino*—Flower of the Alps. Both were made in Asmara and both were excellent.

"The only thing you need to import into this country is whisky," he said. "Nobody can make good whisky outside Scotland, and that stuff that comes like powder is no good at all. But the rest— gin, vermouth, cognac—very good manufactures here."

The Italian newspapers were lying around on the tables, with stories of strikes and industrial unrest. It was news from the un- censored world of anxiety, where everybody worries about every- thing instead of living in censored ignorance.

"Another drink?"

"Yes, but we pay this time."

The Flower of the Alps went down my throat like molten gold.

"There's a lot of bars around here," Angus said.

"Within one kilometre there are forty-six bars and a hundred and sixty girls the *padrone* answered proudly.

"Licensed or unlicensed?"

"Ah! Who knows?"

We left the Villa Verde and drove further down the Bishoftu Road, past the big tanks of Agip and Shell, Mobilgas and Total, until we came to another sign on the left, which said, "Marathon Club." It was a square villa in its own compound like many another in and around town. Several cars were parked outside it, and a kind of red glow came from inside. The red glow and the pounding music gave the impression that inside it a great heart was beating.

But in fact it was a little more ordinary inside. The amplifying machinery for the music was placed on one side, and on the other side was the bar, with decorations behind it that looked very much like characters from a black minstrel show. Between them, in the eye-squinting flourescent light, the dancers shook and gyrated two by two, and sometimes four by four. The men came on their own. Partners were picked from amongst the girls who were already there, not dancing by the ticket as in America, but buying a few drinks and giving a good profit to the bar.

Angus blinked in the strange metallic light of psychedelic dreams and pulled his beard.

"One Melotti beer here," he said, "and we move on."

The music blared forth, the dancers faced each other and shook, often scarcely moving their feet at all. One imagined that the rows of rooms at the back might be put to good use before long.

The next stop, Apollo II, was on the way back into town. The car nosedived down off the tarmac surface of the road on to a track of large stone blocks. Then it veered to the right and entered a compound in which there was scarcely room to turn. A few coloured lights and some green juniper branches testified to the festive season. Apollo II was a tenth the size of the Marathon and twice as crowded. In fact it was hardly possible to worm one's way round the black bodies to the bar.

"One Mehta beer only here," I said *sotto voce*.

"Agreed."

But Madame, our hostess of Apollo II, was immediately upon us, welcoming Angus like a long-lost friend. Having two separate parties at once was no problem to her, but she understood the desire for privacy. She pulled us along the length of the bar into another room, which was empty except for some chintzy arm-chairs and a table or two.

"Diamond Lil's private parlour," Angus said.

"Beck's beer and Courvoisier brandy."

"And the girls all next door."

We slipped away in a hurry and crossed the Bishoftu Road again.

"It's got to be Lucy's bar," Angus said.

"I'm afraid it has."

Back along the Villa Verde road, bumping alongside the railway tracks, we passed a good number of Signor Giargiano's forty-six bars, until at the end of the row, past a little tobacconist's shop, we turned into a compound with a sign on the gatepost which said, in plain letters, "Lucy's Bar."

Lucy, herself, leaped forward when she saw our heads framed in the parted curtain of the entrance. She was dressed in the pure white chiffon dress, with full skirt and bright-coloured border, that is now the traditional Ethiopian national costume. But the other girls had not bothered to put on their party frocks. Three of them were squatting on the floor roasting coffee berries, and effectively blocking the way between the bar, which had been moved from one side of the room to the other, and the door to the interior conveniences. Another three were sitting with some *ferenj* customers in the far corner.

"Happy Christmas," says Angus. "And open up the window before we choke to death. Then it's free drinks on the house."

"No free drinks," says Lucy.

"But it's Christmas Eve."

"All right then. You want beer?"

"Why not Courvoisier?"

"If you pay."

"O.K. Melotti."

We drink our beer peacefully. But we don't remain unmolested for long. A girl with very large breasts filling out a pink sweater is presented to us for our inspection. Another hippy lady sidles silently up. The gimlet-eyed lynx behind the bar pulls out the gin bottle and begins to pour.

"Hold it," says Angus. "Not so fast."

He heads for the door, choking in the smoke of roasting berries. Thinking we are going, Lucy comes running after. Angus stops outside the door and turns to look through the window. But I'm still left inside, so she gets to work on me instead. It's hardly a minute before I have a handful in each hand, and the lynx at the bar is upending the gin bottle again.

"Drink for her too?" Lucy says.

Helplessly I nod. Like an auctioneer at a furniture sale, the lynx takes the slightest nod as a firm bid and sloshes in the Fenili vermouth 'extra' on top of the gin.

I don't feel so mean now. The sleazy gramophone music stirs me up to dance, so I caper about across the floor with Lucy, whilst Angus slips back inside again. Half way through the record she has an idea that accounts for Angus' reluctance to take part. It's not only his cautious desire to hold on to his cash, but also the fact that the other *ferenj* are on the other side of the room, and some of them he may know.

"Come," she says. "*Vieni qua.* Come with me!"

"Madame's private parlour again. Well, it's a change from eating peanuts in the Ras bar!"

We skirt round the coffee-roasters, and into Madame's private room, the space in which is mostly taken up by a large bed and a wardrobe full of clothes, with a trunk on top of it. The girl with the big breasts, a simple, naive lass, who looks as though she is under training in the profession, follows us in. Then Lucy shuts the door, and we have that sinking, but at the same time pleasant, feeling of being trapped.

But a moment later the door shoots open again. The lynx is already there, with more drinks to add to the mounting bill. Useless to resist. Lucy starts a strip tease to give encouragement. Like all her girls she is small. But at the same time she is pliant and pneumatic, like a black rubber ball.

After the lynx has gone, she switches on the radio. But it is a church service in Amharic that greets our ears, no doubt the one that the Emperor is attending at St. Stephen's church. She switches it off with an exclamation which clearly means that, as far as she is concerned, it's a load of cod's wallop. Then, to the beat of the music from the bar next door, she carries on taking off her Ethiopian national costume, which should traditionally be worn for the next fortnight up to Epiphany. No matter. Black underwear against black skin makes it look as though she is wearing nothing at all, but she doesn't seem to feel the cold.

Bang! The door suddenly opens once more, and the lynx is back again with another battery of drinks. At that point Angus leaves with the young apprentice, and Lucy and I are left alone.

Lucy's story was that she came from Asmara, where, she said, she had been married to a German. She had been around with him a lot, she said, even into the closely guarded Kagnew U.S. Air Base, where she had had a lot of fun playing the fruit machines. "Ping! Ping!" she said, pulling at my middle finger. Big joke!

When the German left, he gave her money to set up a bar, so she became one of the many thousands running the girlie houses in Asmara and Addis for the delight of the rogue male.

"Asmara much better," she said. "Good strip-tease. People gay and happy. Here everybody long face. I tell my girls, you want to make good business, you must look gay. Be happy in your work."

"That's what the Japs used to say to their prisoners," I said.

"You must look happy and gay, I say."

"Why did you come south to Addis, then? Why not stay in Asmara?"

"Business. Somebody help me here. I find this house. Four hundred dollars a month I pay. Not cheap. But I have to live!"

"And what about the girls? Where do they come from?"

"Oh, any place. Some Addis girls. Some come from small

country place. Somebody tells them, 'Come to Addis. Get good job.' Then maybe they don't want to work too hard, ask me, 'Why not live here?' I say, 'O.K. If you like it and look happy.' "

"It's a gay life—if you look happy."

"I like white people. If you like, maybe some time I come to your place where you live—if you want—make you happy."

Bang! The door opened again. The lynx came in with four more bottles of beer, and this time the bottle of gin itself.

"There might be less interruptions at my place," I said.

"I like you. Make love too. No pay."

"Free love as well! Lucy, you're wonderful!"

It was well into Christmas day when we left. The lynx had totted up a large bill. We had argued about it. Lucy had started off by being firm, then seeing a dangerous red light, she had beat a tactical retreat and agreed to a reduction. The lynx herself had asked for a tip as a final ploy, and we had all parted, laughing and looking happy. Lucy and three girls, standing on the verandah under the Christmas decorations, had waved goodbye.

"Come tomorrow!" Lucy called. "Come tomorrow!"

The wizened nightwatchman, shrouded in his shamma, opened the creaking gate for us, and received the last gratuity with a dignified bow. Then we were away, bumping back to the main road. Halfway back to Addis we passed a group of white-helmeted armed policemen looking at something in a ditch, with a small crowd of people looking too, from a slightly greater distance. A dead body? An accident victim? We did not stop. One does not stop in Addis at night, if it's possible to go on.

11

The Rock-hewn Epiphany

Up behind Addis Ababa, on the Entoto hills, there is the ruin of a rock-hewn church. One can walk or ride up to it, either past the Italian Embassy, or turning left off the main road just beyond the large compound of the British Embassy and going up through the woods. In either case one must run the gauntlet of children, and idiotic people who should know better, screaming, *"Ferenj! Ferenj!"* as one goes past, begging for money and possibly throwing stones.

The church is sometimes called the Portuguese ruin, though for no good reason. It is probably much older than the time of Portuguese influence, and its other name of St. Michael's is preferable. It lies hidden beside an open pasture, cut deep into a bluff of rock, which has trees on either side. One enters through a tunnel, and inside everything is empty and silent. It could never have been very elaborate and was probably never finished. Rough-hewn and secret, with its concealed position giving it a measure of protection, it must have been something like a primitive catacomb.

A week after riding one of the tough little Ethiopian horses up to this place I went to visit the most famous of all the rock-hewn churches. They are to be found at Lalibela in the northern province of Tigre. It was Timkat, the Epiphany of the Ethiopians, which comes a fortnight after Christmas day, and everyone was preparing for the festival.

Though Lalibela is not particularly difficult of access, it used to take several days to get there by mule either from Woldiya or

Kobbo or Debre Tabor. It is still a day's journey by Land-Rover on the track from Kobbo. But during the dry season the plane now stops daily at the little airstrip that has been levelled out in the fields of sorghum to the west of Lalibela. From there it is under an hour's drive to the village, and I saw that it would be even less after completion of the new bridges being built to straighten out the road.

Lalibela airport must be the smallest in the world. An aluminium tukul houses the office and a bamboo tukul is the lounge for both departures and arrivals. A board proclaims the height—6,500 feet. I had expected it to be cool and damp, for it was raining when we left Addis Ababa, delayed by over an hour and a half because of the departure of the Emperor and the King and Queen of Denmark for Gondar. But a strong sun brought a noontide heat instead, which hardly lessened as we climbed up into the hills.

Lalibela lies on a steep slope at the head of a deep valley. Small town or large village, it is difficult to say which. Perhaps, in spite of the rectangular houses with new corrugated iron roofs that are steadily replacing the round stone tukuls and their coverings of thatch, and in spite of the grand new municipal offices at the top and the fine new school at the bottom, it is still a village, for there are few shops and there is little business except for the churches.

The Land-Rover that met the sturdy old DC 3 aeroplane drove me straight up to the Seven Olives Hotel, which lies right at the top of the village, beside the house of the Emperor's granddaughter Princess Hirut Desta. From this safe haven of comfort, constructed under royal supervision, I went down into the heart of the village, armed with my receipt issued by the priests' office of "Lasta Saint Lalibela".

It was Katera, the Eve of Timkat, and all the priests and precentors, called *debteras*, were preparing for the sunset procession. But walking down the road towards the churches, one saw nothing of this—only a man or two with a donkey and the ubiquitous schoolboys, airing their knowledge of English with pestiferous insistence and wanting to be guides. One did not even see the churches, for they are underground. There is only one which is visible from any distance, and that only from the valley looking up at the hillside.

This, the biggest, was the first one to which I came. Turning left off the road, beyond the tumbledown church office, I reached the entrance to Beit Medhane Alem, the church of the Saviour of the World. Sunk in the pit from which it was hacked out, the situation of the church belies its true dimensions. But in fact it stands 35 feet high and 100 feet long, and its triangular pediments and external columns give it something of the appearance of a Greek temple, though the columns are rectangular, not round.

Nine columns on either side, each one below an elongated cross carved on the roof, and six columns at either end, with connected columns at all four corners, help to hold up the roof, which is carved out, like everything else in the building, from the solid rock. Most of the columns had to be rebuilt in the 1940's, but those round the back of the church are still the original pillars, cut out of the red stone in the thirteenth century, when the village was known as Roha and the saintly King Lalibela of the Zagwe line had the ten rock churches built.

The windows of the church, set between the pillars, reminded me of the shape of the top of the great stele at Axum, crescent-shaped above and then nipped into a narrow waist before reaching the main square-shaped part of the window below. In fact, in these churches there are many reminiscences of the old style of Axum. Some examples are the square protrusions, which seem to imitate the ends of wooden roof-beams, and the protruding courses in the Emmanuel church, which copy the layers of timber that some of the Axumite palaces had let into them.

I walked round the deep trench that surrounds the church of the Saviour, looking up at the walls. The trench was left crude and not even squared off. It was as if all the builders' energies had gone into the building itself, and they had none left for the surroundings.

And indeed, to go inside and see the vault-like pillars dividing the church into aisles and nave, and the cross-shaped stone panels, is to realise how much patient work must have gone into it. Preparations for Timkat were going on. A smell of incense and the sound of chanting were in the air. The white turbans of the precentors were everywhere.

One of the precentors, wearing a yellow satin stole over his shoulders, took me in hand and led me through a tunnel to the next pit in the hillside, containing the church of St. Mary—Beit Mariam. Actually we were going in the reverse direction from that envisaged in the original design, for the flimsy bridge of poles over which I had entered the first pit was clearly a modern innovation. The main entrance was below.

In the deep quarry of Beit Mariam the sound of chanting was louder. It came from the far side, since, coming in the wrong way, I had entered at the back of the church, by the bath-sized font that was covered with bright-green duckweed.

The main entrance to this complex of three churches lies up a flight of steps in a deep trench above the valley of the River Jordan and through a tunnel on the flank of St. Mary's. One imagines, therefore, that this church was the first to be built. The building itself is smaller than Medhane Alem, but the courtyard is more spacious. One can stand back further and admire the many window styles—the square cross and the diagonal cross, the swastika and the four petals. Unlike Medhane Alem it has three double-arched porches, and inside, the walls—unlike the bare, rough walls of the other church—are covered with paintings which, though now much faded, can still be partly discerned. I saw the round face of the sun, complete with eyes, nose and mouth, with discs on either side. I also saw a two-headed eagle and horsemen riding over arches, and saints in their canonicals.

Apart from the curtains concealing the Holy of Holies from profane gaze, a central pillar, left in the original construction of the church, was also wrapped in cloth. It is said that at a certain moment Jesus Christ himself was seen against the pillar, and that afterwards it was discovered that the past and future of the world was written on the stone, though the priests have not thought fit to pass on this useful information to the general public.

Be that as it may, St. Mary's still gives the impression of being the most complete of all the churches. The others are practically bare inside, but, according to the church records, between 400 and 500 craftsmen and artists came from Jerusalem and Alexandria to build St. Mary's and it took them twenty-four years.

In the alcove opposite the main entrance to St. Mary's the precentors were well launched in their chanting, with staffs in the left hand, sistrums in the right hand, and the big drum beating. At first I thought this alcove was the entrance to the third pit, containing the twin chapels of St. Michael and Golgotha. But in fact, as befits the sepulchre of Christ, these two are completely subterranean. My precentor led me through a pitch-dark underground tunnel, which led directly into the nave of St. Michael's, where another chant was in progress and acolytes were vesting themselves for the procession.

The only public entrance to the Golgotha is through St. Michael's. For the moment I happened to be ahead of my precentor, and the door was shut in my face. But they opened up again on his arrival, after some hammering and shouting. I was glad they did, for inside the chapel of Golgotha, where the altars of both chapels are located, there are lifesize statues of St. John and other saints up against the walls, which are most unusual in Ethiopian churches.

But Golgotha holds greater mysteries than the sculptures. Behind a curtain a tunnel goes even deeper into the rock. Only the high priests are allowed to enter. This is Golgotha itself, the Christian version of the entrance to the Underworld.

I returned to the surface, passing by the chapel of the Virgin, Beit Danagel, in which I saw a large painting of St. George slaying the dragon, stretched on a bamboo frame. Then I went down across the road to the one church that stands in isolation. This is Beit Giorgis, St. George's, and not only does it have a cross on its roof, but the tall building itself is in the form of a cross.

At first sight one simply sees a large stone cross flat on the ground, with a trench round it, and another cross carved inside it, and a third inside that. But as one gets closer, one sees first the top layers of the church appearing and then the windows and doors of the lower part. The walls of the pit in which it stands are sheer, and it is wise to walk warily, for there is no sort of protective fence between the hillside and a drop of 35 feet to the hard stone courtyard below. The only thing on the cliff edge is a phonolithic bell stone suspended in a cradle of barbed wire under a juniper tree, though a little back from the edge, in a magnificent position overlooking the valley, a round hall for religious dances, with poles of shining new wood, has recently been built.

There is no way down the cliff. To get down to the church you have to scramble along a trench, cut a short distance from the edge, and through a tunnel with subterranean rooms leading off it. The tunnel brings you to the front of the building, which would be practically a cube if the corners of the cube had not been cut out to give it its cruciform shape. The workmanship is fine and accurate, even though the masons were cutting downwards instead of building upwards, and one imagines that St. George's once enjoyed a higher standard of maintenance than the weed-filled baptismal bath and the three crumbling mummies in a cave in the cliff face would indicate today.

But I was not alone down there amongst the flies and the hot smell of unwashed saintliness. In the room on one side of the tunnel a complete choir was gathered—four precentors with their staffs and sistrums, a big base drum and a smaller drum beating in syncopation. They were building up the atmosphere for the procession to come, and even after I had returned up the trench I could still hear their chanting, coming, as it were, from the bowels of the earth.

The precentor who had shown me St. Mary's and the church of the Saviour, was not with me now; I had acquired a schoolboy, named Asefaw, as a self-appointed guide, and he bombarded me with a continuous barrage of execrable English. He furnished me with a sprig of leaves from a nearby bush to use as a fly-whisk and took me back over the road, which loops around the top of the stream called Jordan, to see the third group of rock-hewn churches, which are carved out of the centre of a hillock of stone.

There are five churches in this group, though two are in one building, like St. Michael's and Golgotha. These two—St. Gabriel's and St. Raphael's—are today entered through a cloister and across a fragile bridge of poles which spans a deep trench. This was clearly not the original entrance, and I suspect that, in former times, one approached up the deep trench from the head of the Jordan, with the stone cross standing in it acting as a signpost. From there one reached the courtyard with the underground cistern below it, in which the level of the water rises and falls with the seasons, and which could be fairly judged to be the source of the holy baptismal stream. I suspect that there was some way up through the rock to the twin churches, which are high above this courtyard, even though, unlike St. Mary's and the Saviour's, they are cut into the hill rather than out of it and so still lie below ground level.

There seemed to be a musty air of antiquity about these crude troglodytic chapels, that reminded me of some of the old cave shrines of Hindu India. And of course the shrine that came most immediately to mind was the great temple of Ellora, cut out of the living rock like the churches of Lalibela, but on a much more grandiose and massive scale. Mysterious tunnels and corridors led off into impenetrable gloom, though fortunately the one that led to the other half of the hill and the other three churches was not very long. Another crazy bridge of poles, across the artificial cleft that divides the hill in two, led me to Emmanuel, which is free-standing like the Saviour's and is also Greek in appearance though not so big and in poorer condition.

I found the whole building, from its almost flat roof down the three storeys of windows to the floor, covered with scaffolding. The sculpturing of the walls was being restored with modern masonry, Inside I found nothing but gloomy pillars and an altar for the tabot, which was bare, since the tabot itself had already been taken out by its escort to join the procession.

It was the same with Beit Mercurios, the church of Mercury. A hall, hewn into the solid rock of the hill, it is now ruinous with age. I saw one painting on a pillar there. It was in three parts. The upper part contained three figures carrying censers and crosses, the middle part had five crowned figures on it, also bearing crosses, and a smaller figure in a white halo-like turban, whilst the lower part was filled by another five figures, one of which was holding a sword and another a book. The crowned figures may well have represented kings of Lasta, crowned here in the church's prime, for a dark tunnel once led away from it in a spiral to a cell in the centre of the hill, which is said to have been the hermitage of the most famous of them all—King Lalibela.

But there was nothing else to see. The famous cloth painting of St. Mary and the holy child, flanked by the horsemen of the day and of the night, had been removed to the safety of the museum in the capital, and the rest of the walls were bare.

In contrast there was a great deal to see at the last of the five churches in this group, which I reached down another steep corridor in the rock. Standing in the open courtyard of the church of Abba Libanos, I watched the debteras and acolytes getting ready to play their parts in the Timkat Eve procession.

The church of Father Libanos is cut into the cliff like Mercury's, but all four walls stand free of the rock and only the roof is attached, so that it looks like a cube slotted into the large box of the artificial cave. Its small size and the narrow doors at the top of somewhat broken flights of steps, leading into the restricted interior, gave it, for me, the appearance of some pink oriental joss-house rather than a building meant for a congregation gathered inside. And the legend of its construction in a single night by King Lalibela's wife can be matched by the tales of the building of many a shrine to Radna and Krishna in the Hindu pantheon.

As I arrived, the last of the little black acolytes from the priests' school was struggling into his vestments of heavy brocade, and the last of the precentors was lifting his bright umbrella aloft. On the bank above the sunken courtyard three young men waited with ancient rifles in their hands, two of which bore the sign of the Lion of Judah both on the bolt action and the butt. A hunting horn was sounded, and amidst the drumming and the chanting, women who were gathered by the stone tukuls, that looked like miniature Martello towers, set up a ululation. Then the procession emerged from the dark church in the cave, like bright butterflies breaking out of the chrysalis.

First in the procession was a small boy ringing a bell. Next came the bearer of the highly ornate bronze cross. After him a debtera swinging a heavy censer spread the scent of incense over all. Then came three umbrellas with their bright gold thread dangling like pelmets from the rich purple cloth.

The umbrellas were followed by the centrepiece and *raison d'être* of the procession. The tabot, wrapped in rich pink damask cloth, ornamented with silvery leaves and flowers, was carried out on a special frame borne on the head of the officiating priest. The tabot, which is the heart of every church in Ethiopia and that which makes it holy, is a tablet of wood enclosed in a casket. It is similar to the Ark of the Covenant but is usually finely carved with the words with which the church was dedicated rather than the Ten Commandments.

I take the evidence of more learned men for this, since such is the veneration for the written word, for the *logos* in a land of illiterates, that no mere layman is ever allowed to see it. Undoubtedly some of them are very old, and the one which came in its bright tinselly wrappings out of Abba Libanos as I watched, could well have been there for 600 or 700 years.

I followed the little procession round the hill. And as I came in sight of the road again, I saw a great procession of all the tabots of the other nine churches advancing down it, with the whole population of Lalibela following in a broad river, of which we were a small tributary.

Soon afterwards the tributary joined the main flood at the junction by the new secondary school, and I was able to merge with the crowd. First came the dancers—youths capering and leaping up and down, lifting up their homemade hockey sticks in imitation of a war dance with spears. Then came the boys ringing bells, dressed in bright vestments—stoles of yellow and blue, with pink and multicoloured skirts. Then the youths in gold-braided cloth of royal purple, wearing the old crowns of the Zagwe kings, with crosses atop and fringes of metal tassels below. Then the debteras in white turbans, the processional crosses, the purple and gold umbrellas and the red, pink and particoloured red and blue ones; and amongst them the ten tabots, wrapped in their different coloured cloths.

The procession went steadily down the road for about a mile until it reached the turning off down the steep, narrow path to the ravine of the River Jordan. It then thinned out into a single file, but not many of the people followed. Those who did so would have to spend the night beside the nine tents, pitched far below on a small plateau above the bank of the river, where the tabots would lie from the setting till the rising of the sun.

I too let them go. But next morning I was up before dawn to go down to the Baptist's stream. Walking through the dark village, I heard the eternal noises of primitive rustic life—the cocks crowing, men and women coughing up the night's phlegm from the smoky tukuls, another kind of cough from someone excreting in an alleyway.

As I emerged on the lower level below the main groups of the rock-hewn churches, I saw the first light of the dawn silhouette the flat tops of the ambas that stood around me. Hurrying down, I met Asefaw and a group of boys with hockey sticks coming up. They had spent the night down there with a few crusts of barley bread in their pockets, but Asefaw immediately detached himself from the rest of them to come with me.

Now, looking down from the point where the path branched off to make the descent, I could see candles flickering round the tents. The sound of chanting came up like prayers rising to the heights above.

I went down. The light increased. The candles were extinguished, and I saw a crowd of people dressed in white, gathered in an arc on both banks of the stream and in it as well. At the top of the arc stood the rocks from which the water came down, and here the baptisms were taking place. The priest took each little black baby from its mother's arms, immersed it in the pool, and handed it back howling, to the sound of the horns and drums.

I walked across the stream and up the other side to where the tabots were. Some of the tents were simple khaki or white marquees, others were more elaborate. St. Mary's was an old pavilion of red, black and yellow cloth, surmounted by a cloth-bound, tasselled cross. Emmanuel's was a very small awning of beige cloth with a red floral decoration, stretched over an oblong bamboo frame. The Saviour's had a second tent for the ceremonial dances. So there were only eight separate establishments in the camp. But of course Golgotha-Michael and Gabriel-Raphael were combined, with two tabots in each tent. St. Michael's would remain there till the following day, which was St. Michael's day.

I watched the churchmen execute the final rites at the rising of the sun, the men with their books and the boys with their bells and candles. Those peasants who could read leant on their staffs and puzzled through the prayer books which they held in their free hands. Then the dancing started again. This time it was the women, shuffling round and gyrating in pairs, whilst the circle of each group set up a ululation and clapped in unison. Then the horns sounded across the still air of dawn, and the beats of the big drums thumped out again.

One by one the tents came down and were loaded on to the waiting donkeys, all except for St. Michael's at the end of the line. The umbrellas were lifted on high, the tabots were raised on to the heads of the priests—pink for Abba Libanos, blue for Mercurios. The procession reformed. The ex-serviceman in his khaki overcoat, the boy in his new sandals and the simpleton swathed in a blue and beige plaid blanket, followed with the rest. People with ailments on their legs and feet paddled in the sanctified water of the stream to make them well. Others filled brass pots to take the water home.

Back on the road the men of the church, the debteras and the acolytes formed up into two lines converging on the high priest, seated on his chair between them. In one line stood the tabots under their gay umbrellas, and in the other the youths wearing the Zagwe crowns and carrying the ceremonial crosses. Next to them two lines of precentors in their white robes and turbans chanted rhythmically, staffs in one hand and sistrums in the other. And with each shake of the metal discs of the brass and silver sistrums, they measured out a pace with their feet, swaying in harmony one side and the other, back and forth. It could have been a scene from ancient Israel, from the time of King David and the Judges.

From there the procession reformed to finish up on the slopes just below the two groups of old churches and repeat the performance. The young men grew more heated in the war dance, shouting "Aha! Aha!" as they raised their hockey-stick spears above their heads. *"Matakkuru! Matakkuru!"* Shoot, shoot! Soldiers in uniform joined in, leaping up and down and shaking their shoulders. When one group was exhausted, others from the circle took their place.

Meanwhile, in contrast with the warriors, the precentors continued their slow, dignified chanting, swaying gently backwards and forwards on their crutched staffs and clicking their sistrums over and back with a rhythmic turn of the wrist.

I left them at it to go and have another look at the churches. They were utterly deserted. In the pit of Beit Medhane Alem there was only the busy buzzing of flies in front of the padlocked door. Pigeons roocoocooed under the heavy roof of Beit Mariam. A lame beggar, left behind by the crowd, came hobbling up for alms, and on the arch of rock between Beit Mariam and Beit Golgotha-Michael sat a lookout man ready for the first sign of the return of the tabots.

He had to wait till noon. Then the tabots dispersed to their homes from the slope below the churches and above the road and Jordan stream, all except St. Michael's, which was still down in its tent beside the ravine, and Abba Libanos, which had already gone up by the other track behind the hill. The Saviour of the World, St. Mary's and Golgotha went one way, Emmanuel and Mercury, St. Gabriel's and St. Raphael's another, whilst St. George's went down below the road into the pit on the bluff above the valley. Once again the church precincts were thronged with people and filled with colour and the sound of singing. The bright butterflies returned again to the chrysalis in the rock.

I too returned to the place whence I had come, saying goodbye to Asefaw, the boy who had stuck by my side through all the comings and goings. And as we bumped our way down to the airfield—with the great flat-topped amba that harbours the church of Asheten Mariam standing up against the skyline behind—the whole Timkat procession seemed to unfold itself once more before my eyes—the boys ringing their bells, the youths in the royal purple and the crowns, the big crosses, the debteras with their censers, the bright umbrellas, the wooden tablets of the churches wrapped in their brocade, the capering dancers with their *genet* sticks.

This, undoubtedly, is the Christian church as it once was; as it was before the Reformation; as it was in Byzantine times—a combination of crown and cross, of bell, book and candle, in a world that was largely illiterate, enacting the Christian year in ritual and processional, richly elaborate or touchingly simple according to the place and time.

In Tigre the Christians delved underground, as they had in the early days in the catacombs of Rome. And in their hidden holy places in the rough, raw mountains they concealed themselves from Moslem and pagan enemies. So nothing changed. All was preserved in its primitive form, with no Erasmus, no Martin Luther to probe and query and put the question, "Why do we do this?"

In Ethiopia they do it because they have always done it. The prince from his palace and the peasant from his hut join in, each in his several degree, before the priest, who holds out this paradox. All shall be unequal in this world in order to be equal in the next.

And in spite of the modern politics of egalitarianism, in spite of the tourists poking their cameras into the ancient Biblical scenes like maggots crawling into an over-ripe apple, in spite of the new generation of English speaking schoolboys without reverence or manners, the church still thrives. New churches spring up. Every year the sanctified water of Timkat is scattered over the crowd on Janhoy Meda in the capital and splashed in the faces of the imperial ministers. As in Greece and Cyprus, the ancient inflexible Orthodox Church of the Eastern Empire retains its close connection with the State, and a mere display of liberal sentiment is unlikely to disturb it.

12

Journey to the East

It was the end of January, and we had already had a taste of the little rains in Addis Ababa when at last I was able to head east to the city where Arthur Rimbaud, the idol of the 'beat' generation, spent most of his working life.

And what a strange life it was! As one of the brightest boys of his generation at school in Charleville in north-east France Rimbaud was already writing poetry of very great promise as well as being a brilliant student. His mother naturally hoped that he would get a safe job in the civil service and rise to high office in government administration. But she was narrow-minded, so narrow-minded that she even objected to her son reading Victor Hugo's *Les Misérables*. The son revolted. His father, an army officer, had already gone away.

So Arthur, aged 16, went off to Paris, having already had a poem published in a literary review. It was 1870 and France was at war with Prussia. He was soon sent home destitute. The following year he sent some more poems to Verlaine, an older man who already had a reputation as a poet, and Verlaine replied, "Come, beloved great soul, you are called, you are awaited."

That was the beginning of the two years of tumultuous Bohemian existence in Paris and London with Verlaine, the seed bed for all the striking and original poetry for which he is famous. A year later it was all over. He abandoned poetry and the company of poets for good, and spent the next five years, 1875 to 1880, in compulsive wanderings in Germany, Switzerland, Italy, Austria,

Sweden, Denmark and Holland, with a short excursion to the
Dutch East Indies, which are poignant enough because nothing
has come out of them to enrich French literature.

But Europe alone could not hold him. From 1880 onwards
Egypt, Aden and Ethiopia set the scene for his life. He became a
trader with his headquarters at Harar.

The city lies 324 miles by road due east of Addis, overlooking
the vast plains of the Ogaden. The first part of the road was
familiar to me. I had already been out as far as Dukam and
climbed the extinct volcano, Zuquala, which fills the horizon to
the right. I had stood under the giant junipers at the top and looked
down at the lake in the middle of the crater. I had looked up at the
Colobus monkeys flashing black and white in the trees, and I had
visited the church of Gabre Manfas Kiddus, the Slave of the
Holy Spirit, which has more than ordinary significance, since a
number of the older men of the realm were educated at the church
school attached to it.

I had already been as far as Debre Zeit too, where another
crater lake is popular for water-skiing and the Imperial Ethiopian
Air Force has its cadet training school. But beyond Debre Zeit
the road was new to me. The ribbon development thinned out.
At Modjo a turning to the right led south to the Rift Valley lakes,
to which Addis citizens drive furiously at weekends with their
camping and boating gear. A little further on, where our road
began to go down into the Rift Valley as well, another turning to
the right went down to the dam across the Awash river, which
supplies Addis with power and the wide Wonji sugar estates with
water. It was built by the Italians as a gesture of peace after the
ravages of war.

All this time we had been bowling along at speed in the Land-
Rover on a good asphalt surface, with the speedometer needle
going past the top point on the scale—120 kilometres an hour—
on the long straights. But at Nazareth, 61 miles from Addis, the
tarmac came to an end. We dropped down on to a familiar kind of
washboard dirt road with a cloud of dust billowing up behind
us.

Now we were down in the Rift Valley ourselves, in a small
section of that extraordinary crack in the earth's surface that
stretches thousands of miles from the Dead Sea in Israel right

down into Kenya. At first there was rough open savannah with few
habitations, but many herds of Galla cattle going back and forth,
on the road and off it. Let Australian cattlemen say what they will
about the plains of the Awash being able to support enough beef
to feed all Africa, the Galla still goes about with his profitless
herds eating the ground dry.

The lonely road, on which we passed another vehicle perhaps
once in a quarter of an hour, went on into drier country. It was the
land of the acacia scrub, and the heat grew more intense. There
were no longer Galla girls with their cattle at the side of the road,
but Danakils with their camels, all armed with knives slung from
their belts and many armed with rifles too.

The day wore on and the sun grew ever hotter, as the Land-
Rover crashed and rattled along. We passed through an area of
volcanic plugs and craters, which left no doubt about it being the
Rift Valley that we were in. A tumbled black sea of lava, encircled by cliffs, supported a bright-green growth of forest trees.
With a little more water it would be the most productive soil in the
world. A little further on a conical slag heap of volcanic cinders
had been cut into to provide road metal for the Imperial Highway
Authority's maintenance works. At one point, just short of
Metahara, the road itself went across a black field of lava, with the
railway running beside it. Then it descended into the valley
proper of the Awash, running alongside a broad lake.

The Awash, which rises in the hills near Addis and winds
through the Rift Valley and the scrublands of the Danakils to
finish up in the mournful desert lake of Abbe, is one of Ethiopia's
major rivers. Like the Omo, it never reaches the sea and has no
navigation, but in its upper reaches it supplies irrigation and power,
and in its lower reaches it is the lifeline of the Danakils. Nevertheless we still had not seen the river, when we entered the area of
the Awash Game Reserve and got the binoculars ready.

We were lucky. Though it was midday, there were oryx on the
march a few hundred yards away, with their long, straight horns
sticking up like slender moving poles and their beautifully marked
beige bodies, streaked with black, merging into the landscape.
Behind them, looking even bigger than the oryx, we saw the round
black bodies and giraffe-like heads and necks of ostriches. Here
and there a delicate little Soemmering's gazelle paused to twitch

its nostrils at us and then turn and show us its white rump and waggling tail.

Past the red tukuls at the entrance to the game reserve we saw baboons lollopping about, showing their black faces and pink behinds, whilst the big males with lion-like manes kept cautious watch. They were not far from the railway-station, which was our unlikely morning's goal.

The dirt road from the entrance to the game park, as I saw on another occasion, leads straight down to the Awash river. A tented camp, run by an American white hunter, is located on the bank in the shade of some large trees. This is the accommodation for those people who do not want to go to the expensive caravans stuck out on the bare cliff overlooking the river further down-stream. One may even pitch one's own tent and cater for oneself, if one wishes, and in that case one may well wake up to find a pair of warthogs nosing into one's provisions or a monkey running off with a packet of biscuits. One is told that the crocodiles only come out of the river on the opposite bank, but I, for one, can affirm that one morning I took the fastest leap backwards of my life when one reared its head up out of the water close to my feet and shut its jaws with a loud snap.

It is a pity that such a charming, sylvan river, with its pic-turesque falls and attractive midstream islets, should be totally taboo to swimming and boating because of these rapacious beasts. Many years ago a Frenchman, named Soleillet, with whom Arthur Rimbaud had been proposing to join forces in leading an arms caravan to Shoa from Tajoura, arranged for a prefabricated boat to be constructed at Nantes for assembly and use on the Awash. But Soleillet died in Aden before the project could be completed, and still, 85 years later, the river runs completely unnavigated.

In Rimbaud's day the banks were well stocked with elephants, but with the advent of the arms and ivory traders like himself the herds were completely destroyed. Now not a beast remains in all that territory. Of lions there was only one, kept tame by the despairing British game warden, until it too was murdered in 1970 by local savages. The herds of oryx, which are the park's chief ornament, have to vie for pasture with the camels of feuding Danakils, who encroach on the reserve in times of drought or stress. It is a melancholy tale, but visitors can still delight in the sight of other animals, such as water-buck and dikdiks too, and of kudu if they are lucky on the slopes of Mount Fantale, the extinct volcano that stands in the middle of the park.

Awash station is a little less than half way from Addis to Harar. It is therefore a convenient stopping place for those who do the ten-hour journey in one day. It is strange to come in out of the wide open spaces of acacia scrub and see the French sign, *"Buffet de la Gare"*, beside the railway tracks. But the station restaurant is, indeed, an oasis. One sits under a shady pergola of vines, beside the potted plants and bougainvillea, and sips one's pastis or some other aperitif whilst waiting to be called to table. Then one goes for one's four-course meal of hors d'oeuvres, lasagne al forno, meat and fruit. The hors d'oeuvres are Greek style—cold vegetables swimming in oil—for the two *buffets de la gare* at Addis and at Awash are managed by a Greek family. But one must be careful to arrive before the train with its passengers who come pouring into the restaurant for their midday meal to fortify themselves for the next stage of the journey to Dire Dawa.

Awash is little more than a railway settlement and a petrol station. The French sign calls it "Aouache" and a short distance past the station on the right, beyond the pole barrier that marks the entry into Danakil country, there is a ruined building with "Campo Auasc" written on it, the remains of the Italian military airfield.

The road itself was better in the Italian days too. Between Awash and Mieso, fifty miles of rough road across the plain, none of the bridges that the Italians built, and then destroyed during the Second World War, have been rebuilt, except for the essential one across the Awash river itself. One has to follow the detours round the remains of the others and drive across the stone fords laid in the *wadis*. Most of the year the *wadis* are dry, but sometimes flash floods can cause serious hold-ups.

We came upon the Awash suddenly, for like most of the rivers in Ethiopia, it flows in a ravine and one cannot see the cleft in the surface of the land until one is close up to it. The road plunged down the side of the ravine, past some of the portable grass huts which the nomad Danakils put up whenever they call a halt. Down at the bottom, beside the broken abutments of the old bridge, were the Danakils themselves, a group of men watering their

camels and a group of bare-breasted women and girls washing out
their shoulder harnesses in the stream.

The new bridge was much narrower than the old one, so the
road had to swing back to the narrowest part of the defile to cross
it. Thereafter the ascent was as rough as the descent had been,
until the lip of the ravine was reached and the river disappeared
again as if it had never been.

So we went on until we reached the little railway village of
Mieso, which boasts a mosque with a minaret that looks like a
lighthouse, and stopped to fill up with petrol. At this point there
should be a choice of roads. The most direct route to Dire Dawa,
where we had decided to stay the night in preference to Harar,
follows the railway line through the semi-desert of the low lands.
But for the fifty miles or more to Gota the road is so bad that,
even with a Land-Rover, little time is saved. Besides, it is considered dangerous, and if one has to stop for some reason and get
out of the car, one has to face the possibility of attack, not from
wild animals but from wild men.

We were unarmed. We had not even a sword-stick or a loaded
cane between us, let alone a gun, so we decided on the upper road,
which climbs out of the Rift Valley into the Chercher hills to
the south, and runs along the ridge line high above the hot
deserts.

This road was built by a British firm, appropriately named
Marples-Ridgway, at a cost of several lives and a bill still not
fully paid by the Ethiopian government. And some might wonder
why the long route was chosen, soaring up into the high hills,
sweeping into valleys and out of them again, and running along
the topmost trails, with the land of the Danakils to the north and
the vast expanses of Somali country to the south. Part of the
reason is in the latter names, for the Chercher hills, with stands
of giant juniper on their well-wooded slopes and fertile fields in
their folds, are well settled by the Amharas. The road links up
these settlements along the eastern finger of the Amharic empire—
Asbe Teferi, Hirna, Deder and, most important of all, Kolubi.

A large sign at the point where the road leaves Mieso and begins
to climb into the hills says, "This is the road to Kolubi," and even
as far back as Awash I saw a handwritten Shell sign which said,
"Kolubi 267 kms." For Kolubi, perched on the last of the heights

before the British road descends towards Harar, occupies a key position in the myths of the Amharas.

The mythology is centred round the church of St. Gabriel, which we reached in the middle of the afternoon. Passing through the first part of a typically decrepit Amhara village, one takes the track to the right and follows it for a couple of kilometres up to a shallow dip in the high ridge. There stands the square church crowned by a silver dome, towards which tens of thousands of pilgrims converge every year by every means of transport on 28th December, the feast of St. Gabriel.

On that day the slopes of the surrounding hills are covered with tents. Mothers bring their babies for baptism, young men seek inspiration to make the right decisions in life, and the sick crowd close in the hope of cures, together with the beggars seeking alms. The people bring their *silet*—gifts for the church in search of divine favour, or offerings vowed in return for favours received. The *silet* are as likely to be cattle, goats, sheep, hens or donkeys as sums of money, but all are converted into cash. The total sum realised for 1969 was reported to be the equivalent of over £10,000, not counting the gold and jewelry received as well.

It is a considerable harvest, and the popularity of this Ethiopian Lourdes is apparently increasing. As travel becomes easier, more and more people make the trek to Kolubi. Yet a hundred years ago there was nothing there. In 1887 Menelik's army of warriors marched eastward through the Chercher hills. They were marching against Harar, then in the hands of the last of the emirs, in an action that was not entirely naked agression, for Menelik's purpose was partly to forestall the Italians, who were said to be planning the city's conquest from Somaliland as a reprisal for the massacre of Count Porro's exploring expedition.

Menelik defeated Emir Abdullahi at Chalanko in a lightning battle lasting a quarter of an hour, and marched on to Kolubi. He gazed down at the hills below, falling away to the ancient city of the Aderis and gave thanks for his victory. But it was the subsequent governor of Harar, Ras Makonnen, who actually erected the original church after another, later victory, having put his trust in the archangel and vowed his own *silet*.

And thus the new church stands there too, celebrating the conquest of the east. As we descended past a lake and into the lower, drier hills of the prickly pear and the euphorbia cactus, I looked back time and again. From more than 10 miles away I could still see the dome of St. Gabriel's church like a little pimple in the dip in the high ridge behind.

Legends are now connected with the church, which are typical of peasant mentality the world over. It is said that a poor farmer and his wife—Iyakken and Hannah—were childless for many years, so they made a vow that if ever they had a child they would devote it to St. Gabriel's at Kolubi. After that a girl was born and named Mary. She served the church, and in due course she too gave birth. This time it was a male child and she was still a virgin. Naturally, the child was christened Jesus, and the girl became St. Mary.

We came down off the ridge through Galla country, dotted with plantations of yams wherever there was enough water to make them grow. The drier, rockier areas were speckled with *chat* bushes, and their dark green leaves, somewhat like tea, broke up the barren appearance of the bare slopes.

It is these leaves that the easterners of Ethiopia, like the Eritreans, love to chew. Some take the chat with sugar in order to masticate better, but the majority just pick the leaves off the branches, which are sold in bunches in the towns and villages, and ruminate. They say it gives them powers of endurance beyond the norm and also keeps the brain clear and alert for study and for passing examinations. Consequently when I tried chewing *chat* on a visit to Jimma, I expected some kind of invigorating euphoria to ensue. But perhaps I did not persevere for long enough, since the opposite symptoms appeared. I began to feel irrepressibly sleepy.

The fact is that chewing *chat*, like chewing tobacco, is a pleasurable activity which easily becomes a habit. The drug in *chat* is no more harmful than nicotine, and the habit has such a firm hold in Arabia as well as in Ethiopia that there is a brisk trade in the export of *chat* leaves through the Red Sea ports across to the Asian shore. The *chat* plantations of Eritrea and Hararge province do not only cater for indigenous consumption.

It was getting dark as we approached the end of the Marples 'ridgeway', but there was still enough light to see the white buildings of Dire Dawa far below. We turned left to go down into the lowland warmth, along a good tarmac road which looped down the mountainside into the valley of a dried-up *wadi*, crossed the *wadi* by a wide ford and then cut through a narrow pass to debouch, after some 13 miles, on to the Dire Dawa plain. It led us past a series of petrol stations to the Ras Hotel and a little town with streets adorned with pavements and electric light, and laid out at right angles to each other like a colonial cantonment.

And indeed the railway town of Dire Dawa was, in its heyday, as French colonial as Djibouti away down below on the shore of the Gulf of Tajoura. The new town grew up entirely as a result of the construction of the railway, which started creeping forward across the wild hills of the Danakils in 1897, and finally reached Dire Dawa in 1902.

The imposing railway station of the Compagnie du Chemin-de-fer Franco-Ethiopien was then built. For many years it remained the terminus, because when Menelik heard that the company was about to pass out of private hands and come under the control of the French state, he stopped further work. The railway did not, in fact, reach Addis Ababa until 1918, twenty years after the first rails were laid, by which time the company was under new management.

Strolling through the streets of Dire Dawa before dinner, we might have been in some little town in the Mediterranean. There were shops with French signs on them, café tables on the verandahs of hotels, the offices of Greek forwarding agents, and even an office for the "Liberation Movement of Free Djibouti." The station itself, crowded twice a day when the trains come in, looked like some small provincial junction in India, with tattered timetable posters and the list of special trains for the Kulubi festival a month ago still stuck on the wall, whilst a shunter clanked away in the darkness of the sidings.

Not far from the station the bungalows of the railway employees and the railway club completed the picture of an African Bhowani Junction, with Ras Makonnen's high palace and its arabesque gateway in the place of a maharaja's seat, and lean women of the Somali breed instead of Indians in the street. The two-wheeled rubber-tyred pony carts were even called by the Indian name of *gari*.

That night I slept under a fan, and was woken in the small

hours by a chorus of dogs barking under a full moon. Their wild howling put me in mind of the other, older Dire Dawa on the far side of the wide wadi, which sprawls across the plain as far as the surrounding hills.

Next day we went to see it and found it much larger than we had expected. It was almost an Arab town, with the formless dirty white cuboid houses of the poorer quarters of countless cities of the Middle East. Camels were as conspicuous as donkeys, and the rough road led past the whitewashed cubes and a village of huts made of flattened kerosene tins straight into a scrubland of prickly pear.

Here, beside the lower reaches of the wadi, a large Christian cemetery had been laid out with an eye to a more and more predominantly Amharic future, whilst, close by, blue and white maribou storks strutted about on the city's refuse piles. After that there was nothing. We followed a rough road, which climbed a low ridge, leaving the railway line on the lower ground to the left. The town disappeared behind us, and at once we were in a complete wilderness of acacia scrub and dry camel thorn.

The road was no more than a track, rising and dipping over bumps in the landscape and crawling painfully through gullies that would be full of flash floods it if ever rained. The crest of each ridge simply revealed another jumbled, flat valley with an identical ridge beyond. And so it would go on, for in 140 miles up to the point where the track regains the railway at the tiny settlement of Aysha, there is absolutely no staging-post or group of permanent habitations.

Yet this is the main road to Djibouti, fallen into such disrepair that no one but a fool would attempt it without a couple of Land-Rovers and a useful armament. It is in striking contrast with the fine new road built across the Danakil desert to Ethiopia's own port of Assab, further north just inside the Red Sea.

Arms are advisable, for although there are no habitations, the scrubland is by no means uninhabited. In the short distance that we penetrated into the wilderness we passed a dozen or more conveys of camels heading for Dire Dawa. The nervousness of the beasts, when our Land-Rover closed with them, showed that they were very unused to traffic.

The camel drivers were the slim, wiry Danakils of the desert,

the African counterparts of the Arabian Bedouin. All were armed
with the ubiquitous curved Danakil knife, slung from the waist in
a leather sheath. Many carried rifles over their shoulders as well,
some had spears, and others electric torches, showing that they
expected to be still on the road after dark. Most of them also had
hair-picks stuck into their tight curls, which looked like single
horns on the tops of their heads. They were not at all inclined to
hurry off the track to let a mere vehicle pass. Holding up a hand in
a gesture that seemed to be a mixture of a greeting and a threat,
they made us wait until their camel trains had moved comfortably
aside before letting us proceed.

I was not keen to tangle with them, for in their own territory we
were completely at their mercy. Though their reputation for
savagery and as collectors of testicles has somewhat abated in the
twentieth century, they are still renowned for their quick tempers
and jealous independence of spirit. They are the people of whom
Shakespeare writes, when Othello beguiles Desdemona with tales
of his experiences as a campaigning soldier:

> The Anthropophagi, and men whose heads
> Do grow beneath their shoulders.

It is not the "anthropophagi"—the cannibals—who are the
Danakils, but the others. For the fierce Danakils, whom Arthur
Rimbaud and the traders of the nineteenth century came to dread
as slaughterers of merchants and plunderers of caravans on the
terrible trail from the coast to the highlands, had the custom of
squatting on the ground, ready to leap up at any moment and
spring an ambush. Whilst in this posture their bodies, except for
their eyes and mops of black hair, were almost completely covered
by their big shields. The black leather shields were decorated with
patterns of white, which often had the appearance of eyes and noses
And so, as they sat motionless on the ground, they looked at a
distance as though their faces were on their chests.

Apart from this they had an unenviable reputation for ugliness,
which was probably exaggerated because of the fear they engen-
dered by their savage customs. Those that I saw had quite fine
Arab-style features, though I must admit that their grimaces were
so ambiguous that it was impossible to say whether they were
smiling in friendliness or scowling with suspicion.

There was no doubt about the women, however. They were naked to the waist, and their quick, flashing eyes, beneath their neatly braided hair, showed wit and intelligence as well as a fine appearance. Though their looks soon faded, the young girls were beautifully formed creatures, built on a small scale and moving with the grace of gazelles.

We were quite relieved to get back to Dire Dawa out of the Danakil country with our anatomies still intact and our voices still deep and manly, for though they are friendly and hospitable enough to those who go amongst them with the right introductions, they are still people it is dangerous to trifle with. But as for me, I admired their nomadic independence of spirit and their belief that a man with a camel is just as good as a man with a motor-car. It was good to see them on the move with the curved frameworks of their grass huts slung on either side of their camels, to wave to their little children tending their goats and their goat-like Danakil sheep, and to see their high-spirited, small-breasted girls washing in the wadi and delighting in their short lives under the sun.

K

13

The City of
Arthur Rimbaud

Next morning, as we drove back up the escarpment towards the junction with the ridge road, it seemed to me that we had already delayed far too long on our way to the ultimate goal of my eastern journey—the fabulous old walled city of Harar. But now it was not far away, only another twenty miles beyond the road fork along the flat surface of a plateau and past two lakes, the first of which is said to contain the sunken tomb of a Moslem leader, Sheik Adeli, and the second of which has the Agricultural School of Haile Selassie University beside it.

The lakes with their reed beds and flocks of coot and hern and the avenues of eucalyptus trees bordering the fields, all bright in the fresh sunlight of the hills, made a delightful approach to the ancient city. So when we came down over the last rise and looked down on the buildings of Harar, standing at 6,000 feet above sea level on the sun-drenched southern slope of the hills, it was difficult to imagine the sinister reputation of the place in the past.

Yet, like Shiraz in Persia and many another place enjoying a perfect climate and surrounded by fertile lands, Harar has not escaped evil times. It's remote past is lost in obscurity, but it may well have been a Christian city before it was taken over by Moslems from South Arabia not long after the death of Mohammed himself. In the sixteenth century Ahmed Gragn, the 'left-handed',

issued forth from Harar and became the deadly scourge of the
Ethiopian Christians until he was finally killed with the aid of
Portuguese soldiers. After that the Galla tribes poured up from
the south and surged round Harar. As a result the Moslem capital
was moved to Aussa in the heart of the desert to the north.

Harar became the capital again after the pagan Gallas had been
pacified and converted to Islam. But for centuries the city was
closed to Europeans. Richard Burton's journey from Aden,
finally entering Harar disguised as an Arab merchant after two
months on the way, has become famous. He was the first known
European to set foot in the city in modern times, and his descrip-
tion of it as it was in 1855, in his book *First Footsteps in East Africa,*
gives the impression that it had become considerably run down
under the government of a vicious and autocratic emir.

> The present city of Harar [Burton says] is about one mile
> long by half that breadth. An irregular wall, lately repaired, but
> ignorant of cannon is pierced with five large gates, and
> supported by oval towers of artless construction. The material
> of the houses and defences is rough stones, the granites and
> sandstones of the hills, cemented, like the ancient Galla cities,
> with clay. The only large building is the Jami or Cathedral, a
> long barn of poverty-stricken appearance, with broken-down
> gates, and two white-washed minarets of truncated conoid
> shape. They were built by Turkish architects from Mocha and
> Hodaydah: one of them lately fell, and has been replaced by an
> inferior effort of Harari art. There are a few trees in the city,
> but it contains none of those gardens which give to Eastern
> settlements that pleasant view of town and country combined.
> The streets are narrow lanes, up hill and down dale, strewed
> with gigantic rubbish heaps, upon which repose packs of mangy,
> one-eyed dogs, and even the best are encumbered with rocks
> and stones. The habitations are mostly long, flat-roofed sheds,
> double-storeyed, with doors composed of a single plank, and
> holes for windows pierced high above the ground, and decorated
> with miserable woodwork.

As we came down through the woods into the town, I was
curious to see how modern Harar compared with the city Burton
saw over a hundred years ago. But of course the first impression
was completely different, as we were approaching the city down

the straight dual carriageway of the new town without the city wall, with its military academy, its provincial government offices, its Ras Hotel and its large equestrian statue of Ras Makonnen, father of the Emperor of Ethiopia.

It was not until we got to the gate of the Duke of Harar, named after the Emperor's eldest son, who was killed in a motor accident in 1957, that I got my first glimpse of the old town which Burton saw. But the Gate of the Duke, itself, is a modern addition, a breach in the walls cut for the convenience of motor traffic, and in effect a sixth gate added to the other five, which are still in use. The nearest of the original gates is a short distance to the right. Called the Shoa gate, it stands above the Christian market, which is outside the walls like the modern government buildings, but it has been sadly defaced by an indiscriminate plastering of white-wash.

By this time I was fortunate in having the company of an Irish-man, named Dan O'Dowd, who was working as a trainer of tea-chers in Harar and was so enthusiastic about the antiquities that he had even tried to get donations of cement to help rebuild the crumbling walls. He took me straight to the central piazza of the city, which is called the Faras Maghala, the 'Horse Place'. Though I doubt if one could hire horses there now, it may well have been the horse-dealers' preserve in Burton's day.

However, it is certain that Burton would not have seen the church of the Saviour of the World, which stands on the eastern side of the square, for it was built by the Amharas after Menelik's conquest. Abdullahi, the last of the emirs, who had been ruling the city under Anglo-Egyptian protection, had refused to recognise Menelik's overlordship unless he became a Moslem. Menelik's answer was to knock down the mosque and build a Christian church over its ruins.

But this was not the Jami mosque that Burton mentions. The mosque by the Faras Maghala was put up by the Egyptians in 1875 after Raouf Pasha's 4,000 men had taken over the city and forced the emir to recognise the Khedive of Egypt as overlord. To reach the Mosque of Assembly, which Burton calls the "Jami or Cathedral", we drove further on towards the Erer gate on the eastern side of the city.

We did not enter, but it did not look as if it had changed much.

The whitewashed minarets of truncated conoid shape were still there, looking like lighthouses on unimportant Irish coasts, and the building still had its poor, barn-like appearance. We turned up a narrow lane such as Burton has described, but without the rubbish heaps and packs of dogs that he mentions, and skirted the mosque to reach a gateway, which led into a modest courtyard surrounded by unpretentious single-storey buildings covered with the universal whitewash.

Dan was evidently well known here, for a small boy led us willingly to the open entrance of the building on the far side. We took off our shoes and entered. Inside, half of the square room was occupied by a low, carpeted dais, on which we were invited to sit. Below the dais a row of ageing women had come to squat and see the visitors. They wore the thigh-length tunics and tight, tapering trousers in flowered prints of the Aderi—the native families of Harar.

"You are now sitting on the throne of the emirs," Dan said.

A young man came forward and offered us biscuits. I looked around. The three white walls beside and behind the 'throne' were adorned with enamel washbasins, tacked on in pairs. There must have been close on a hundred of them, bottoms up, painted in broad strokes of pink and yellow, blue and green. They looked weird and garish in such a setting. But no doubt as the first, most coveted products of the manufacturing nations, brought up on camel back from the sun-scorched coast, such things were highly prized in their day and fit for a king to fasten to his walls as his first trophies from the industrial world.

We rose to go. "*Shukriya*" (thank you in Arabic) we said to the young man. "*Salaam aleikum!*" (Peace be with you), the old women murmured. The little children leapt up to escort us to the gate and beg for alms. It seemed a miserable come-down for a once noble family, though I was told that some of them were still well-to-do through trading with the Galla. Yet even in Burton's days the emir was no more than what he describes as a "petty prince". This is how he kept his dignity at that time:

> The Emir Ahmed is alive to the fact that some state should hedge a prince. [Burton says.] Neither weapons nor rosaries are allowed in his presence; a chamberlain's robe acts as a spitoon; whenever anything is given or taken from him, his hands must be

kissed; even on horseback two attendants fan him with the hem of their garments. . . . He rides to mosque escorted by a dozen horsemen, and a score of footmen with guns and whips precede him: by his side walks an officer shading him with a huge and heavily fringed red satin umbrella—from India to Abyssinia the sign of princely dignity. Even at his prayers two or three chosen matchlockmen stand over him with lighted fuses. When he rides forth in public, he is escorted by a party of fifty men: the running footmen crack their whips and shout '*Let! Let!*' (Go! Go!) and the citizens avoid stripes by retreating into the nearest house or running into another street.

But twenty years later the emir's wings were clipped. Ahmed's son became a mere puppet of the Egyptians, and Raouf Pasha built himself an imposing house that was far superior to Abdullahi's 'palace'. At that time, so the story goes, the women took to wearing tight trousers to give themselves a line of defence against the lubricity of the soldiers. At that time, too, the first Frenchman came to live in Harar. His name was Arthur Rimbaud, and he arrived from Aden in December 1880. He was followed three years later by his compatriot, André Jarosseau, who became Bishop of Harar and lived there for fifty-eight years.

Dan took me from the throne of the emirs eastwards along another narrow lane to reach the former house of the French bishop, who started life in Harar as third apostolic vicar to the Gallas. We found a two-storeyed building in poor repair, and were greeted by an African priest, who said that it was decaying because it had to be left exactly as it was when Jarosseau was living there. But the church, with its Latin quotations on the twin doors— *Tu es Petrus* and *Tibi davo claves*—and its altar screens of carved black local hardwood, was better kept. And there was even a little school in session beyond the convent for the African nuns and up against the northern wall of the city.

Nevertheless in the eighteen years that had elapsed since the Free French Forces nailed their memorial plaque for André Jarosseau to the wall by the church door, the whole of the Catholic compound seemed to have fallen on poor times.

"The present Bishop of Harar lives at Nazareth," the priest said. "Perhaps he stays there so that he can be near Addis Ababa, the capital."

It seemed that his absence from his flock was felt, and I was not sorry to return from the quiet sadness of the seminary to the bustle of the town. We went out by the Erer gate, past a spirited gang of young Galla girls, and skirted the insubstantial walls to re-enter them elsewhere and make our way to the Moslem market.

The scene was a lively one, with nearly every square yard of space taken up by the little piles of wares that the Galla women bring in from the surrounding villages to sell in the town. Small heaps of potatoes or onions or yams were close by bundles of firewood or bags of peppers or chillis. One had to step over them to get from one side to the other.

But the market women and girls did not seem to mind. They laughed gaily. Unveiled and free, with golden and silver fillets round their hair and necks, chunky bangles and bracelets, and gold and silver ear pendants, they looked happy to be alive. Dan went up to one or two of them and tipped them under the ear. They did not seem offended, and he was only looking to see whether they were wearing Maria Theresa silver dollars or gold sovereigns or rare coins from Arabia.

This, at any rate, was a far cry from the scene reported by Burton, and a change for the better, even though Harar remains under the foreign rule of Addis. For in his day the market was in slaves.

Harar is still, as of old [he says] the great half way house for slaves from Zangaro, Gurague, and the Galla tribes, Alo and others: Abyssinians and Amharas, the most valued, have become rare since the king of Shoa prohibited the exportation. Women vary in value from 100 to 400 Ashrafis, boys from 9 to 150: the worst are kept for domestic purposes, the best are driven and exported by the Western Arabs or by the subjects of H.H. the Imam of Muskat, in exchange for rice and dates. I need scarcely say that commerce would thrive on the decline of slavery: whilst the Felateas or man-razzias are allowed to continue, it is vain to expect industry in the land.

Though some, like the tougher gun-runners and traders, might have regretted the passing of the bad old days, the ending of the trade in human merchandise must have been regarded by most as a milestone on the road of human progress. Indeed the strangest thing of all about the slave trade is how long Africa remained a source of human goods for both white man and brown man alike, when the rest of the world had stopped selling their neighbours into slavery centuries before. It seems as though the African was apt for slavery, just as the Slav was apt for torture and the German for the sado-masochistic syndrome.

Slavery, of course, still exists in pockets in the back alleys of the world, and is widespread under other names in other climes. But when Arthur Rimbaud first reached Harar, it was still a routine affair of whips and fetters and half-naked black bodies, though already regarded as a vile business by most of the world. Dr. Enid Starkie, in the third edition of her full-length study of the French poet, published in 1961, even claims to have proof that he, himself, was "in some measure implicated in the traffic in slaves". And in so doing she has set us an enigma.

It is an enigma of considerable importance, for her absorbing work *Arthur Rimbaud*, first published in 1938, is undoubtedly the main source of information for most English-speaking students of the poet. When, in the first edition of her book, Dr. Starkie referred to one of Rimbaud's employers, César Tian, she described him as a gun-runner and perhaps a slaver. This provoked an angry reaction from the dead man's son, as a result of which she wrote an open letter, dated 30th June 1939, to the editor of a French literary review, which was to be inserted in the French edition of her study of the poet. This letter I have translated as follows: "I said that most of César Tian's money was made from gun-running. This remark is not founded on any document, it is simply a personal supposition. . . . To the supposition about gun-running I added the following phrase: 'and perhaps even of slave-trading—for the two traffics were inseparably linked together'. This hypothesis is not founded on any document either. . . . The supposition about slave-trading came from me alone."

The surprising fact is that, even after these words had been written, Dr. Starkie retained her remarks about César Tian and slave-trading in the third English edition of *Arthur Rimbaud* without any qualification at all. In fact she goes further, stating that amongst Rimbaud's private papers, which she had been permitted to consult by Henri Materasso, she had found "further and conclusive proof that he was, in some measure, implicated in the traffic of slaves".

The proof she gives us is contained in a letter to him from Emperor Menelik's Swiss engineer, Alfred Ilg, dated 23rd August 1890 from Entoto. Ilg says, according to Dr. Starkie, "as for slaves, I cannot undertake to procure them for you. I have never bought any and I do not wish to begin. Even for myself I would not do it."

The enigma is presented by the fact that a significant sentence has been left out of the quotation. The relevant portion of the original manuscript reads as follows: *"Quant'aux esclaves pardonnez-moi, je ne puis m'en occuper, je n'en ai jamais acheté et je ne veux pas commencer. Je reconnais absolument vos bonnes intentions, mais même pour moi je ne le ferai jamais."*

I suppose we shall never know what Rimbaud put in his letter to Ilg, which provoked this reply, but one would dearly like to know why those significant words, "I entirely appreciate your good intentions" were left out by Dr. Starkie, for they throw the quotation into a completely different perspective. Is it conceivable that Ilg would have written, "I appreciate your good intentions" if he had been asked to buy slaves for the slave trade? It is far more probable and far more plausible to anyone who appreciates the social conditions that obtained in Ethiopia in those days, that he had been asked to buy some people for Rimbaud's own establishment, where he expected that they would be properly treated.

It may seem carping to dwell on this point, considering that the events concerned took place eighty years ago, but at that time slave-trading was already considered evil, though gun-running was becoming more and more respectable so that today it is an important business of governments and civil servants. Therefore it is of some concern to all lovers of poetry that the popular image of Rimbaud in Ethiopia as a disreputable dealer in human flesh should be dispelled. For the evidence of those who knew him in Harar is that he tended to be unusually sympathetic towards the primitive negroes of the kind who were sold into slavery, and regarded them compassionately as ignorant children.

Unfortunately Dr. Starkie had little first-hand knowledge of the setting for Rimbaud's life in Harar, and due to ill health she was unable to accept the British Council's invitation to lecture in Ethiopia in 1969 or 1970. I had already prepared my notes for a letter to her, saying how grateful I would be if she would let me have her own views on the matter and help me to solve the puzzle she, herself, had set me, and also asking whether she had any further evidence on which to base her allegation against Rimbaud of slave-trading other than the, to me, flimsy deduction from two sentences in a letter; when I heard of her sad death. It seemed, then, that the enigma would never be solved.

Yet we have only to read Oliver Bernard's *Life of Rimbaud* in the Penguin Books edition of the poet's works, first published in 1962 and reprinted without amendment in 1966 and 1969, to see how this English *canard* has followed the French poet into the second half of the twentieth century.

Under the heading 1881-91 Bernard writes, "He obtains a licence to sell arms and ammunition and also helps in the slave traffic to Turkey and Arabia."

Henri Materasso, who obtained Rimbaud's papers in 1938, says nothing in his *Vie d'Arthur Rimbaud* about the letter which mentions slaves, though he quotes two other letters from Ilg. Dr. Starkie, herself, quotes Bardey as saying that Rimbaud "was the embodiment of loyalty and integrity. Nothing that he ever did was contrary to honour".

Furthermore Rimbaud, himself, writing to his mother in November 1890, claimed that, "No one in Aden can say anything bad against me. On the contrary, for ten years now I have been highly considered by everyone in this country." And six years earlier, when his mother had written complaining of gossip and slander, he had replied with these words: "My reputation stands high in these parts, and will permit me to earn my living decently anywhere. If I've had bad times to go through in the past, I've never tried to live on anyone else nor by evil means."

It was nothing less than the truth. Henri Materasso gives us an impressive list of Europeans who knew Rimbaud as a respected merchant. They included Jules Borelli, the explorer; Armand Savouré, a well-known trader in East Africa; Pinot, a retired army officer; Zimmermann and Appenzeller, who were working with Ilg; and many Italian travellers such as Cesare Nerazzini, Pietro Antonelli, Luigi Robecchi-Bricchetti, Ottorino Rosa and Armando Rondani.

In fact Rimbaud, as Materasso says, "was part of the European family in Abyssinia". Not one of these people, to my knowledge, has ever suggested that Rimbaud was connected with the slave trade in any way. Are we, then, to imagine a conspiracy of silence on the part of all the European residents of Ethiopia and travellers in those regions at the end of the nineteenth century?

Robecchi-Bricchetti first met Rimbaud in 1888 at a party in the Harar premises of the Italian merchant house of Bienenfeld and Co., which were located on the Faras Maghala. He was lodging there during his first stay in the city.

"*Della colonia europea l'italiana e la francese erano au complet,*" he says in his account of his travels in East Africa entitled *Nell' Harrar*, which was published in 1896. "All the Italian and French members of the European colony were there. Bidault and his friend, the polyglot Rimbaud, who used to be a man of letters in France, and then abandoned the muses, put criticism on one side, threw away his pen, and came to Africa plucking out his ideals and drowning his winged verse, epic poems and artistic articles in the prosaic but lucrative bath of an import export business. He was spirited and witty and had a truly French conversational ability."

This picture of Rimbaud shows him as neither the social outcast nor the taciturn misfit of popular legend. Towards the end of his book Robecchi-Bricchetti makes some remarks about the future of Harar and about its trade with Djibouti. "One must admit," he says, "that French aspirations have not remained in the realm of ideas, but have crystallised in such a way that their trade and commerce are building up and expanding there every day, as I said, thus making the English government uneasy and jealous."

Could it have been British jealousy that coloured the reports of British Red Sea officials to the Foreign Office, on which Dr. Starkie based so much of her original assessment of Rimbaud's activities in Ethiopia?

The reason advanced by Dr. Starkie for the inevitability of the European gun-runners being involved in the slave trade was that they could do nothing without the co-operation of Abou Bekr, Pasha of Zeyla, who was the slaver-in-chief of the Gulf of Tajoura. It is a neat equation, but I would suggest that a more accurate assessment could be deduced from the records. The well-known explorer, Soleillet, who knew Rimbaud and who also saw nothing wrong in supplying arms to the King of Shoa, states explicitly in one of his letters sent to France in 1883, that Abou Bekr had a mortal hatred of the Europeans because he was afraid that they would put a stop to his trade in human flesh. It is just not credible that the Abou Bekr clan, already generally regarded as the assassins of two Frenchmen, would have welcomed Europeans into their own cherished preserve or even permitted them to muscle in on the slave trade.

Rimbaud, himself, has given us a clue concerning his caravans to the coast in the last words he ever wrote. As he lay semi-conscious and dying of cancer in a hospital in Marseilles, he asked his sister to send a letter for him to the director of Messageries Maritimes. But before starting the letter he dictated the following words in his delirium:

"Un lot: une dent seule
Un lot: deux dents
Un lot: trois dents
Un lot: quatre dents
Un lot: deux dents."

They were not human teeth but elephants' tusks to which he was referring, and the heavy lots that the caravans of the Europeans took down to the coast were not slaves but ivory.

A more recent visitor to Harar, who has gained fame in his time, has also fogged the picture rather unnecessarily. Evelyn Waugh's *Remote People* was published in 1931, and in it he describes a visit to Bishop Jarousseau:

I went to the cathedral and there met the Bishop of Harar, the famous Monsignor Jerome [sic] of whom I had heard many reports in Addis Ababa. He had been in the country for forty-eight years. . . .

I steered the conversation as delicately as I could from church expenses to Arthure [sic] Rimbaud. . . .

He used to live with a native woman in a little house, now demolished, in the square; he had no children; probably the woman was still alive; she was not a native of Harar, and after Rimbaud's death she had gone back to her own people in Tigre . . . a very, very serious young man, the bishop repeated. . . .

It was rather a disappointing interview. All the way to Harar

I had nurtured the hope of finding something new about Rimbaud, perhaps even to encounter a half-caste son keeping a shop in some back street. The only significant thing I learned from the bishop was that, living in Harar, surrounded by so many radiant women, he should have chosen a mate from the stolid people of Tigre—a gross and perverse performance.

So we have one respected author accusing Rimbaud of being in the slave trade with little reason, and another assuming that his housekeeper was his 'mate' or mistress and assuming that she was unattractive with no better reason. Others have called him homosexual on equally fragile grounds and yet others impotent.

Poor Rimbaud! At this distance of time I, myself, did not hope to find anything new, but I had a burning desire to try to form some idea of how he lived in Africa. So Dan and I left the market-place to look for his house. Perhaps it was a futile quest, yet the poet had been a part of my mind for so long that I could not leave it alone.

The fact is that he moved house several times. So those who point to the various claimants of the honour of having accommodated him as creating a ridiculous confusion may, themselves, be confounded. It seems pretty certain, however, that his first residence in Harar was the most imposing. On his arrival in 1880 Raouf Pasha, the first Egyptian governor, had left, and no succeeding governor, even in the brief spell of British indirect rule between 1886 and 1887, would occupy the so-called palace that he had built. Thus Bardey, the Aden trader who was Rimbaud's employer, was able to rent it as a branch of his store, a warehouse and a suitable abode for his branch manager.

It was a large house built in a sort of seaside chalet style that can only have come from France via Alexandria. Walking up a short alleyway behind the white tomb of Aba Said Ali on the northern side of the market-place, Dan and I reached a modest doorway, through which we entered the walled compound.

The chalet, which we had already seen from the market, on the hill behind the Said's minaret, now towered above us, complete with fan windows under gables pointed with wooden spikes, and fretted woodwork over panes of glass in a false collonade of arches. It was quite startling to see something so thoroughly Victorian in the midst of the traditional Moslem style of the horn of Africa. The tall house, with its wooden facade overhanging the ground floor and giving it a shady verandah, was quite the highest in the old city of Harar. A 5-foot terrace, with steps leading up to the downstairs rooms, made it look higher still.

The building seemed to fit what I already knew about Rimbaud's early days in the strange city of his self-imposed exile. But if I still had some doubts in my mind, the inhabitants of the house clearly had none. A woman in a loose white dress came forward out of the main doorway and nodded and smiled when Dan said, "Beit Rimbaud?" She was followed by a plump schoolgirl and a young boy.

A pair of pyjamas and a towel were hanging on lines slung between the wooden posts of the verandah, and a chicken was pecking about on the stone floor. I peeped into the downstairs rooms before following the boy up to the second storey. Each one appeared to be occupied by a separate family, and the walls were plastered with various garish pictures, culled from calendars and posters and colour magazines.

I could dimly visualise the former comfort of the house from the neatly carved banisters that ran alongside the flight of stairs. But the first floor had the same appearance of a Gorbals tenement. This time the inhabitant was an old man, surrounded by his cooking paraphernalia and family photographs.

"Photos of Rimbaud? Writing? Letters?" Dan asked.

The negative reply was predictable. So we followed the bannisters up to the third storey, which was untenanted. But the stairs went still further, since above the third storey there was an oval balcony, giving, in effect, four floors in all. Up on the balcony one could either look down over a ring of bannisters at the floor of the third storey, or out through the dormer windows at the extensive view, or up at the painted ceiling. There was nothing on the balcony except for some bundles of grass of the kind used in Harar basket making, and some spilt grain.

I looked up at the tattered ceiling. Against a predominantly green background there were naive paintings of what must have been the epitome of modern life in the late nineteenth century—a new mosque, a church, an ornamental pond, a little railway with a light engine on it of the kind that was used in the early days of the run from Djibouti to Dire Dawa. These, surely, were not

Rimbaud's work. They may have been commissioned when Raouf Pasha built the place, and now the oiled canvas on which they were done is hanging down in shreds.

The young boy threw open one by one the battered window shutters facing north, south, east and west to catch the four winds of heaven. Then he let us rest for a while admiring the various views. That to the south was the most extensive, since looking over the white minaret and dome of the Said, the cream-coloured tower and barracks of the market place and the lower part of the city wall, where a strange individual feeds the hyenas every night at dusk, we could see the opposite hillside. On its wooded slopes are the houses of the more prosperous people of more recent times, and two large buildings which stand out from the rest—the church of St. Michael and the dome of Ras Makonnen's memorial.

The latter was intended to be a mausoleum for the great Ras, similar to the mausoleum of his uncle, Menelik II, in Addis Ababa. But Ras Makonnen died before it was even begun, and was buried in St. Michael's. When the mausoleum was completed, the priests would not give up the body, so the building remains there, glistening silver in the sun—a tomb without a corpse.

The young boy banged the shutters back and bolted them again. We returned downstairs and out on to the stone flats of the terrace. I still could not quite imagine what the house must have been like when Rimbaud lived there, but clearly he was living in some style, at any rate in comparison with the people who surrounded him, and by no means in the pinched and desperate circumstances some have imagined.

When Rimbaud left France, virtually for good, to seek his fortune in the East, he was still only twenty-four years old. He had already written his epitaph on the sentimental adventure with Verlaine, which earned him the reputation of being a homosexual, in *Une Saison en Enfer* (A Period in Hell), and at the age of nineteen he had burnt his papers and renounced poetry. After that, apart from possibly some of the prose poems later collected together under the title of *Illuminations*, he wrote no more verse and wandered over the face of the earth, a would-be man of action, who could never quite shake off the mantle of the dreamer.

After he had roamed Europe like a nineteenth-century hippy,

the East was the great magnet of his dreams. The Dutch army
took him as far as Java, but he deserted and returned round the
Cape of Good Hope in a British windjammer. Then he set out
again and reached Alexandria, where he worked on a large
farming estate. His name is still there, in Egypt, for all to see,
carved high up on a pillar of one of the principal temples at
Luxor.

From Alexandria he went to Suez, where he was employed for
a while looting a wrecked ship. Then he crossed over to Cyprus,
where he was engaged more respectably as a foreman on the
construction of the governor's summer palace in the Troodos
mountains. A plaque commemorates his presence there. He moved
from Cyprus down the Red Sea, and finally fetched up in Aden at
the end of his tether.

It was in Aden that his East African adventures began, for
Bardey, a trader in coffee, hides and gum, gave him a job there.
Bardey, who was accustomed to buying these products either in
Aden or in Zeyla on the African side of the gulf, decided that there
was money to be made in opening a branch closer to the source of
his goods.

After making his own reconnaissance, Bardey rented Raouf
Pasha's former palace and sent Rimbaud up to Harar to manage
the store there. At first Rimbaud assumed that it would not be
long before he was moving on again, as he had moved on from all
his other jobs and all the other places he had been to. "I don't
expect to stay here long!" he wrote to his mother in Charleville
after he had been there only three months. He was thinking at the
time of going to America to try to get work on the construction of
the Panama canal.

But strangely enough he remained at Harar on and off for the
rest of his short life, and when finally he was at death's door, a
desperately sick man with an artificial leg, back in his mother's
home, his passion to return was so great that he insisted on catching
a train for Marseilles and trying to book a passage for Aden. He
died at thirty-seven years of age in the Hospital of the Immaculate
Conception, still in the French port, unable to embark.

Rimbaud's eleven years at Harar were, of course, broken by
long and arduous trips to Zeyla and Aden, by the terrible hardships of the gun-running expedition from Tajoura to Ankober and

(*Left*) A Moslem girl
from Bale

(*Right*) Gurage girls near
Lake Zwai

Pilgrims on the road to Sheik Hussein

on to the embryo Addis Ababa on the side of the Entoto hills, and by journeys into the Galla country and the Ogaden, which would undoubtedly have earned him fame as one of the significant explorers of his day, if he had cared to go methodically about publishing his experiences.

He was hardened to rough living, to violence, to the harsh lives of the gun-runners and slavers. Yet his life at Harar was by no means sordid or debauched. On the contrary he looked back on his hippy period in Paris and London as the episode of debauchery and drunkenness in his life. In Harar he lived as a respectable bourgeois merchant, just as respectable as those government officials and manufacturers who run guns to the Middle East today. It was bad luck when he caught syphilis, not an indication of a depraved existence, though it could be an indication against the homosexual school of critics. He had a Harari mistress, and later on a Tigre woman looked after him. This was, of course, normal for single men in the East. Meanwhile his poems had been 'posthumously' published in Paris by Verlaine and were being talked about in literary circles as if he were dead.

Reverting to the careful husbandry of his peasant forefathers, Rimbaud, in spite of some very damaging setbacks, eventually made enough money to live reasonably well. He was accepted amongst the local pillars of society. Bishop Jarosseau, with whom he was quite intimate, considered him to be a sober and careful man. Ras Makonnen regarded him as a friend. He wrote a letter to him, dated 12th July 1891, in which he addresses him in the warmest terms of personal friendship.

"How are you?" the letter runs. "As for me, thank God, I am well! I learnt with horror and compassion that they had been obliged to take off your leg. From what you tell me, I gather that the operation has been successful. I thank God for that! I hear with pleasure that you are proposing to come back to Harar to resume your business. I am glad of that. Yes! Come back quickly, and in good health. I am always your friend."

Alas, the operation was not successful, and four months after the letter was written, he was dead. When Ras Makonnen heard of his death, he wrote to France again to say how upset he was. It was as if "his soul had left him."

Rimbaud's house in fact became a place where visitors knew

they could find friendship and hospitality. Traders, explorers and globetrotters bear witness to his wit and urbanity and sincerity. In the later years, of course, he had been obliged to move, as Ras Makonnen decided he wanted the former governor's 'chalet' palace for himself. It may have been in one of the two-storeyed houses, with overhanging verandahs, on the other side of the market-place that Rimbaud played out his last years in the city, noted for his charity and for his compassion for the poor negroes, or it may have been in a building that is no more.

Yet all the time he kept himself close and revealed little of his true heart to his friends and associates. Not a word about those magical lines, thrown off like a halo of heat from an overcharged engine, which he now regarded as the aberrations of a crazy, mixed-up teenager. Not a word about those profound *Illuminations* that were to change the course of twentieth-century poetry. Not a word about his passions and desires. Simply a brief remark to Bardey that he had known "writers, artists and so on in the Latin Quarter", but he had "seen enough of those birds". His affection for Djami, his young Harari retainer, has been made much of by the homosexualists, but there is no evidence to indicate it was any different from the fatherly feeling I have seen in many an Indian Army officer towards his faithful servant.

Of course it still seems incredible that one so gifted as Rimbaud was should have turned his back so rigidly on creative writing. It is tempting to think that he was still writing in secret, as many people secretly write poetry today, relieving their tensions with their own illuminations. A pile of manuscripts in the back room of his house might account for his desperate anxiety to get back to Harar, when he was a dying man.

But, as far as is known, nothing was ever found. Not a page, not a line, not a word of the old magic that made the *Drunken Boat*, *A Season in Hell*, and the *Illuminations* was ever discovered. Naturally, this does not mean to say that Rimbaud never wrote again, but unfortunately the one person who could have told us the truth, the one person with whom he might have left manuscripts, died almost at the same time as he did. Rimbaud's faithful and beloved servant, Djami, did not even survive his master long enough to receive the legacy he sent him, and the manner of his death is unknown. He could have died in the disastrous famine of 1891, in which the hyenas swarmed into the city, eating up the putrefying corpses, and Gallas were executed for consuming their own relatives.

As we left Beit Rimbaud and returned to the market-place, some lines I had translated from the *Drunken Boat* many years before, kept hammering at my brain:

> *Si je désire une eau d'Europe, c'est la flache*
> *Noire et froide où vers le crépuscule embaumé*
> *Un enfant accroupi plein de tristesses, lâche*
> *Un bateau frêle comme un papillon de mai.*

> I want no water of Europe but the cold,
>   black pool a sad-hearted child squats by,
> And launches out into the scented dusk
>   a boat as frail as a May butterfly.

And again the well-known words from *Une Saison en Enfer*:

> *Je reviendrai avec des membres de fer, la peau sombre, l'oeuil furieux, sur mon masque on me jugera d'une race forte. J'aurai de l'or: je serais oisif et brutal. Les femmes soignent ces féroces infirmes retour des pays chauds.*

> I will return with limbs of iron, bronzed skin and fierce of eye, from my mask I will be judged to be of a mighty race. I shall have gold: I shall be idle and brutal. Women take care of these ferocious invalids returned from hot countries.

For fifteen years the frail butterfly was crushed in the vice of iron limbs and withered under the gaze of the fierce eye. And when Rimbaud finally reached home after leaving Harar a "ferocious invalid", carried on a rough stretcher by relays of sixteen men, it was not the woman of a man's dreams who tended him, but his own sister, Isabelle. As far as we know, the mask never slipped, and his poetry remained to him a 'Season in Hell' until the bitter end.

As we went back that night down the hill from Harar, and the hooting laugh of a hyena came across the moonlit bushes of chat, snatches of the whole poem came back to me. It was the longest poem that Rimbaud ever wrote, that he wrote before he had even seen the sea, when he was scarcely seventeen. With echoes from Baudelaire and Poe, with snatches from Figuier's *Ocean World* and

Michelet's *The Sea*, and possibly even from Coleridge's *The Ancient Mariner*, the images of the sea are nevertheless transformed by Rimbaud's personal alchemy into both a testament on the maelstrom of his adolescence and a prophecy of the world-wanderer of the future, ever seeking the "million golden birds".

In my attempts to translate the untranslatable I hope I have not done too great a disservice to his memory.

The Drunken Boat

As I was floating down impassive Rivers,
　I did not feel the towmen leading me:
Gaudy Redskins had taken them for targets,
　Nailed each one naked to a coloured tree.

I cared not once for all those other craft,
　Carrying Flemish wheat or English ware.
When all the shouting with my towmen ceased,
　The Rivers let me go down anywhere.

More self-absorbed than children fixed in thought
　I ran, last winter, into fierce tide bores!
And all the headlands, floating from their chains,
　Have never heard more fine, triumphant roars.

There was a storm to bless my new sea life.
　Lighter than corks I danced for ten long nights
On waves that men call rollers of the dead,
　With no regrets for stupid harbour lights.

Sweeter than sour apples are to children,
　The sea-green water lapped my pinewood hull,
Washing away blue stains of wine and vomit,
　Carrying helm and grapnel off as well.

And then I bathed in the Poem of the Sea,
　Filled with the stars and drinking the milky foam,
In which, like pale flotsam held entranced,
　A dreaming, drowning man sometimes goes down,

Where, suddenly dyeing the expanse of blue,
　Under the gleam of daylight from above
Slow rhythms, more than music and alcohol,
　Ferment the bitter rednesses of love.

I know the lightning-cracked skies, the waterspouts,
 The breakers and the currents. I know the evening lore.
I know the dawn, rising like a flock of doves.
 Sometimes I've seen what men have thought they saw.

I've seen the sun far down, flecked with mystic horrors,
 Lighting long streaks of blood that fill our minds
With actions in some ancient tragedy,
 Whilst distant waves sound like rattling blinds.

I've dreamed of a green night with dazzling snows,
 Of kisses in the sea's eye, rising slow and long,
Of juices circling in undreamt of ways,
 Of yellow phosphorus awake with song.

I've followed months on end the heaving swell,
 Battering the reefs like herds of maddened cows,
Never dreaming that the luminous Marys
 Could muzzle the snorting Oceans with their vows.

I've struck Floridas, where panthers in human skins
 Have eyes of flowers, indescribable in words.
I've seen rainbows under the sea's horizon
 Stretched out like bridles to sea-green water herds.

I have seen mighty swamps like seething traps,
 Where whole Leviathans rot amongst the wrack,
Waters that pour down in the midst of calm,
 The distance rushing into one vast crack.

Glaciers, silver suns, pearl waves and red-hot skies!
 Hideous wrecks deep in brown holes in the seas,
Where giant snakes, eaten away by lice,
 Fall down, stinking black, from twisted trees.

I would have liked to point out to a child
 The blue wave dolphins and the fish that sing—
My driftings have been rocked in foam of flowers,
 And puffs of wind have set me on the wing.

Sometimes, with sobs that gave me a soft roll,
 Like martyrs tired of poles and zones, the seas
Raised up dark flowers with pale suckers to me,
 And I remained like a woman on her knees . . . .

Almost an island, whilst clamouring, pale-eyed birds
  Were tossed up on my beaches to brawl and weep.
And I was sailing fair, when across my frayed, old ropes
  Drowned men sank backwards into their last sleep. . . .

But now, a boat lost under hair of coves,
  Hurled by the hurricane into birdless space,
I, for whose carcass, sodden drunk with water,
  Never would salvage skipper turn his face;

Free, smoking, risen up from violet fogs,
  I who bored through the red sky wall the spot,
Which bears a jam that all good poets love,
  Lichens of sunlight mixed with azure snot. . . .

Who ran, speckled with electric sparks,
  A crazy plank, escorted by black sea-horses,
When Julys were cudgelling skies of ultramarine
  And funnelling them into narrow, burning courses;

I who trembled fifty leagues away
  From rutting Behemoths and the fell whirlpools,
Eternal spinner of motionless blue dreams,
  I long for Europe and its ancient walls.

I have seen archipelagos of stars!
  And islands with open skies of pure delight.
Are you sleeping in those bottomless nights,
  Oh million golden birds, oh future Might?

But I have wept too much. Dawn breaks the heart.
  Every sun is bitter and every moon a stink.
Sharp love has puffed me up with heaviness.
  Oh let my keel split! Oh let me founder and sink!

I want no water of Europe but the cold
  Black pool a sad-hearted child squats by,
And launches out into the scented dusk
  A boat as frail as a May butterfly.

No more can I, bathed in the listless waves,
  Sail in the wake of the carriers in bulk,
Nor submit to the pride of ensigns and of flags,
  Nor pull past the horrible eyes of a worn-out hulk.

14

Arnold in Ethiopia

I had already travelled over 4,000 miles in Ethiopia and visited over 100 schools when I headed south for the southern colonies of the Amharic empire. As far as the Central Highlands, which are the core of Ethiopia, are concerned, Addis Ababa appears to be very much off centre to the south. But the empire of His Imperial Majesty extends far into the lowlands of the south as well, including Gallas and Gurages, Sidamos and Wollamos, Gemus and Gofas, and many another tribe that has hardly moved a fraction up the evolutionary scale in half a million years.

The roads penetrate into these territories from the capital like tentacles from the head of an octopus. In some directions the tarmac lasts for 150 miles or so before giving place to the dirt surface and the dust clouds; in others one goes on to the gravel after only 50. The road with the longest stretch of good, smooth tarmacadam, and the one that has become most popular in recent years, is undoubtedly the road that heads due south down the Rift Valley into the land of lakes. It is also the road of the future, for it will be the first part of the highway to Kenya, which is now being constructed with the help of German aid.

I set out on this road one morning in February, and with me went Alan Moore, vigorous and active radio officer of the Educational Mass Media Centre, who wanted to visit the southern regions in order to see what sort of reception his radio programmes were getting. From Modjo the road starts off through dry acacia scrubland, which stays with it for well over 100 miles, so the views of the lakes, when they appear across the parched landscape, have the attraction of magical mirages in a thirsty desert.

The first of these lakes, and a foretaste of things to come, is an artificial one, created by the dam across the Awash river at Koka. I found it had already reached the bridge across the river and was spreading out on the right of the road as well, drowning trees in its progress. It was already full of bird and animal life. On one side there was a large flock of Egyptian geese, and on the other a colony of black and white storks was settled on a marshy island in the new waters. Some way out across the placid lake some dark humps breaking the surface showed that the hippos had not been slow to find the new paradise either.

From the new Koka lake the road goes down to the next one in long, straight stretches, with the wall of the Rift Valley showing like a blue-grey cliff to the left. Under the flat canopy of the acacia trees the land is dotted with large anthills, made by termites, some twice the height of a man. In some parts they are so densely concentrated that it looks as if the insect world has taken over.

This type of country continues as far as Lake Zwai, and the town on the flat lakeside land, which bore all the signs of modern development—dual carriageways marked out, corrugated iron roofs on the houses and, rather surprisingly, a church training school. The white dresses of the Amhara women were still much in evidence here, so I suppose the place has become a kind of southern outpost of the Amharic people, though Zwai is already quite low, a mere 5,000 feet above sea level.

But beyond Zwai one is clearly in the territory of the southern tribes. A white dome on the left of the road, surmounted by a crescent, shows that the Moslem world has penetrated even as far as these inland areas. Small, dark women, wearing leather skirts, with necklaces of cowrie shells, brass bangles and bare breasts, offer some primitive baubles for sale, made of dark-blue braided fibres, buttons and beads. In the old days the white men bartered beads to the natives, and now it was the other way round, a reversal of the old ways of the traders.

It is still mainly flat land, which makes all the more prominent the hill that dominates the village of Adamitullu, half way between

Lake Zwai and the next two lakes in the chain, which stretches right down into Kenya. The slopes of this hill are covered with prickly pear, and there are the ruins of a house on top of it, which used to belong to a German settler, named Goetz. During the troubled times of the Italian intervention he was burnt out. Whereupon he went to live on one of the five islands of Lake Zwai, where he was still residing when I passed that way. A very old man, who lived as a recluse, he nevertheless had the reputation of welcoming hospitably anyone who cared to brave the journey across the water to his retreat in a frail reed boat.

Past Adamitullu it was the same acacia scrub again, but this time I was driving between two lakes—Langano on the left and Abiata on the right. They are the traditional names in spite of their Italian sound, and from time to time I glimpsed the waters of Lake Langano through the acacia trees. But it was not until the road rose beyond the little village of that name that I was able to see its wide extent, stretching as far as the cliffs of the Arussi highlands on the other side.

The lake had a brownish colour, derived from the minerals contained in the metamorphosed sandstone that surrounds it. Yet it is the cleanest of all the Rift Valley lakes because, apart from Awassa, which was recently given a clean bill of health by a special survey team, all the others suffer from that scourge of African waters—Bilharzia, the deadly blood fluke that matures from an embryo into a fish-like form in the body of a snail, and then enters man, if it can, through the feet and legs.

For this reason a hotel and a camp site and holiday bungalows have grown up on Langano's shores. But they are still few and far between, and the peace of the lakeside, with its white salt spits and sandstone cliffs, is hardly disturbed even at weekends.

From the hills beyond Langano I could see Lake Shala on the right as well as Abiata. Its peculiarity is that it is a soda lake, fed from hot springs, and is consequently a favourite haunt of the flamingoes. They were, of course, too far away to see from the road, but the water itself was visible, looking placid and serene below the western cliff of the Rift.

From Langano onwards the scenery changed. The countryside was greener and more hilly. The acacia woods were gradually replaced by great baobab trees and by the euphorbia cactuses, looking like giant green candelabras. The village tukuls were surrounded by false banana trees.

Shashamane, 155 miles from Addis, stands at an important cross-roads, with a trail coming in from the remote Galla country of Bale to the east and another going off to the west to Wollamo and Gemu Gofa. But the dirt roads are so unfrequented that they hardly increase the motor traffic, and Shashamane still looks like a frontier town in the Wild West, with a wide main street flanked by shacks, rough stores and bars, and full of horses, cattle and donkeys.

I had to drive carefully through a mass of schoolboys, who were hogging the road in arrogant disregard of the rights of motor vehicles. Some held up their books, wanting to hitchhike down the road to their homes, for it was the midday break, and those who did not live too far away would be going back to their living quarters. Others just sauntered down the centre of the road, four abreast, without the slightest consideration for other road-users.

I was glad to get through the straggling market town and escape back to the open road. Shortly afterwards I saw from the crest of a hill the lake beside which I had decided to stop. At the end of a long, gentle descent through an extensive plantation of sisal, Lake Awassa lay in a basin in the hills.

A lot of the sisal was in flower, and the tall stems shooting up from their matrix of dark green, sharp-pointed leaves, looked like a forest of prehistoric trees, two or three times the height of a man. They stayed with me until the road was almost down to lake level and curved through the little village at the head of the water. Suddenly a child careered across the road, and I had to slam on the brakes. At the same moment I realised that it wasn't a child at all, but a big brown baboon lolloping over into the bushes on the other side.

It was a fitting introduction to Lake Awassa and to the Oasis Hotel, at which I stayed. For the glory of the lake is its wild life, and in particular the birds. I saw more varieties of birds there in one day than I had seen elsewhere during the whole of my stay in Ethiopia.

The first to meet the eye, as I drove along the sedgy shore of the lake, were the waders. They were huge—far bigger than any of the lakeside birds one is accustomed to seeing in England. The one that immediately caught my gaze, with its superb lack of any kind of camouflage colouring, was the saddle-billed stork. There was only one, strutting through the marsh water after eels, but that one must have been over 5 feet high. It was a tall black and white bird with a long red bill, barred with yellow and black, and it looked as though it was feeling supremely secure and safe as it stalked about scarcely 100 yards from the dusty road.

And of course it was safe, for shooting and hunting are prohibited on the shores of Lake Awassa. Those who want to go after game birds must shoot on the sisal plantation, with the permission of the owners, or further afield. I went and installed myself in one of the hotel chalets, and then walked out again to the lakeside in the late afternoon to bird-watch at leisure.

Now the great pinky–white pelicans, which I had seen earlier bunched up on the remains of a ruined causeway beyond a broken gate, were out on the lake, swimming about like boats, with their big beaks tucked into their chests to look like the bows of high-prowed ships. The saddlebilled stork was further along the shore, but another giant bird was standing almost opposite the archway entrance to the hotel. It was the goliath heron, grey-blue, motionless, with its long curved neck making it almost as tall as the stork, and a long, thin, sword-like beak.

The heron's mate was standing just beyond it, similarly motion-less. The pair of them dwarfed by their size the lesser brethren of the heron breed—the handsome egrets that peppered the lakeside with white dots. But in size, if not in height, they were equalled by another big bird of the lake—the sacred ibis.

I had never imagined that I would ever see this beautiful bird, so rare in Egypt that the ancients worshipped it as a god, in such profusion. Yet there they were before my very eyes—a whole flock of them, with their striking colouring of white bodies, black curved beaks and necks, and black feathers on their wingtips. They too scorned camouflage, fed calmly on the marshland, and simply flew a few hundred yards away and settled down again, if one approached too close. Their plainer cousins, the wattled ibises, were common on the lakeside as well, but I had already seen such birds in Addis and consequently they did not have, for me, the sharp impact of novelty.

These were the great birds of Lake Awassa. But they were far from being the majority. On other patches of marshland there were flocks of black geese, and there were also flocks of Egyptian geese, which looked black and white on the wing but brown in repose on the ground. Some way down the lake to the south there was a group of black cormorants, with white cheeks and necks, standing close to their fishing grounds, whilst nearer at hand a fish eagle was perched on a tree stump, with its white bird of prey's head, white chest, back and tail, chestnut shoulders and black wings.

These were the medium-sized inhabitants of the lakeside bird world. In amongst them hopped and skipped and jumped the little coots and plovers, the stilts and crakes, whilst the swifts and swallows flew over them in their eternal quest for insects. Who knows whether some of them were not refugees from the winter of Europe?

I was so satiated with the birds of the lakeside that evening that I had no appetite left for the rest of the feast. Yet the lake birds are only half the story of Awassa, as I realized very quickly when I I awoke in my chalet next morning to a symphony of birdsong in the acacia trees opposite my front door.

The most striking feature of the concert was the extraordinary variety of the instruments in use. The deep bass came from the thick-billed ravens and the low 'kkrrkk, kkrrkk' sound they made as they flopped from tree to tree or hopped heavily on the ground. I was surprised to find these parrot-like black creatures at such a low altitude, but a colony of them had taken over the Oasis, scavenging from the pigstyes and the refuse dumps, and they had become quite tame.

The tenor came from the 'do do de do do' morse code cooing of the pigeons, and the score was completed by a large number of intermediate notes that I was not expert enough to identify. However, I could distinguish the birds themselves when I was able to see them flitting amongst the branches of the trees. Their colours were so vivid and so striking that they seemed to be a different type of creature from the birds of England. Or was it simply the bright sunlight that made their feathers flash with such brilliance as they moved about?

Surely it was more than this, for even the humble starling had a sheen of glossy metallic green, which verged on blue or gold according to the angle of the light. And its eye was bright orange and under-belly violet, so that it looked as if it had been called down from a rainbow. Its Latin name, *Lamprocolius chalybaeus*, gives no indication at all of its shining beauty.

And the starling was plain compared with the Abyssinian roller, with its light-blue body and back of dark blue and green, brown and black, and the two dark feathers sticking out behind its tail like long shafts. In repose on a branch its many colours melted miraculously into the dappled interplay of light and shade, but on the wing it was a sudden flash of brightness.

So was the most superb of all the smaller birds, the paradise flycatcher. I saw it in the upper part of one of the acacias, and then it came down low past a row of papaya trees, and up again on to another branch. It was not so much its colour that caught the eye, although the interplay of black and white, grey and brown, was attractive enough, but it was its shape that was its glory. The long white tail streamers, trailing behind like the vapour stream from a plane high in the sky, showed immediately how it got its name, for it could be compared to nothing else but the birds of paradise of the New Guinea islands, that are even now still fighting for survival.

Apart from these there were many more varieties of small birds in that precious patch of woodland round the Oasis hotel and the municipal headquarters of the growing town of Awassa. The smallest was the African equivalent of the South American humming bird, a tiny creature with whirring wings and a beak curved like that of a miniature ibis, called a sunbird. Marked with daubs of brilliant colours like an Impressionist painting, it was difficult to detect in repose, but on the wing its metallic hues made it flash like fire. Above these little creatures of the forest sat the big birds like the auger buzzard and the pied crow, and, fortunately at some distance away, I saw the black shapes of vultures in an isolated tree, their ugly pin-heads on the look-out for carrion.

That same morning we went back up to Shashamane in order to visit the schools there. There were two of them—a new junior secondary school for children in grades seven and eight and an old elementary school for grades one to six. Walking into these country schools with my letter of introduction from the Ministry I wondered if the poet, Matthew Arnold, had felt the same way as

I did on his pioneering inspection tours of schools in Victorian England, apprehensive of what to expect and wondering how big the classes would be and how bad the sanitation, whether the staff would be full of enthusiasm or sunk in apathy, and whether the headmaster would offer a warm welcome or one of deep suspicion.

Now, under American influence, the headmasters of the Ethiopian schools are called directors, and few of them teach at all except in the very small schools. The Shashamane Junior Secondary School had been built with Swedish help and had only been open for a year. The young school director, a university graduate, had already made a good start with his 220 boys and 80 girls, mostly of the Galla, Wollamo and Amasien tribes. He had even got one of his teachers planting gardens round the bare buildings, but as usual there was no water to flush the nice new lavatories.

In the older school buildings nearer the centre of the town, however, classrooms were crowded and teachers harrassed. The dresser, for whom no medical supplies had been provided, and the storekeeper had been roped in to teach. But even including them there were only thirteen teachers to cope with 1,200 elementary-school children. And there might have been 900 more if the school director had not closed the doors and fled from the irate parents who were clamouring for the admission of their offspring at the beginning of the school year.

I suppose Matthew Arnold would not have flinched. Classes of 100 or more were not unusual in his day, with monitors keeping discipline in the serried ranks of sweaty children. But my stiff upper lip twitched when I considered the problem of applying the ultra-modern playway methods set out in the new English course to this seething mob.

The director, however, took it all calmly and even mildly, sitting safely in his office and immaculate in a dark serge suit in a temperature high in the eighties. A narrow black bow tie, winkle-picker shoes and a pink plastic brocade handkerchief in his breast pocket completed his gear. He had previously been a school supervisor in a place called Hosaina, and he clearly regarded his new post as another desk job.

We left the Prince Naod Elementary School, Shashamane in time for a lunch of tagliatelli and beefsteak at the Bekele Molla hotel, which is one of a chain spread over southern Ethiopia, giving adequate bed and board at moderate prices. And after lunch we took the right-hand fork on the dirt road to Soddo.

The road ran across the plain, broad and straight like a motorway, and although it had only a rough surface, we kept up a good speed against the non-existent traffic, with our dust cloud billowing up behind us. It led us past candelabra cactus and acacia trees to the western side of the Rift Valley, and up into the higher country of the first ridges between the Rift and the gorge of the Omo river. From here we looked back at Lake Shala, encircled by its cliffs, and into the blue beyond. Ahead lay the country of the Wollamo people, who were independent until their conquest by Menelik II in 1894 and trace a line of seventeen kings back to 1580.

Our first encounter with these people was with a funeral party that straddled the road in front of us. A line of men with linked arms stretched from side to side of the road. They plunged forward rhythmically, step by step, letting out a grunting, chanting, shouting groan as they did so. The coffin, raised on high by the pallbearers, was covered with red cloth, and in front of it women pranced and danced to the beat of the drums. In front of them a line of caparisoned horses showed that this was a chief on the way to his last resting place.

We edged forward little by little, and they let us pass. A few miles further on Lake Abaya came into view below, stretching out into the cloudy distance. It is the largest of the Rift Valley lakes of Ethiopia, 45 miles long and full of fish, including Nile perch weighing up to 100 pounds. Like the two southernmost lakes, it has a European name as well as an Ethiopian one. When the explorer and big game hunter, Count Teleki, passed through these regions in 1888, he called the two stretches of water on the border of Kenya and Ethiopia Lake Rudolf and Lake Stefanie after Prince Rudolf of Austria and the Archduchess Stefanie. Lake Abaya, with its brown water the same colour as that of Lake Langano, he called Margherita.

When we reached Soddo, 75 miles from Shashamane, more of the lake was in view, with some of the islands on it. For some distance we had been passing through archways made of corrugated iron and of bamboo, which had been put up as triumphal arches for the Emperor's tour of the Wollamo district in the previous month. One village, freshly whitewashed, with a school newly painted red and blue, reminded me of the stories told of some of Catherine the Great's tours of Russia, in which new model villages were put up specially for her inspection.

We observed with interest what the Emperor must have seen in Soddo—dual carriageways still being bulldozed out of the red earth, a new Commercial Bank, the new Damtse Abegaze Hotel, where we found rooms for the night, another new hotel and a petrol station still a-building. And we drove across a stream to the decrepit old town with its open market on the bare earth between rows of shop huts, and its line of men with sewing machines patching the seats of trousers in bright reds and blues.

Soddo, the capital of Wollamo district, was slated for development. Perhaps it was high time, for the Wollamo people resisted Menelik three times, and when, in the third attack, they were defeated, their thatched *tukuls* were set ablaze and their people enslaved and scattered to other parts of the growing empire. There is many an Amhara household in the highlands that still keeps the children of the Wollamo slaves as servants. Legally they are free to go, but in practice they have never seen the land of their origin and have nowhere to go to. Some of them, indeed, are related to the master through the so-called 'servants of the thigh'.

We took second-class rooms in the hotel, as the first-class ones with showers were all booked. Then we settled down for the evening. A fresh lake fish, gleaming white under its golden fried crust, made an excellent supper, after which the red light of the neighbouring *tej beit* failed to lure us out of the hotel. So we went to bed early after a game of chess, Rain fell during the night, and next morning I was up early too, looking for the first-class amenities that were not provided in the second-class rooms. The green hills behind Soddo were covered with mist, and the lake looked as shadowy and dour as a Scottish loch.

Breakfast over, we drove over the earth surface of one of the dual carriageways to the Soddo schools. There were 1,300 students in the Ligaba Bayenne Secondary School, and most of them still had not moved into the new school buildings, put up with Swedish help, because the classrooms were not big enough to accommodate the large classes made necessary by the shortage of teachers. Entering the elementary school I found the classes even bigger—

(*Above*) The author outside a Sidamo tukul

(*Below*) Derbaw, Said and the mules in Kundi on the Way of the Cross

(*Above*) The gateway to Amba Gishen

(*Below*) Pages from the Holy Book

eighty or ninety children sitting on benches in mud and wattle huts. Even Matthew Arnold might have flinched at that. And yet I don't know. In his day the advocates of education for the masses were still saying that a good barn would make an excellent school.

Leaving the schools behind us we drove along another straight dual carriageway, which dipped through a valley and then rose up the hill to the Y.M.C.A. compound at the highest point of the development area. The corrugated-iron sheathe of a giant *tukul* flashed like a shining light above us. It was the library and reading room, built inside like a traditional Sidamo *tukul*, with bamboo matting and poles bound together with cords, but covered with iron instead of the perishable thatch.

Beside it, in a smaller *tukul*, which did have a thatched roof, was the folk museum, which must have considerable importance in restoring a sense of identity to the Wollamo people. The Y.M.C.A. man took us into it to show us round, and we saw that it had been set out just like the hut of an old-time Wollamo chief. To the right of the door his walking-out dress of wide red trousers, speckled white, was laid out, together with his lion skin cape and his lion's mane headdress. On the other side of the doorway his spears were ranged against the wall behind the drums of his heralds. Further back stood his throne bench of webbed hide stretched over a wooden frame, and near it were circular seats made of reeds with lion skins thrown over them.

Behind these seats were ranged shell-shaped black pottery implements for tearing the raw flesh off the carcasses of animals, and to the right of them, between the men's and the women's quarters, was the raised platform for storing the maize cobs and the millet. In the women's section behind the partition dividing the tukul in half, stood earthenware pots and polished gourds, together with brooms made of strips of *enset* dried white. Head fillets for the girls, made of cowrie shells strung together, were hanging on the walls.

The Y.M.C.A. man was very helpful. He took us from the museum to the large hall, which included a cinema, ping-pong tables and huge charcoal drawings of the Emperor, done for his recent visit.

"Do many people visit this place?" I asked.

"Very few," he answered. "The people are lazy. But the new

M

Fituwari, the new Governor, is very strict," he added. His eyes gleamed in his black face. "He makes them shake. Whipping was good for them. But," he went on sadly, "difficult in present times."

"Anyway," I muttered, "you've been building for the future. The people will come in time."

"We are trying."

"Good."

We left for lunch, and then we started on the eighty-mile journey down south to Arba Minch. To tell the truth I had been more interested in the museum tukul than in the ping-pong tables, and soon after passing the airstrip and climbing into the hills on the other side of it, I had the opportunity to see with my own eyes that it had been laid out true to form.

We stopped at the roadside beside a field of maize, with the domed thatched roofs of the Wollamo people's houses peeping out above the high green stalks. A man wearing a singlet and shorts beckoned us towards his own tukul, and we went with him. White bolls of cotton were drying in a basket tray beside the doorway, which was made of stout wooden beams. Inside, the tukul was surprisingly spacious, perhaps nearly three times the height of a man at the centre. Just like the museum building it was divided in half by a screen and to the right of the screen stood the raised platform for the cobs and grain. A woman was throwing a little wooden tub backwards and forwards to churn butter, and beside her stood a charcoal-burning pipe.

Our host did not beg, and wondering what we could give him, we decided that a box of matches would be the most useful thing. He took it in both hands, and we continued on our way, with the broad lake filling the middle distance on our left.

About half way the road came down to the lake's level, and we had to face the hazard of the fords, of which there were four in all. The first two presented no problem, but the third was high with rushing water, for it had been raining in the hills to the right. Little boys waded across to show us the depth and the best route between the rows of sticks. Then we took the plunge.

The fourth ford was not so wide, but deeper. All went well until the engine almost stalled in a deep dip just before the steep ascent on the other side. Luckily at the last moment it recovered, and we carried on until, a mile or two further on, we saw a crowd of baboons running into the forest, and Alan, the radio officer, shouted, "Stop!"

It was easy to stop but impossible to start.

"Water in the carburettor," I said.

"Maybe it's just overheated," Alan said.

I lifted up the bonnet and saw pools of water on the air filter.

"It isn't just overheated," I said.

I cleaned off the water, drained the carburettor, replaced the drain plug and tried the self-starter again. There was no response from the engine. Alan tried as well with the same result.

"Don't run the battery flat," I said.

" What about the electrics?

"What about them?" I said.

We stood back from the car, listening to the baboons crashing about in the branches of the trees and feeling that a screwdriver and a pair of large pliers were insufficient tools for our task.

"There's a man and a woman coming up the road," Alan said. "Let's get them to push."

Pushing was no better than using the self-starter, however, and the prospect was looking bleak when a cream-coloured Volkswagen came up to us from the direction of Arba Minch and stopped just past us. Out stepped an athletic young Ethiopian, who introduced himself as Sergeant Amara Abebe, a dresser in the army. He went to work without delay. First he wanted to dismantle the petrol pump, then take off the distributor and then remove the plugs. I had visions of all the parts of the engine being scattered over the road with no instructions as to how to put them together again.

But after these false starts had been tactfully headed off, he got going in the right direction. He opened up the distributor, cleaned it out in a very competent way, rubbed down the points with emery paper, then replaced the rotor arm and leads, closed it up again and said, "Start please!"

Miraculously the engine started. Sergeant Amara, well pleased with himself, offered us brake fluid to clean the grease off our hands, replaced all the tools, shook hands and said farewell. We hardly knew how to thank him and said we hoped to be able to offer him a drink in Arba Minch.

Half an hour later we were at the T junction where the road

divided, right to lower Arba Minch by the big government farm, and left to the upper part of the new provincial capital of Gemu Gofa. We took the left-hand fork and found another of the unmade dual carriageways which seem to be the hallmark of the developing bush towns. The buildings, roofed with corrugated iron, were strung out along a ridge, and a second dual carriageway took us out of the town to the Bekele Molla Hotel, beside the modest villa residence of the governor.

The hotel was superbly placed, overlooking a steep jungle-clad slope and facing the hill dividing Lake Abaya from Lake Shamo, the next one in the chain, which was said to be full of crocodiles. The rain that had swollen the rivers in the fords was still hanging around the encircling hills. At dusk, shortly after our arrival, it fell, hammering on the iron roof of our large communal room. We wondered whether we would be able to get back or whether my car was trapped until the next dry season.

Next morning I was awoken by another hammering on the roof. Two large ravens were hopping about on it, croaking at one another. They were joined by another pair, and between them all they effectively banished sleep.

Lake fish for breakfast fortified our visit to the Arba Minch secondary comprehensive school, which was down the hill by the lower town, and had originally been built as an agricultural school to be linked with the farm that had been bulldozed out of the lake plain. I knew the school director, who had been beaten up during the student troubles that had been engineered from the university earlier in the year. He had been transferred to Addis, and no replacement had yet been appointed. Consequently this senior school of over 500 students was now being run by the unit leader, an American who had first come to Ethiopia in the U.S. Peace Corps. Though a classroom teacher by preference, he was working hard to keep the school on an even keel.

This was the only senior school in the whole of the bush province of Gemu Gofa. It had previously been located up in the hills at Chencha, but when the administrative capital was moved to Arba Minch the school moved with it. The children of the Amharic colonists and the Gemus and Gofas come in from the junior schools in the country districts and club together to live in communal huts and look after themselves with supplies sent by their parents, often by air. In such circumstances there is not much order and discipline, and they become easy prey for the troublemakers.

I saw a Philippino teacher with an unusually small English class of twenty-seven students, and talked to the other four English teachers—the acting director of the school, a married couple of the U.S. Peace Corps with a Polish name, and an Indian. Then we went back up the hill to the Fituwari Haile Degage elementary school, in which about the same number of children were crammed into the original school buildings of the town.

The school secretary welcomed us and told us about the self-contained classroom grades one to three and the departmental grades four to six, designated according to up-to-date American terminology. But I was more interested in the green electric-light flex, partly covered by a sheath of pink plastic tubing to make a handle. The business ends of the flex were bared down to the wire to give a useful sting to the whip when used on tardy children. Would Matthew Arnold have winced now? I still doubt it. He was well aware of the dominie's strap and the methods of chastisement of his day.

The school director took me to a class being conducted by a young graduate from the teacher training institute in Harar. There were three boys in front of the class. "This is a small boy," the teacher was saying. "This boy is smaller. This boy is the smallest." I seemed to have heard it all before.

The Provincial Education Officer, Ato Mebrate Ashagre, kindly lent us a Land-Rover for the afternoon. It had been our intention to continue southwards to Gidole at the southern end of Lake Shamo, but according to Ato Mebrate the rain had turned the track into a quagmire.

"Then we'll go to Chencha instead," I said. "It's only forty kilometres."

"The road is rough," warned Ato Mebrate.

"How long will it take?"

"Perhaps an hour and a half."

"Then we can go and come back today."

"Perhaps you can."

And so we set out after our lake-fish lunch and headed back to the last of the fords with Abebe, the Education Officer's driver, at the wheel. The Land-Rover passed through easily where the Opel Kadett had nearly foundered, and a short distance further on we turned left, crossing another stream, in which branches had been laid to give the wheels of passing vehicles a firmer grip. From there the track went straight and gently rising to the foot of the hills. We passed brown crested hammerkopf birds and women and girls wearing red headscarves plodding along with heavy sacks of greenstuff on their backs.

The track then climbed into the hills. It was so steep and rough that I remembered Ato Mebrate's "perhaps." "Perhaps an hour and a half." "Perhaps you can."

He had clearly been placed in an awkward position. If he had refused to let the Land-Rover go, he might have been reported back to Addis as being obstructive. Nevertheless he had to warn us that twenty kilometres on a rough mountain track were not the same as twenty kilometres on a main road. This was the reason for the 'perhaps'.

Perhaps we would not have gone, if we had realised how rough and slow the going was to be. After an hour we were still below the village on the crest of the hill to the right, which I thought must be our destination. We passed through a rocky area of pillar-like outcrops amongst false banana and bamboo. The village remained on our right.

"Ocholo," said Abebe. It was clear that this was not the one.

Half an hour later we reached what appeared to be the crest, slithering through thick mud in a Scotch mist. A village green appeared, with rows of stones set on the ground for the weekly market.

"Dorze," Abebe said. Obviously this was not our destination either.

Our track then continued along the ridge, dipping down into gullies from time to time. We passed another village, with all the tukuls in their own compounds behind woven bamboo fences which made lanes and avenues leading from the main track. There were few people about in the drizzle. We passed two distinguished-looking men on horseback, wearing overcoats and Bombay bowlers, which they doffed as we went by. We also saw a man wearing wide red trousers like the ones we had seen in the museum, with a retinue of half a dozen retainers. Other folk were presumably sheltering from the mist and rain behind their bamboo fences.

A stretch of open grassland was all that remained between this village and Chencha, but we had already been on the road for two hours when we passed under the festive archway and reached the outskirts of the settlement. Over the fence to the right the staff and children of the Sudan Interior Mission school were standing outside for the flag-lowering ceremony marking the end of the day's work. We knew that, by the time we reached the government school at the other end of the town, it would be closed.

Luckily, however, the District Education Officer, Ato Awalee Negusse, was still in his office, and he took us to meet the school director, Ato Hailu Maskal Burge, who was playing basketball on the court behind the school buildings. He broke off from the game to tell us about his school of 674 pupils.

It sometimes happens that the more remote the school, the better managed it is. An isolated community has to help itself, and the people have either to co-operate with one another or live in squalor. In this case, in the false banana and bamboo stone-age civilization of Chencha, the staff of the school were obviously co-operating to make it a tidy, well run concern. And so was Ato Awalee, who had to spend a lot of time out of the office on muleback visiting the elementary schools in his district.

Ato Hailu, who came from Debre Sina in the Amharic heartland, said that the Chencha people were mostly poor cattle-herders, ill-nourished on the false banana and subject to many diseases. But they were lucky to have two doctors in the town.

We waited some while for the office clerk to complete certain despatches, which were to be taken down to Arba Minch by our driver, and to put them in their red official envelopes. Then we set out again on the return.

The mist lifted, but it very soon gave place to the failing light of dusk. We saw a pair of buck, which scattered off the track at our approach, and the women and girls we had passed on our way to Chencha were still toiling upwards, bent under their loads. By the time we got to the bottom of the hill it was completely dark, and we ran down the last straight to the main road under the Southern Cross and the Great Bear.

All seemed well. But the last hazard—the ford with branches

thrown across it close to the main road—proved to be fatal. Our driver plunged in, scarcely pausing to consider the consequences, and the Land-Rover became firmly stuck between the logs that had been thrown in with the branches. The chassis became suspended on the logs, and the wheels spun ineffectively in the mud.

We laboured for two hours to release it, digging, heaving, pushing, rocking, roaring the engine and trying both forward and reverse gears. It was all in vain. The Land-Rover remained firmly stuck. So we had to leave it and start walking the 12 miles back to Arba Minch.

Tramping through the noise of running water, the croaking of frogs and the bell note of the cicadas ringing in the maize, we marched steadily ahead. The candles were alight in the roadside tukuls. From some came the noise of muttered conversation, from one the sound of a gentle song. A man crossed the road with his spear glistening in the moonlight and stopped to challenge us.

A little further on, just short of the ford, we stopped by a parked bulldozer at a wayside inn that sold Coca Cola and Melotti beer. Whilst Abebe sought out friends to help him with the problem of the Land-Rover, Alan and I sat on rough chairs with my black briefcase between us. But a few moments after the first bottle of beer had been opened by the woman of the establishment we heard the roar of an engine coming from the direction of Soddo. I ran out into the road to stop a heavy lorry and have our plight explained. A few seconds later I was climbing up into the cab and the two passengers who were already there were making room for me.

Alan gulped his beer down and came rushing out of the humble pub just in time to prevent the lorry driver starting off without him. We then negotiated the narrow Bailey bridge, a relic of the British Army's aid to Ethiopia in the 1940s, and ploughed through the ford on the other side of it. Twenty minutes later we reached the *T* junction at Arba Minch. But the lorry was turning right instead of left, so we again found ourselves out on the open road at night without a weapon between us, only a black briefcase, and this time in lion country.

The hill seemed very steep as we tramped up the embryo dual

carriageway past the skeleton of the new hospital that was being built on our right. But our luck held. Less than half way up we were overtaken by one of the Indian schoolmasters. He stopped his car for us and drove us back to our hotel, leaving us to order a late fish supper in our mud-caked clothes.

"What happened?" asked the Italian manageress.

Next morning we went to see Ato Mebrate in his office, and he told us that he had been up half the night trying to get the Land-Rover out of the stream, still without success. So we left Arba Minch, the place of 'Forty Springs', commiserating with him in his difficulties. But when we reached the bulldozer again, we found that the Land-Rover had at last been rescued. It was standing, covered with muddy finger-marks, in front of the pub, and Abebe, the driver, was with it.

All was lightness and laughter now. We shook hands and went our ways. Skirting round the cliff, beside which the ferry-boat, the only craft on Lake Abaya, was moored, Alan and I came to the village of Lamte. We stopped there to visit the new six-classroom school.

There was a tree, called Duduba in the language of the Gemus, in front of it, and the children were playing under the big sausage-like, but inedible fruits that were hanging down from its branches. The director came from behind the tree to greet us. He was a man from Harar, having been trained at the teacher training institute there. He was also a man of ideas, and the most enterprising feature of his school was the large vegetable garden behind it, in which the children were cultivating cabbages, tomatoes, beetroots and lettuces, and through which the parents were introduced to types of food that they had never known before.

But the director was facing a serious problem too. When the government had opened the new school, they persuaded the people of Ocholo, the village on the crest of the hill that we had passed on our way to Chencha the day before, to come down to Lamte to live. The villagers had built themselves square houses of mud and wattle on the flat land beside the road, but as soon as they had settled in them, they started getting malaria. So before long they returned to their hill village, leaving the new houses at Lamte empty. Every day they tramped for three hours down to their fields and for three hours back again up to their village. Of the

200 children at the school there were always about forty away with malarial fever.

This melancholy tale, alleviated only by an inadequate little bottle of mepacrine tablets on the director's desk, showed the folly of moving people about without proper planning. At Soddo we met a German over lunch, who had recently arrived under World Bank auspices to create the infrastructure of agricultural development. He told us that the malaria eradication programme was about to start. It seemed a pity that the authorities had not waited for this before moving the people of the hills into a malarial area.

That afternoon, after changing a wheel with a punctured tyre, we made our last stop of the day at a place called Kolito. It was half way between Soddo and Shashamane at a point just before the road changes direction eastwards to descend into the Rift Valley.

Kolito is also called Alaba, as it is the administrative centre of the district of Shoa province of that name, and the Atse Iyasu Alemseged elementary and junior secondary school has been established there for some time. It is the first building on the right as you turn off the main road at the petrol station.

Indeed it is so old established that we found many bottles of chemicals there, that had been supplied by a London firm as part of a science teaching aid programme of twenty years ago. They were carefully stored on the shelves in front of a row of large bottles of Stephen's ink and they had never been used. As each item had been carefully entered in the storekeeper's register, they had never been disposed of either.

The school director, Ato Kinde Getahun, was a man from Gondar. "We have nearly a thousand library books too," he said. "Would you like to see them?"

"Where are they?"

"In the store."

"Do the children read them?"

"No. We have no library, where we can keep them safe, so we keep them in the store."

We went to look at the store.

"The store is not very safe either," the director said, pointing at the little window eight feet above the ground. "I am sorry we have not arranged the books yet."

"What's the gun for?" I said, indicating an old Italian long-muzzle rifle that was leaning against the wall.

"It is for the protection of the store. But," added the man from Gondar, "I am sorry there is no ammunition for it."

We visited the classrooms, but found few children there. Ato Kinde explained that this was because it was market day. So since there was little we could do at the school, we persuaded him to take us to look at the market instead.

It covered a large area, and according to Ato Kinde it was one of the four largest in Ethiopia. Most of the large crowd were Moslem Gurages from the surrounding areas, bartering for salt and oil and other necessities. On one side there were large sacks of maize waiting to be transported to the railhead at Modjo, from where they would be railed to Djibouti for export. On the other side were the merchants of cheap cloth and clothing. I bought a wicker-work sunshade of rather Japanese appearance for a dollar from a lantern-jawed little man in an old battledress blouse, and a little later I heard his wife screaming at him for letting it go so cheaply.

We stopped briefly at Shashamane to have our punctured tyre repaired and then we drove on towards Langano, where we proposed to stay the night. But just before reaching Neghele we stopped again to photograph a circle of old gravestones with geometric patterns on them, that had survived from pagan days.

Two students, walking home from the Neghele school, stopped to greet us. They were in the eighth grade, they said, and they hoped to go on to the senior school at Nazareth next school year. They wanted to know what we were doing and where we were going. We wanted to know how far they had to go to get home. Then they wanted cigarettes. Then, not getting cigarettes, they wanted money for exercise books. As usual the *ferenj* was the target for a soft touch.

We left the boys on the road and went on to Langano, where we spent the night at the lakeside. Next morning we stopped again on the road back to Addis, this time at Adamitullu, the village domina-ted by the ruined house on top of the hill. Alan wanted to see what the reception of the elementary schools' broadcasts was like. So we turned off the road and headed for the national flag, which was a kind of beacon above the roofs of the houses, marking the school's position.

Whilst the radio officer discussed the school timetable and the question of erecting aerials to get better reception, I went to listen to the children chanting their Amharic syllabary and their multiplication tables. The school director was a gentle, mild man, who was suffering from trachoma, for which he intended to seek hospital treatment when the school term ended. He told us that he could not start school earlier to fit the broadcast timetable because many of the children had to walk long distances from their villages.

It was the acacia scrub, being remorselessly cut down by the charcoal burners, that the children would have to walk through. Less than twenty years ago it formed a thick canopy of trees, through which it was impossible to see the lakes. Now it was semi-desert, and still the piles of wood and big bags of charcoal were being stacked on the roadside for the Addis men to feed the voracious appetite of the city.

Dry and dusty Zwai was an object lesson to show the sad effects of random deforestation, and Zwai school was the last one on which we called on this southern tour. The school director was not there.

"He has gone to the District Education Office," an assistant master said.

A boy took us to the District Education Office, where a conference was in progress.

"He is at the school," the District Education Officer said.

What, I wondered, would Matthew Arnold have done now? I think he would probably have sighed and sat down to write a few more stanzas of the *Scholar Gypsy*. We, instead, returned to the school, where we listened to the moans of a university student doing his year's national service as a teacher. He grumbled about the staff, the children, the school books and even the school chalk in an orgy of self-pity.

Finally Alan exploded. "You can blame everybody and everything else," he said. "But please don't blame the chalk."

And he proceeded to draw a picture of a fish in crisp white lines on the blackboard.

The undergraduate was somewhat chastened for a moment, whilst I suggested that he might have preferred to do national service in the army and receive about $1 a month in pay instead. But he soon returned to the attack. He had never wanted to be a teacher and never intended to be a teacher, so it was painful for him to be a teacher.

On that note we left Zwai and continued our journey back to Addis. Half way to Modjo we made our last stop to buy a sack of charcoal and thus make our own small contribution to the future desert of the Rift Valley.

We had seen good schools, bad schools and indifferent schools. But one thing was certain. Education was in big demand. The most striking feature of any village was the groups of school-children walking along the road morning and evening with their books in their hands. Everybody wanted to learn. (See page 77.)

15

The Way of the Cross

The big rains come in the summer in the highlands of Ethiopia.
They start in July and carry on into September with much noise
of thunder, thudding raindrops and rushing torrents. As the rains
peter out the sun shines again, spring is in the air, and on 27th
September in the first month of the new year, the Ethiopian
Christians celebrate the finding of the True Cross at the festival
of Maskal.

The central feature of the Maskal ceremonies is the great
pyramid of wood that is erected in every town and village of the
Amharas and set ablaze. The green branches of juniper and
eucalyptus ensure that there will be plenty of smoke with the fire.

This is important, because a smoke signal plays a significant
part on two different occasions in the ancient legend. When
Helena, mother of the Emperor Constantine, who made the
Roman Empire Christian, went to Jerusalem to look for the cross
on which Christ had been crucified, she lit some incense and
prayed for divine guidance. Smoke from the burning incense rose
up into the sky and then curled back again towards the earth,
pointing to the ground at the spot where the cross lay buried.
The cross was then unearthed, and Saint Helena went to the top
of the nearest hill and lit a signal fire to announce her success to
the Emperor.

So the signal fires continue to this day, and the crosses move in
procession round them. But it was not until the end of the
fourteenth century that Ethiopia received her own piece of the

cross. The Emperor David I was on the throne, and he was called upon to help the Christians of Egypt and the Sudan against the Muslims. In return he was offered gold, but instead he asked for a fragment of the True Cross, which was kept by the Patriarch of Alexandria. The relic was sent to him, together with paintings attributed to St. Luke and St. John, and the receiving of the relic is still celebrated at the Imperial Palace in the ceremony called Atse Maskal, a week before the bonfires are lit.

According to the fifteenth-century chronicle called the *Tefut*, a beautiful volume hand-painted in Ge'ez, which is kept in the monastery of Gishen, David's fourth son, Zara Yakob, who became emperor in due course, dreamed a dream when he was a very old man. He dreamed that God was ordering him to "place his cross upon a cross."

Pondering the significance of this dream, he fasted and searched for two years until he found a mountain shaped like a cross. On the top of this mountain in the wilds of Wollo he built a church called Eghziab, or God the Father, and in it he placed the piece of the True Cross in a golden casket, to be looked after by the monks of Gishen Mariam. Pilgrims go there shortly after Maskal for the feast of the Virgin Mary on 1st. October.

I myself remained in Addis Ababa, where Maskal is nowadays celebrated with the greatest pomp and splendour. When I reached Maskal square early in the afternoon, it was already crowded with onlookers. The crowds in their new *shammas* on the bank by St. Stephen's church looked like a patchwork of black and white, and the leaders of church and state were assembling in marquees erected on the traditional platform on the other side of the square.

Between the two groups stood the tall pyre of poles and branches, called the *demera*, that had been erected the day before. It was festooned with sprays of the yellow daisies that bloom all over the hills at the end of the rainy season, and beside it stood the choir in their white robes and turbans ready to sing and dance. Further back were assembled the high churchmen of Addis Ababa in their cloth of purple and gold under the pelmeted umbrellas.

As the precentors chanted and swayed back and forth, members of the diplomatic corps, generals and ministers arrived in their official cars. Then the Emperor himself appeared, and shortly afterwards the *demera* was lit and flames lit the darkening sky.

This was followed by the appearance of the carnival procession coming down the avenue from the west. Horsemen in the lion's mane headdresses and epaulettes of the old-time warriors mingled with displays by the modern armed services and their bands. Church groups carrying candles twinkled in the dark. Floats bearing tableaus of old-style village life and new-style crosses of electric light bulbs drove past. Then came one of the Emperor's lions sitting on a float and viewing the mortals around him with something like disdain. After that there were more horsemen with spears, a Red Cross display and men with flaming torches, which they threw on to the pyre as they went by.

Meanwhile the *demera* was belching smoke up into the sky, together with fragments of leaves which fell back on to the crowd. As soon as the procession was past and the Emperor had gone, people broke through the police cordons and rushed forward to throw their own sticks and bunches of daisies on to the blaze. There was a general melée, and the party over, I made my getaway through the hubbub of the streets.

But somehow, like someone on Guy Fawkes night, who has had to leave the firework display before the best and most impressive Roman candles have been lit, I felt that the whole thing was incomplete. And as it turned out I had to wait until the following spring to comlete the experience with a visit to the place where the Ethiopian True Cross is reputed to lie, high up in the mountains of the Amhara land.

My first negotiations were with Professor Chojnacki of the Institute of Ethiopian Studies, for it seemed necessary to have a *warakat*—a letter of introduction—that I would be able to present when I reached the place. He kindly agreed to have my petition translated into Amharic for me to present it to the Secretary of the Patriarchate in his office behind St. Mary's church.

The letter stated that, being interested in the cultural traditions of Ethiopia and a Friend of the Institute of Ethiopian Studies, I was keen to visit the church of Gishen Mariam during my forthcoming tour of Wollo province, and I would be grateful for assistance in my project and for an introduction to the abbot of the monastery there.

It may be asked why a letter should be necessary at all in order to be permitted to visit a church. But this was no ordinary one. It was perched high up on an almost inaccessible *amba*, and the sole path of access was guarded night and day against unwanted intruders. One might, indeed, have been admitted without a *warakat*, but it was better to have one.

So on the afternoon of 3rd May I took my letter to the block of wooden ecclesiastical offices to look for someone who could help me. But the little rains were pouring heavily down, and I failed to find anyone. I went round the back of the offices to a somewhat imposing stone building fronted by a terrace of steps, but a *zebegna* shooed me away, saying that there was nobody there.

Next day I returned to the stone building to find a complete contrast with the previous afternoon. There was much activity outside. Little groups of white-turbaned clerics clustered amongst the parked cars, a black-coated man moved hither and thither briskly amongst them, and the khaki-clad *zebegnas* and ushers looked full of importance. I was surprised to find myself eagerly ushered forward through the big doorway and into a hall with rows of chairs in it.

As soon as I saw who was there I realised why. Abuna Teophilos, with his distinctive black hat ringing his head, emerged from a side room and spoke to those people who reverently approached him. I was clearly in the Patriarch's palace, and things were moving forward towards his investiture on the following Sunday in place of the late Abuna Basileos. He was holding audience.

When I stated my business the black-coated secretary smartly ushered me out and back to the wooden offices. There he read my letter. But although he was full of goodwill, it was clearly not his responsibility, so he took me across the passage to the office of the Vice-Minister for Religious Affairs, Ato Makonnen Zawde. He introduced me to the minister's clerk, gave me his telephone number and said, "Just keep phoning till you find him in. Then you can make an appointment to see him."

I went away and tried phoning that very afternoon without success. The next day, Wednesday, was a holiday in remembrance of the Emperor's triumphal return to Addis in 1941, and obviously no minister would be found in his office then.

On Thursday morning I again had no success. I was beginning to get anxious, for I was due to leave for Dessie on the Monday,

N

and I doubted whether, with all the preparations afoot for the Sunday celebrations, I would ever find him in. But that afternoon I was lucky at last. I was ushered into the thick-set minister's office by a rather frightened secretary, and we sat and had a chat. He then agreed to write a letter to the senior church official in Dessie, Memher Aberra Tilahun, who would facilitate my journey. I was to return to collect it next day.

Next day, however, it was written but not signed, either in the morning or the afternoon. Saturday morning would be my last chance to get it, yet at ten o'clock on that day the secretary told me that it still was not signed. She would see to it as soon as he came in.

I grew angry. Clearly she had been too timid to put it in front of him the day before. How could I spend all my time coming and going when I had a hundred other things to do? She became apologetic and asked me for my home address. As it was all her fault, she would bring the signed letter to my house after the office closed at one o'clock.

At that I relented, saying that I would return to her office at twelve thirty. When I got back there at the appointed time, I found that it had at last, been signed but that it had to be sent to the registry to be booked out and dated. This took an exasperatingly long time, but finally, just as everyone was packing up to go home for lunch, I got it in my hand, signed and delivered. I hoped that all the time-wasting delay had been worth the trouble.

I duly set out for Dessie by Land-Rover on the Monday, passing through Debre Berhan, the Mussolini tunnel and Debre Sina on the route I had followed over a year before. On closer acquaintance Dessie did not look quite as bad as it had done in the first flush of cultural shock, though it still seemed very nondescript for the third city of the empire. With the Crown Prince as governor of the province one would have expected it to show more signs of nobility and progress.

I stayed at the quiet touring hotel away from the main road. The Italian proprietor being away in Addis and the manageress away in Asmara, it was run by three Tigre women in nurses' caps and was almost empty. But the unvarying menu of spaghetti or *pastini in brodo*, *vitello arrosto* or beefsteak and papaya or cream caramel suited me whilst I presented my letter to the Memher and went about my business in the schools.

Memher Aberra Tilahun, in his creaking office of religious affairs tacked on to the Wollo treasury, was affability itself. He wasted no time in getting a letter written, addressed to the Abbot, Memher Tekle Markos. But he warned me that the abbot was away in Addis for the patriarchal investiture. However, some deputy would deal with it, he assured me.

It was Tuesday. I had my letter the same day, unsealed so that I could open it and have it read to me. And the next day I went out to visit a school in the direction of my objective at a large village called Kutaber.

Dessie, although it lies in a dip with mountains all around, is itself a high place, and there is no further ascent on the 15 miles of road to Kutaber. The crumbling track, which is still signposted to Addis Zemen and Gondar, was a fine road across the uplands of their Amhara province when the Italians built it in their brief years of glory. It starts off from the main road to Asmara through an avenue of eucalyptus trees and then skirts a beautiful highland vale called Kala Meda before reaching the village. Now all the bridges are down, and only some 60 miles of the road from Dessie are motorable with difficulty. Various contributions from the Wollo people towards its reinstatement do not seem to have yet been put to use.

At the school at the northern end of the wooded village I found that the *zebegna*, a little old man named Ayele, who had lived all his life there, was willing to arrange for mules for me. So before leaving Kutaber to return to the touring hotel for my spaghetti I met the mule man in the village square and put two dollars deposit on two mules to be ready on Saturday morning.

The same afternoon I found a twelfth-grade student of the senior secondary school in Dessie, who had completed his school leaving certificate examination and was willing to go with me. His name was Derbaw, and he was well used to the hardships of the trail as his home village was three days' walk to the west of the town.

So on the Friday evening the two of us went back to Kutaber, I with my rucksack stuffed full and a sleeping-bag, and he only with his *shamma*. It had rained hard that afternoon, but the

weather cleared as we neared the village, and there were hopeful
signs that it would be fine next day.

Ayele had appropriated the only room in the only hotel for us.
It belonged to one Ato Yimer, a 49-year-old stalwart who spoke
Italian well enough to yarn to me about the Second World War
and about how he and fifty men had defected from the Italians with
all their arms and gear to join the British and the Emperor in
Khartoum. He was the big man of the village, with two bars in
his establishment, one containing the Melotti beer and Fanta
orange of the advertisements on its shelves and the other stocked
with bottles and flasks of orange-coloured *tej* and earthenware jars
of brown *talla*. He it was who was the entrepreneur and raiser of
subscriptions to pipe the drinking water down from the hillside
behind the houses into the centre of the village, which naturally
also happened to be opposite his place.

Yet he had no lavatory, not even a latrine dug in a corner of the
compound. One had to ask where to go, using the word *shinta*,
and was directed to a couple of trees or a place behind a low
haystack, which was nevertheless still well within view of people
in daylight. Such primitive arrangements do not seem to worry
village Ethiopians much. By European standards they are mostly
constipated, and their bowels do not usually move more than
about twice a week. But it took me some time to get used to
public defecation.

That evening Yimer, Ayele, Derbaw and I drank *tej* in the back
room and discussed the expedition. Both Ayele and Derbaw had
been to Gishen Mariam in the past at the time of pilgrimage on
the feast of St. Mary, but they were curiously vague about the
details of the journey and of the *amba* on which St. Mary's of
Gishen stands. Derbaw thought that there were *shiftas* in the
Kuskus 'desert' but that they only attacked local merchants, not
foreigners. Yimer said it was altogether a twelve-hour trip through
the village of Kundi, but on the return Gishen to Kundi was four
and Kundi to Kutaber was only three, so it looked as though the
way back was very much more rapid than the ascent.

In fact, having read the literature on the subject, I felt that I
knew considerably more about Amba Gishen than they did. Apart
from having the reputation of being the home of the True Cross,
it had, in the Middle Ages, been one of those strange mountains

on which the sons of the emperors were incarcerated in order to avoid fighting over the succession. Alvarez, the Portuguese priest who spent six years in Ethiopia from 1520 to 1526 as chaplain to a diplomatic mission sent by King Manoel 1, described it, according to information received, as two days' journey round.

The above-mentioned valley [he says in the words of his translator, Lord Stanley] reaches to the mountain where they put the sons of the Prester John. These are like banished men; as it was revealed to King Abraham, before spoken of, to whom the angels for forty years administered bread and wine for the sacrament, that all his sons should be shut up in a mountain, and that none should remain except the first-born, the heir, and that this should be done for ever to all the sons of the Prester of the country, and his successors, because if this was not so done, there would be great difficulty in the country, on account of its greatness, and they would rise up and seize parts of it, and would not obey the heir, and would kill him. He being frightened at such a revelation, and reflecting where such a mountain could be found, it was again told him in a revelation to order his country to be searched, and to look at the highest mountains, and that mountain on which they saw wild goats on the rocks, looking as if they were going to fall below, was the mountain on which the princes were to be shut up.

The last prince, who succeeded to the throne, to be incarcerated at Amba Gishen, the 'grassy mountain', was the Emperor Naod, who reigned from 1494. By this time it was already known as the home of the Cross, though strangely enough Alvarez, who contradicts himself later on as to its size, does not mention its cruciform shape.

Shortly after the Portuguese visit Ahmed Gragn came to plunder the land of the Amharas with his Moslem soldiers. But Amba Gishen was too much for him. According to the Chronicle of Gragn the soldiers:

travelled by a difficult road across mountains and rivers, and arrived at the *amba* in question. They saw that it was a tall and steep mountain which could only be reached with the aid of ladders. On top there were more than one thousand houses inhabited by the children of kings; there were rivers there as well as houses. . . . When a king had male children he sent them to this mountain so that they should not be the cause of conflict in the kingdom. When the king died one of the princes was brought down and invested with royalty. There were 2,300 princes and princesses on the *amba*; the king supplied them with food and clothing.

As he found that the mountain was almost impossible to capture, Gragn left it and went on to the area of Lake Haik, where he made boats and crossed the 200 yards of reedy water to loot the church and monastery on the small island there.

I only mentioned all this in passing as we talked whilst the sun went down. As we sat drinking our *tej* the women walked past with their evening pots of water supported on their protuberant rumps, and the shouts and yells of the children suddenly rose to a scream as a bush buck foolishly ran through the village from one side to the other. Then there was silence whilst the early country night came down with no light except for a paraffin lamp on the table in the back room. Later the silence was broken by the shouting wail of an Amari singer in the nearby rival bar.

Next morning the mule man, a well-built youngster in a red headcloth, reached us at about a quarter past six and handed over to us two of his mules, together with Said, a young muleteer, who wore a check dishcloth with tassels on it on his head. Ayele gave us the name of his friend in the next village and then we were away.

For the first part of the journey the road led steadily downwards from the headwaters of the Kuskus river in Kutaber itself into the deep gorge which the torrent has carved for itself on its north-westerly descent towards the Blue Nile. In many places broken bridges had been replaced by rocks and stones stacked up closer to the mountainside, and as is the habit of mules my animal invariably walked as close to the unparapeted edge as possible.

It was a sunny, warm day, and by the time we got down to the first ford the gorge was becoming something of a heat-trap. I got off my mule to walk and stretch my legs and found that the mules had to trot to keep up with me. But it was necessary to speed things up with a twelve-hour journey to complete, so I could not worry about the looks of passers-by, seeing me on my feet whilst the mules went unmounted.

Many of the people were going to Kutaber, which was the parish headquarters, to pay their taxes, striding along with their sticks across their backs. There were also merchants coming up out of Delanta with their mules and donkeys laden with *teff* and lentils. They all knew the different cries of the road—*muj* for a mule, *wash* for a donkey and *che* for a horse, whilst *hij*, meaning 'go!' was used for all the beasts, a corruption of the word *hid* as used with people.

There was no sign of the *shiftas* that Derbaw had worried about in the 'desert' of the Kuskus, but many men were armed. One such—a government official with pistol and bandolier—had a retinue of three riflemen. He nodded as we passed. Others raised their hats or their right hands in a gesture of greeting.

And so, after nearly three hours, we came to Kundi, where a few *tukuls* serve as resting places for merchants and pilgrims. The mules ran off to the river, and in our concern at catching them we neglected to ask for Ayele's friend to make arrangements for our return. We were still in a hurry. Even when the mules had been chased back on to the road again we did not stop.

"Let's have a rest under the next tree," I said, though trees were rare indeed in that deforested land, where the only ones left were generally clinging to inaccessible cliffs.

"Let's go on to Talayyan," Said said.

It was the place of parting, according to Derbaw. But the way was long and hot above the wide, stony bed of the river with its thread of water running through the stones, and splashes of green where the *teff* was growing that would have to be harvested from the irrigated reaches before the big rains. We passed a wide oak tree and a row of eucalyptus that were too tall for their roots and leaning over the shingle like drunkards on a beach. And still we plodded on, Derbaw and I riding the mules now, whilst Said walked beside us.

"How far now?" I said after a long pause.

"Just past that patch of green," Derbaw answered after consulting Said.

We reached the patch of green in another quarter of an hour and rounded a protruding hillside. Then another quarter of an hour brought us to a junction of our torrent with another, wider one coming in from the right. This was clearly the 'place of parting', but it was yet another quarter of an hour before we reached the ford of the combined torrents, with a row of trees and an orange grove beside it, which is called Talayyan.

Here at last, after six hours on the march, I was allowed to rest. I got some biscuits out of my pack and passed them round. Then I drank deeply from my water-bottle, so that by the time my interpreter and muleteer had had their gulps too it was empty, and I was too late to stop Derbaw filling it up with river water. It would have been better to replenish it from the *talla* sellers in their rough shelters of sticks and straw beside the road.

A short way downstream stood the six piers and two abutments of the seven-span bridge that the Italians had built over thirty years before. Now not a vestige, not a scrap of wood or bolt or metal bracket of the carriageway remained, and when the big rains came and the torrent was in flood all traffic would cease.

After fording the river and passing the end of the ruined bridge on the right bank we took a sudden turn away from the road and up the mountainside to the right. The track wound steeply upwards through a dessicated, eroded landscape, where, apart from the *teff* and barley fields, little had been left to grow except for the indestructible agaves, the apples of Sodom and the candelabra cactus. The stones were gathered into piles, and the fields were then steeply cultivated like those of the Gurkhas in Nepal, but not nearly so neatly terraced and preserved.

Now I was glad of my mule taking me up the stony track out of the gorge, though the shortness of the leathers, which proved to be non-adjustable, soon caused my hunched-up legs to ache. Said's cries of *"muj"* and *"hij"* became more and more frequent as we climbed towards the saddle on the skyline, outtopping several lesser crags and ridges.

Three quarters of the way up our path merged with one that came along a higher trail under the sheer cliff of a flat-topped peak, and striding along it, using his *maquamma* as a staff, was a priest from Addis Ababa, who was also on his way to Amba Gishen. He stayed with us for a while, but he doubted whether we would get into the *amba* after midday, as he did not think that they would admit us from the afternoon onwards.

This worried me a little, but not much. There had been so many conflicting opinions as to what time of day one would or would not be let in that I put my trust in my *warakat* from the Memher in Dessie and was content to wait and see. One educated lady, back in Addis after two years in America, had even told me that I would not be admitted at all.

"Why not?" I had asked.

"Well, you see, Mr. Forbes, up there they believe that God is black," she had answered, implying that for this reason white men were not welcome.

After an hour's hard work with the beasts we reached the saddle and the cool breeze on the pass. Derbaw pointed across a deep re-entrant with its sides built of sheer precipices 1,000 feet high and said, "Look, Amba Gishen."

But he spoke too soon. The flat-topped peak with the shining roof of a house amid the dark green of the trees on its summit was not our ultimate destination. It was the last staging point—the false Amba Gishen—before the true goal beyond. We had to make a long traverse up to the head of the re-entrant before we could head in the right direction again, and then there was a steep climb similar to the one leading to the saddle.

I felt a raging thirst after over nine hours on the trail, and I asked Derbaw what the river water was like.

"Somewhat good," he answered.

I unscrewed the top of the bottle and looked at it and smelt it. It was yellow and it stank so much that, in spite of my desire, I could not touch it.

"I should say somewhat bad," I said irritably.

I was annoyed at my companions for taking my water so improvidently. We asked for *talla* at the *tukuls* we passed without success, whilst a large family of baboons stood looking at us from the edge of the ravine, clustered behind their big lion-maned leader. Though at this time of year all the *medas*, or flat parts of the uplands, were a rich green, here, even after the little rains, the mountain slopes were still arid and baboon-coloured—simply a little lighter than the dun ploughed fields. And from field to field the cries of the farm boys went up, now calling to each other, now singing the wailing shouting songs of high Africa.

We clattered across the stony dry ford at the head of the re-entrant, and shortly afterwards I heard a blessed trickling sound coming out of a rocky cleft to the right of the path. My two thoughtless guides would have quite happily walked straight past, but I insisted on stopping, emptying the muck from the water-bottle and slowly refilling it with the clear spring water using a leaf to guide the precious drops in the right driection.

Then the second steep climb began, zigzagging up to the house on the ridge. It was five in the afternoon by the time we got there, and the mules were spent. But the scenery around us was so grand and strange that I gained new energy as I contemplated it.

We were standing in the dip of a broad ridge on the edge of an open field. On one side of the dip there was a village, and on the other, southern side stood the house with the shining roof in its grove of eucalyptus trees, with servants' *tukuls* and the cliffs of a higher mountain behind it. Behind us, to the west, was the deep gorge of the combined torrents, joined by a third in the distance, out of which we had so laboriously climbed. Part way up the hill on the far side of the grey snake of the river shingle a splash of green marked the village of Tenta, and behind it stood the flat-topped massif of Magdala, on which the great mortar 'Sebastopol', which the Emperor Theodore hoped would defend him from the British, still stands.

But our eyes were mostly turned onwards towards the west, for there, appearing to rise quite gently out of a high plain, was the wooded hill of Amba Gishen with its church buildings light against the background of trees. To me, at that moment, it did indeed look a little like that place described by Milton in *Paradise Lost*:

> Nor where Abassin Kings their issue Guard,
> Mount Amara (though this by some supposed
> True Paradise) under the Ethiop line
> By Nilus' head, enclosed with shining rock
> A whole day's journey high. . . .

For us it had been a whole day's journey already, and the giant crevasses of the cracked and fissured tableland all lay below us. The evening cool dried the sweat on my back, freeing my shirt from sticking to my skin.

"The big man here is Ato Abegaze," said Derbaw after making some enquiries. "Let us go and ask him if he can give us somewhere to sleep. It's too late to get into the *amba* now."

I left myself in his hands, so he asked a boy how to get into the estate. But, deeply suspicious, the boy would not tell him. Then, after searching round the wall of the compound, we finally found the gate to one side, placed there no doubt judiciously away from the main pilgrim trail. Standing just short of the threshold for fear of the guard dog, we called out to some men who were hay-making in the home paddock. After some persuasion one of them came reluctantly over to us, and told us that the master was away up the mountain, so there was nothing that could be done for us.

We turned away, disappointed, with the night chill already descending. But Said, the simple Moslem mule boy, was more sensible than the twelfth-grade high-school student.

"Why don't we go on to the Gishen?" he said. "It's only one hour, and there are places to stay there."

I agreed. So we set off again. It looked quite close to us on the horizon, but again the *amba* played us false. Hidden between it and us there was a deep ravine that had to be skirted on one of the familiar tracks that run along the top of a precipice. But at least there was no more climbing to be done. I let my mule go at its own pace, and watched the *amba* gradually reveal itself to me as it emerged out of the surrounding gorges.

As the sheer cliffs of the *amba*'s sides came into view, I could see the shape of the cross materializing. One arm, the southern-most, lay diagonally across our path, whilst the western arm was illuminated a dusty grey by the last pale rays of the setting sun. The eastern arm was dark with trees, but for the time being I had to take the northern one on trust. Now the gateway and the steps leading up to it became clearly visible. The extremity of the southern arm had crumbled, leaving a jagged pinnacle of rock and a knife-edge ridge between it and the flat top beyond. The steps were built on this ridge, with the gateway at the top on the edge of the flat surface. In spite of Alvarez's mention of three entrances, I was subsequently told that there was now no other way up.

Our own trail led us to another ridge which opened out onto a tiny plateau just below the cliffs of the rocky pinnacle. Here stood the cluster of *tukuls* that Said had told us about. Derbaw went to the first one we came to and asked for shelter. The owner told us we could sleep in his field further up, but that his house belonged to God. We shrugged our shoulders and went on up the path to the top end of the little settlement to enter a walled compound on the left.

Is this the field? I wondered. At least the walls would be protection against hyenas if not leopards, and I had my warm sleeping-bag.

But suddenly, with one of those dramatic changes of fortune that are part of the fascination of travel in wild places, we were honoured guests. At that moment a priest was emerging from the *tukul* at the bottom of the compound to go up the *amba* and take part in early mass next morning, Sunday. He bade us welcome in his home and left his wife and son to look after us.

I walked past the growling guard dog into the *tukul*, where a fire was already burning in the open hearth in the middle. Even so, it was difficult to see in the sudden gloom. I was directed to a sleeping platform on the right—the marital couch—which was covered with fresh dry hay on which an oxhide was laid. I sat there resting, and as my eyes became accustomed to the dim light I made out the other features of the big circular room—the kitchen part screened off at the back, the lower sitting and sleeping platforms closer to the fire on one of which the good wife was reclining, the storage corner, the three-pronged hayforks and the sacks of grain.

A small boy brought in some sticks, and the fire was blown and coaxed into a respectable blaze. Then the young man brought *talla* in pint glasses, which we drank greedily, spitting out the fragments of hop leaves. After that he brought a red plastic bowl and water in a plastic jug of the same colour and washed and massaged my travel-sore feet and legs. It was a touching, biblical gesture, completed by a ritualistic light kiss on the toes when the task was complete. The young man wanted to wash Derbaw's feet too, but he declined being waited on and insisted on doing his own.

Then the *masob* was brought, piled high with *injera*, together with a tasty lentil *wat* of which we ate our fill. The simple courtesy and generosity of our country hosts seemed to undo all the unkind words I had ever said about the city customs of Addis people.

Eating my supper I cracked jokes with our hostess, who said that she wanted to come to England with me. "Marry me first and you can come," I joked, "but what about your husband?"

But the talk, conducted through my student interpreter, did not last long. Without light except for the flickering fire or the rare luxury of a candle, village people turn in early. Although they rise at six, they still get more sleep than the average city dweller since they are usually curled up in their *shammas* by eight or nine at night, Besides, after our twelve hours on the road to get "a whole day's journey high" I could hardly keep awake myself. Stretching out on the oxhide I closed my eyes.

It was Derbaw who awoke me, scratching at fleas that had started infesting his *shamma*, and rather unkindly rolling over closer to me on the oxhide than before. In spite of the application of the insecticide spray that I had brought with me he continued to scratch, and I was lost to sleep. The tukul's cock started crowing without waiting for the dawn, whilst the donkeys in the nearby stall gobbled away as if they had been turkeys. I watched the first light come like leopards' eyes in the holes in the walls, and then the dawn lighting a hundred cats' eyes in the cracks in the woven roof.

We were up at six, though Derbaw, the eternal pessimist, now doubted whether we would be admitted to the *amba* before morning mass was over. However, there was no sense in waiting. The priest's son came with us, guiding us round to the right of the terminal crag of the *amba* and up a steep path on its eastern wall, which brought us, after ten or fifteen minutes, to the steps below the gate.

There are twenty-seven *zebegnas*, who take turns at this part-time duty in recompense for the use of church land in the vicinity, so there was no chance of finding the gate unguarded. But at least we found it open—a double barrier, part sheet iron and part iron bars, below a thatch-roofed room.

Once through the square gateway we entered another world. A flat expanse of green grass, leading up to the central hill of the *amba*, stretched in front of us, with sheer edges like the deck of an aircraft-carrier. It was a perfect landing-place for a helicopter. To the left stood the watchmen's *tukul* and beyond it the house of the guardian of the gate.

We waited whilst the *zebegna* on duty sent a man for the guardian, and after a few minutes a frowning, hollow-cheeked toothy individual arrived, who seemed little pleased to see us. He

examined my *warakat*, but declined to open the envelope. I needed
to be firm and compel my youthful interpreter to state not only
that I had a letter from the Memher in Dessie but also that the
Memher had received a letter from the Vice-Minister in Addis.

The gatekeeper softened and detailed an armed man to escort
me up the hill in search of the man who was *enderassie*, or acting
commander, of the *amba* in the absence of the abbot, or alternatively of the abbot's father. So we left him to cross the green
aircraft deck and climb the hill.

There was a cluster of *tukuls* at the foot of the hill, which Derbaw
could not remember having seen on his previous visit, but there
were nothing like as many as the 1,000 houses mentioned by
Gragn's chronicler. In fact we were not shown any remains of the
habitations of the imprisoned princes, which have long since
perished. Nevertheless there would have been ample space for
2,000 or 3,000 inhabitants, provided their supplies were sup-
plemented with food from below, for each arm of the cross is a
quarter of a mile long.

Ignoring the sour-sweet smell of human excrement, which so
often surrounds places of pilgrimage in peasant communities, I
walked on up the right hand side of the hill in a loop to reach its
flat top—a miniature *amba* on an *amba*, as it were. There stood the
church of Gishen Mariam, shaded by the trees in its churchyard,
facing us.

For the time being we did not stop. My rifleman led me past the
church and a rocky pond to the church of God the Father, Eghziab,
a few yards away to the north-west. Here, in the churchyard, we
found Ato Abebe Sege, *enderassie* of the *amba*. He took the envelope, which I had sealed up before entering the gate, opened it
and read the *warakat*. As he did so a kindly-looking old man
emerged from a house in the corner of the churchyard and
joined us. He was the abbot's father.

They discussed the letter together, and I then announced that
I would like to make a donation. This I did, presenting it in a
plain envelope to the venerable doyen of the small band of monks.
All was then in order for the tour to be conducted by the
enderassie.

We started with Beit Eghziab, since this is really the heart and
core of the religious settlement, although the goal of the modern

pilgrims is Beit Mariam. The reason is that, although the *Tefut* claims only a fragment of the True Cross, the traditional oral legend claims it all. It is said to be buried on the cruciform amba under the cross-shaped church of Eghziab, which marks the spot, or alternatively there are three stone cubes in a row between the gatehouse of the church and its front door that may mark the spot. Each one is about 2 feet high and has a cross of Axumite style carved on it, and they may have belonged to the original church of Zara Yakob, for the present church is much more recent, having been built, it is said, in the reign of the Emperor Bakaffa in the eighteenth century.

Basically it is a stone church, with plastered and cream lime-washed walls, of the normal circular kind, but four gable-end extensions built at opposite corners give it its cruciform shape. Mass had been over for some time when we reached it, so it only remained to unlock the blue and red door and let us in after we had taken off our shoes at the threshold.

However there was nothing of any great interest inside. The curtained doorway to the holy of holies was flanked by two paintings from Addis Ababa by a modern Ethiopian ecclesiastical artist, beneath one of which stood a five-branched candlestick of Judaic appearance. In the gable-end on the right a second link with the Gondar dynasty apart from the Emperor existed in the tomb of Abuna Michael, and in the same room the processional crosses for the Maskal festival were stacked up against the wall. They were crudely nailed planks of wood, with variegated cloths tacked on to them. Ato Abebe pointed somewhat mysteriously at the uppermost.

"That one is the shape of the True Cross," he said.

It differed from the others in having some extra pieces of wood fixed to the main planks to give the corners a curved appearance instead of a sharp right-angle. Presumably it was in imitation of the cruciform shape of the *amba* itself.

From this church we went past the railed-off pool of holy water, which is used mainly at Timkat, and past the drinking water pond again and a corrugated-iron generator house between them, which the *enderassie* proudly pointed out. This path led us to the inspection of St. Mary's.

It was a more modern round church, built of unfaced dressed

stone with a tabernacle in the centre presented by one, Woizero Mamite Bayenne "and her husband," which contained a silver ikon of the Madonna and child obtained, I was told, from Jerusalem. The other ikon, hanging on the right of the interior doorway, also seemed to have come from Jerusalem. It was another Madonna and child with the faces framed in gold brocade.

Apart from these showpieces Italian-style tapestry rugs completed the picture of the church's sparse embellishments. In fact its bare curved corridors were not half as colourful as the scene outside in the churchyard, where a priest was expounding the gospel to a group of peasants sitting on the ground wrapped in their white *shammas*.

Actually the treasures are kept away from the churches in a separate building on one side of the churchyard of Beit Eghziab. We went there next, now followed by a crowd of boys from the church school who were free on their Sunday holiday. Climbing up to the first-floor verandah of the treasury, we waited for the key, and were then ushered into a large room full of ceremonial umbrellas and vestments and articles bundled up in coloured cloths.

We were made to sit down on heaped up carpets. Then one of the bundles was brought to us and unwrapped. It was a large book, with board covers overlaid with striped yellow satin—the famous *Tefut* of Zara Yakob, containing the Old Testament story, the gospels and the story of the Ethiopian church. We looked at page after page of tiny, neat hand-writing illuminated with scrolls in pale greens and yellows that looked as fresh as the day they had been painted, and at page after page of cleanly and clearly executed pictures of Moses, of Aaron with his burgeoning rod, of Christ on the cross, of the gospel writers, pen in hand, bent over their work, of the twelve apostles and of many another man of God. The sweat of the journey would have been worth it to see this book alone.

After leaving the treasury we went round the corner to the abbot's house, and from there it was possible to see the northern arm of this extraordinary *amba*, which appeared to be almost equal in length to the southern one. At the far end of it stood the most modern of the three churches—the circular St. Michael's— and beyond that lay the jumbled landscape of *amba* and ravine leading away towards Lalibela and the fastnesses of Lasta.

I turned away reluctantly from the view as Ato Abebe led the

way to his own house in order to do the honours of host. I must
have mopped my brow on the way, for as soon as we got inside his
tukul a glass of water was offered to me. Clearly it came from the
scummy pool with the cross in the middle of it between the two
churches, for in spite of the fact that they try to freshen up the
supply with a conduit from the gutters of St. Mary's, the liquid
was so thick that I could hardly see through it. I asked for *talla*
instead and gulped down my pint of mild beer with relief.

We then had *injera* with a hot *berbere* sauce, followed by coffee.
But all was not well in the household. The good woman of the
house was lying on a sleeping platform groaning with toothache,
and with no dentist anywhere near there was nothing they could
do about it. All I could do was to offer aspirins to help soften the
pain and to thank the *enderassie's* pretty daughters for their
hospitality.

Then, after all too short a stay, I started on the descent. Now
that I had been identified and accepted the hollow-cheeked gatekeeper was much more friendly than he had been on our arrival,
and I was sent on my way with many expressions of goodwill.

Said, being a Muslim, had not come up the *amba* with us, and
when we got back to the *tukul* where we had spent the night we
found him ready with the mules. But first we had to have a
second breakfast of *injera* and *wat*, and I made a donation as a
small token of gratitude for their hospitality. Then, at about
eleven o'clock, we set out on the return journey. It was, of course,
much less arduous than the ascent, though we could not ride the
mules down the two steep sections and had to walk instead. In
this way we got to the river crossing at Talayyan before three in
the afternoon and were able to snatch a short rest before tackling
the tedious river gorge section up to Kundi.

The road was quite crowded, since it was the day after the
Saturday market in Delanta, and the merchants were taking
country produce into Dessie. This was the Via Dolorosa of the
poultry of Daont, for the wretched white creatures were tied
together by their legs in bunches and carried with heads hanging
downwards on the jogging donkeys. If it was found that one had
died of its sufferings on the two and a half day journey, it was
thrown into the ditch, for they had to be sold alive in the
Dessie market to satisfy the town's appetite for fresh meat.

o

Of course, where the life of man himself tends to be nasty, brutish and short, there is usually little sensitivity towards beasts, and the raw-backed mules and donkeys were scarcely happier than the pullets. I was glad, in the end, to reach Kundi at a quarter to six and dive into the hut that Ayele's friend provided for us whilst the merchants unloaded their wool mats and bags of grain at the other end of the village.

We were hard up against a thick grove of bullrushes in which a colony of weaver birds had made their nests, and the air was loud with their twittering as the sun went down. Said spent fifty cents on fodder for the mules, which he tethered to a log, whilst Derbaw and I drank *talla* served in a Spanish olive oil tin.

Then, after eating a tin of baked beans, we turned in early once again, and once again I watched the dawn creep through the chinks in the hut like eyes lighting up one by one. We left the insecticide spray with Ayele's friend, Yilma, so that he might have at least one glorious flea-free night in his grey life, and set out in a light drizzle, which the green parrots near the roadside seemed to enjoy tremendously.

There was no hurry to cover the last 10 miles to Kutaber, as the daily bus that was to take us back to Dessie was not due to leave the village till two. So we went forward gently, enjoying the cool damp air, and I put my umbrella up and rode along holding it over my head. By the time we reached Kutaber the rain had stopped. A small welcoming committee, consisting of Ayele and the mule man escorted us back to Ato Yimer's hotel, and shortly afterwards the owner and driver of the bus arrived.

He was a huge Italian, named Giuseppe Aretuso, but known by everyone as 'Pipo', who had been in Ethiopia for thirty-seven years, most of them in Dessie. Had we but known it and had my plans fitted his schedule, he could have driven us to a much closer starting point for Amba Gishen, since every Friday he bulldozed his big converted Viberti deisel lorry through to Delanta for the Saturday market.

As he sat sharing his ham rolls and tinned peaches with me in the pub he told me how he himself "adjusted" the road with a gang of local helpers whenever rocks or landslides blocked it, and he showed me faded photographs of his road gangs to prove it. So this is how I came to return from the cross-shaped *amba* with Italian arias ringing in my ears above the roar of the engine and sitting beside a 16-stone man who tickled the babies and even made the Ethiopian women laugh with his primitive Amharic and his practical jokes on the men.

After one more night in Dessie at the touring hotel I flew back to Addis from the little airport which still has the rusty litter from its former life as an Italian military airfield alongside it. On the plane they had the latest edition of *Paris Match*, and I read the story of Operation Dewey Canyon III and America's agony—the Vietnam War. All the anxiety of the space-age world seemed to be crowding in on me again after my brief retreat back into a more ancient era, in which news travels only with the speed of a mule, or at most a galloping horse.

16
The Czar of Africa

It was May when I moved in next to the big house. The estate manager doffed his soft felt hat and bowed. The servants and the watchmen looked on. The children of the servants paused to look up.

The big house had belonged to a Polish Jew who had made a fortune out of the Ethiopian trade in coffee and other commodities. It was built of grey stone, and although it had only one storey it looked higher because of the terrace on which it stood. Purple bougainvillea grew up the walls, and if it had not been for the corrugated-iron roof, it would have looked like one of the more expensive older villas in the South of France. A Bechstein grand piano stood on the floor of the main salon, the dining-room was almost filled by a large black mahogany dining-table, the beds were all double size, and every bathroom had its separate bidet.

The surrounding park contained juniper trees as well as the ubiquitous eucalyptus, and it supported a fabulous variety of bird life, including mouse-birds and paradise flycatchers. Green and yellow bee-eaters built their nests in the bank of the mountain stream that circled the servants' village and the rose-garden, whilst sheep and goats grazed amongst the eucalyptus saplings on the slopes on the other side of the murmuring waters. At the top of the slope stood a native village, and usually the only thing that disturbed the tranquility of the park was the barking of the villagers' dogs.

Sitting on the terrace of the big house, where we were the ever-welcome guests of 'squire' Moore and his talented Finnish wife,

Eine, we used to watch the alsatian and the dachshund playing together on the grass of the park, which was laboriously cut from time to time by the gardeners with little sickles, so that the cuttings could be gathered up to spread on the earth floors of the servants' *tukuls*. They would not pass the terrace without making a series of respectful bows.

At half past six, when the quick dusk of the tropics came, a servant would come into the salon and the other rooms to close all the shutters, and a nightwatchman, clad in an ancient khaki greatcoat, would post himself at the entrance door. And we would sit in the salon talking about London and Rome like characters out of Chekhov with their minds on Moscow.

Standing in the middle of the park you could see nothing but the big house, the small villa and the trees. But when the Moslem gatekeeper had opened the main gates for you and bowed you out with a nod of his round white cap, you found yourself immediately in the heart of the city on Teodros square half way up Churchill Street. There was usually a beggar at the gate, sometimes a naked man, frequently a group of donkeys being beaten on their way to or from the *mercato*, often a sheep slung round a man's shoulders or a clutch of chickens with their feet tied together hanging upside down in a man's hand. Occasionally a man or woman would be urinating by the roadside. You felt you had emerged from a haven of peace into a maelstrom of pullulating humanity, and in a second you had entered the stream of motor traffic going up and down Addis Ababa's main thoroughfare.

Early in June I emerged from behind the iron gates to make the last of my trips before the big rains made travel in the highlands a wet and muddy business everywhere and an impossible business off the main roads. I went north again as far as Debre Berhan, the 'Mount of Light', and on into Menz, and then I went off on the gravel road that leads to Ankober.

To get to Menz you go north from Debre Berhan as far as the tunnel. But you do not go through it. Instead you turn right on a road that curves back over the tunnel and then continues along the edge of the escarpment instead of plunging down into the valley below.

Although it was not yet time for the big rains, clouds were continually swirling across our path, slowing us down like fog.

Men with their brown woollen blankets wrapped tightly across half their faces emerged out of the mist like sentinels guarding the approaches. Others were ploughing the steep fields and we could hear their cries and grunts at the oxen although we could not see them.

Every now and then the mist cleared, giving us a glimpse down the escarpment into the abyss, and then the road veered westward from the edge on to a stony tableland, where the round houses were also built of stone. This is the hard land where a high proportion of the leading families of present-day Ethiopia have originated. It is the homeland of the Emperor himself, the harsh land in which parents christen their children with names meaning such things as 'Wipe him out', 'Powerful', 'Smash him', 'Thrash them', 'Let them bow', 'Hacker', 'Shover', 'Squeezer'. Names for a ruthless warrior breed.

A high plain entirely surrounded by escarpments, Menz's villages are still small and undeveloped, and the feudal life continues scarcely touched. After three hours' hard driving we reached Molale, the end of the road on that particular track. It is one of the Menze centres of population, but it is still no more than a village with a miller and a few weavers, sitting with their feet in holes in the ground, and a school on top of a small hill, built some time ago when things were built more solidly but still uncrowded. The people of Menz are conservative in education as in all things. They live out on their farmsteads and do not crowd into towns. But they know it is their folk who rule. The story is told of the time when local elders were asked to nominate a representative to the new parliament. "What do we want with this?" they said. "We've already got our representative—the Emperor."

My companion, Ato Asmelesh, being a man of Tigré, was as much a stranger to the Menzes as I was. They considered us with a slow, cautious courtesy, such as one might find in the Scottish highlands—eyes weighing you up first to find out what makes you a man.

The road from Debre Berhan to Ankober is shorter, and in contrast we swept up over the open highlands on it under a clear blue sky. Half way it descended a high valley, that was bright with white heather and purple thyme, which would have made me think I was in Glencoe if it had not been for the spikes of the giant lobelias on the skyline.

But the road does not go down far. A little further on it goes near the edge, and you see a great cliff thousands of feet high with lammergeiers coasting along its face. Then it rises and falls again but maintains its height, for Ankober, 26 miles from Debre Berhan, is 9,000 feet above sea-level and stands sheer above the Danakil desert which in parts is actually below sea-level.

Ankober today is no more than a large village. But in the nineteenth century it was the capital of the Kingdom of Shoa, the mountain eyrie of Sahle Selassie, leader of the Amharas, and after him of Menelik II until, with waxing power, he moved his headquarters to the more accessible Debre Berhan and subsequently to the area of Addis Ababa.

It is thus of peculiar historical significance, for the leaders of the Amharas, the men of Ankober and of the highlands of Menz, are still the men who wield the power in Ethiopia today. But you will not find any castle or mountain fastness in Ankober, not even a walled darbar hall such as the kings of Gorkha had before they conquered Nepal. All the royal buildings were made of wood and thatch and have gone long ago. Only their site remains, and St. Michael's church, which contains the tomb of Sahle Selassie's father, standing in the dip between Menelik's mount and the present-day village.

It was from this hutted camp that Sahle Selassie sallied forth every year after the Maskal ceremonies at the end of the big rains when the fields are covered with daisies. With the Christian blessing conferred by the tabot, the holy ark of St. Michael's, he led his warrior braves in the annual foray against the Gallas, who occupied the country south of the Chacha river and the slopes of the Entoto hills, where Addis now stands.

Major W. C. Harris of the Bombay Engineers was the leader of a British mission sent to the King of Shoa in 1841, and he has described one of these forays, which he accompanied, in his book *The Highlands of Aethiopia*. It was the King's custom to send out false information about his intended line of march, feint in a certain direction and then suddenly wheel about and descend upon some unsuspecting part of the country in a surprise attack.

Embosomed between the isolated peaks of Yerrur, Sequala [Zuquala] and the far-famed Entoto, lay the wide plain of

Germama, thickly peopled by the Ekka and Finfini Galla, upon whose doomed heads the thunderbolt was next to fall; and full in its centre two placid lakes, like great mirrors, reflected back the rays of the morning sun across sheets of luxuriant cultivation, extending for miles, nearly ready for the sickle. Far beyond, the long wooded line of the Awash, rolling its troubled waters towards the plain of Adel, loomed indistinctly through the haze; and in the extreme distance, the lofty blue range of the Arussi and Ittoo Galla, skirting the mysterious regions of Gurague, bounded the almost interminable prospect. . . .

The luckless inhabitants, taken quite by surprise, had barely time to abandon their property, and fly for their lives to the fastness of Entoto, which reared its protecting form at a distance of a few miles. The spear of the warrior searched every bush for the hunted foe. Women and girls were torn from their hiding to be hurried into hopeless captivity. Old men and young were indiscriminately slain and mutilated among the fields and groves; flocks and herds were driven off in triumph, and house after house was sacked and consigned to the flames. Each grim Amhara warrior vied with his comrade in the work of retributive destruction amongst the execrated Galla. Whole groups and families were surrounded and speared within the walled courtyards, which were strewed with the bodies of the slain. Wretches who betook themselves to the open plain were pursued and hunted down like wild beasts; and children of three and four years of age, who had been placed in the trees with the hope that they might escape observation, were included in the inexorable massacre, and pitilessly shot amongst the branches. In the course of two hours the division left the desolated valley laden with spoil, and carrying with them numbers of wailing females and mutilated orphan children, together with the barbarous trophies that had been stripped from the mangled bodies of their murdered victims.

Thus were the first steps taken in the reconquest of the lands usurped by the Gallas. It was total war, and Major Harris makes it clear that the Gallas were just as bad when their turn came.

But it is only fair to quote another resident of Ankober, the Birmingham naval surgeon, Charles Johnston, before leaving the subject of King Sahle Selassie. He calls him "the most accessible, the most patient listener, and the most upright judge that I ever heard praised by word of mouth, or read of among the most laudatory history of kings. . . . . The Dankalli may well style Sahle Selassie 'a fine balance of gold,' for even now, when thinking of his character, the most lively pictures recur to my mind of instances of his kindness and feeling for the happiness of his subjects, which I have witnessed myself."

Menelik's methods were more diplomatic than Sahle Selassie's and more successful. Though on the whole the Amharas gained the ascendancy, there was intermingling with the Gallas, and Shoa became relatively peaceful at last. Barbarities that never reach the files of the United Nations Secretariat still occur from time to time, but they are rare. In our day it is the northern Muslims who are trying to break the hegemony of the Amharic empire. The southern Gallas no longer have a chance.

Meanwhile the old Czar of Africa perseveres in his role of benevolent autocrat to his loving people, whilst massive injections of foreign aid have the effect of enabling development to take place without disturbing too much the pyramid of power, and of maintaining the *status quo*.

Returning from the village of Ankober to the city of Addis Ababa it was impossible not to be impressed by the astounding change in the status of the Ethiopian capital that has taken place over the last eighty years. But at the same time it seemed as though the countryside had hardly changed at all. In the stony hills they still built their little round houses out of scarce wood and thatched them with grass, they still tended their cattle and sheep on the unfenced open slopes.

As I returned through the iron gates into the private park in the centre of the city and the gatekeeper bowed low as my car went past, I thought of the old Amharic proverb that seemed to sum up feudal Ethiopia on its painful journey into the twentieth century: "He who bows lowest farts loudest."

And then I thought of that other one, equally and sometimes painfully applicable: "Keep your mouth shut or the flies will get in."

INDEX

Aaron, 208
Abaya lake, 175, 180, 185
Abbai river, 31
Abbai Minch, 38
Abba Libanos, 127–30, 132
Abba Pantaleon, 82
Abbe lake, 136
Abdullahi, 140, 148, 150
Abiata lake, 136
Abou Bekr, 155, 156
Abraha Aria, 57
Abraham, King, 197
Abunas, 27, 78
Abyssinia, 10, 50, 92, 150, 151, 155
Achangi lake, 56
Adamitullu, 168, 169, 187
Addis Ababa, 12–24, 27, 28, 32, 40–2, 47, 49, 50, 52, 58, 59, 62, 64, 65, 72, 89, 91, 98, 103, 104, 111, 113, 115, 119–22, 134, 135, 138, 142, 150, 156, 159, 161, 167, 170, 180, 187–9, 191–5, 200, 204, 207, 213, 215, 217
Addis Zemen, 97, 98, 105
Adel, 216
Aden, 81, 135, 147, 150, 154, 157, 160
Aderis, 140, 149
Adi Abun, 76
Adi Arkai, 88
Adigrat, 62
Adowa, 15, 20, 60, 62, 76, 77, 82, 88
Adulis, 66, 77
Aedisius, 78
Afe Negus, 46
Afework Tekle, 95, 105
Africa, 15, 18, 19, 38, 42, 43, 50, 55, 66, 77, 90, 105, 136, 151, 155, 157, 201, 217
Africa Hall, 105–8, 110
Agaus, 36, 37, 39, 50, 98

Agordat, 65
Ahmed, Emir, 149, 150
Ahmed Gragn, 28, 61, 146, 197, 198, 206
Aida, Princess, 58
Alaba, 186
Alamata, 54, 55, 60
Alata river, 99, 100
Alexandria, 27, 78, 79, 124, 157, 160, 191
Alitalia, 19
Alula, Ras, 68
Alvarez, 29, 83, 197, 203
Amasien, 174
Amba Alagi, 54, 56
Amba Gishen, 196–210
Ambas, 36, 88, 132, 193
Ambo, 34, 68
America, 18, 42, 75, 160, 201, 211
Americans, 14, 70, 137, 180
Amhara, 54, 89, 195
Amharas, 10, 11, 36, 48–50, 53, 58, 62, 139, 140, 148, 151, 168, 176, 190, 197, 215, 217
Amharic, 10, 11, 14, 20, 29, 31, 36, 42, 43, 49, 53, 60, 114, 119, 143, 167, 188, 192, 211
Angareb river, 88
Ankober, 20, 48, 59, 160, 213–15, 217
Antonelli, 154
Aosta, Duke of, 33
Appenzeller, 154
Aqaba, Gulf of, 72
Arabia, 78, 79, 141, 144, 146, 151, 154
Arabic, 83, 149
Arabs, 50, 65, 67, 104, 105, 143, 151
Arat Kilo, 17, 18, 41
Arba Minch, 178–80, 183–5
Ark, 128, 215

Arnold, Matthew, 173, 174, 177, 181, 188
Arussi, 169, 216
Arya Selassie, King, 59
Asbe Teferi, 139
Asfa Wossen, Crown Prince, 42, 53, 87, 194
Asheten Mariam church, 132
Asmara, 12, 14, 32, 47, 50, 52, 55, 57, 63–9, 74–7, 116, 119, 194
Assab, 49, 51, 53, 143
Athanasius, St., 78
Atse Maskal, 191
Aussa, 147
Australia, 11, 136
Austria, 134
Awash river, 49, 135–8, 168, 216
Awassa lake, 169–72
Axis powers, 16
Axum, 14, 47, 59, 75–7, 123, 207
Aysha, 143
Azezo, 97

Baboons, 29, 137, 179, 201
Babylon, 77
Bahar Dar, 37, 97, 98, 101, 102
Bakaffa, King, 91, 93, 95, 207
Bale, 10, 170
Bantu, 50
Baratieri, General, 76
Bardey, 154, 157, 160, 162
Basileos, Abuna, 27, 193
Baudelaire, Charles, 163
Bedouin, 144
Begemder, 39, 88, 99
Bekele Molla, 174
Belaya, 26
Bernard, Oliver, 154
Bidault, 155
Bilharzia, 38, 169
Bishoftu, 114
Blue Nile, 25, 27, 30, 31, 35, 37, 39, 87, 98, 198
Bole, 15
Borelli, Jules, 154
Borkenna river, 51
British, 16, 26, 56, 69, 72, 75, 83, 91, 92, 139, 155, 157, 196, 202, 215
British Council, 153
Bruce, James, 92–4
Bulgaria, 11, 58
Buna, 35, 88

Bure, 35, 36, 39
Burma, 33
Burton, Richard, 147–9, 151
Byzantine, 59, 84, 96, 132

Cairo, 14, 93
Catherine the Great, 176
Catholics, 29, 62, 63, 66, 67, 150
Ceylon, 76, 77
Chacha river, 215
Chalanko, 140
Charleville, 134, 160
Chat, 141, 163
Cheesman, Major, 98, 99
Chencha, 180, 181, 183, 185
Chera Chera, 98
Chercher hills, 139, 140
Cherkos, St., 61
Cherkos island, 84
Chika, 30
Chojnacki, Professor, 192
Choke mountains, 37
Christianity, 61, 71, 77, 78
Christians, 10, 13, 61, 65, 70, 71, 81, 125, 132, 143, 146–8, 190, 191
Christmas, 114, 118, 121
Churchill, Sir Winston, 26
Churchill street, 16, 104, 107, 110, 112, 213
Coleridge, Samuel Taylor, 164
Colbus monkeys, 135
Constantine, Emperor, 101, 190
Constantinople, 80, 97
Copts, 27, 59, 67, 70, 74, 94
Crocodiles, 137
Cushitic, 10, 50
Cyprus, 133, 160

Dabat, 88
Daga Istephanos, 101
Dahlak islands, 70, 74, 75
Danagel, Beit, 125
Danakils, 48, 50, 53, 136–9, 142–5, 215, 217
Dangila, 37, 98
Daont, 209
David, Emperor, 101, 191
—— King, 96, 131
Dead Sea, 135
Debarek, 88
Debre Berhan, 47, 48, 50, 62, 194, 213–15

Debre Berhan Selassie church, 95
Debre Damo, 62
Debre Libanos, 27, 28
Debre Mariam, 101
Debre Markos, 27, 31–5
Debre Sina, 48, 49, 83, 183, 194
Debre Tabor, 54, 92, 97, 122
Debre Tsehai, 94, 95
Debre Tsighe, 27
Debre Zebit, 54
Debre Zeit, 114, 135
Debteras, 122, 127, 131, 132
Decamere, 62, 63, 67
Deder, 139
De Gaulle square, 16
Dejen, 31
Delanta, 199, 209, 210
Delphi, 85
Demera, 191, 192
Denmark, 122, 135
Dervishes, 57, 96
Desdemona, 144
Dessie, 47, 51, 53, 54, 59, 193–5, 200, 206, 209–11
Dire Dawa, 138, 139, 142, 143, 145, 158
Djami, 162
Djibouti, 21, 142, 143, 155, 158, 187
Dogali, 68
Dongollo, 68
Dorze, 182
Doxiades, 82
Dukam, 135

East African Airways, 19
Economic Commission for Africa, 18, 105
Eghziab, Beit, 191, 206–8
Egypt, 27, 31, 39, 59, 68, 69, 77, 78, 83, 100, 135, 160, 171, 191
Egyptians, 27, 50, 69, 71, 148, 150, 157
Eilat, 72
Ekkas, 216
Elizabeth II, Queen, 82
Ella Amida, 78
Eltham Palace, 83
Emmanuel, Beit, 123, 127, 130, 132
Enda Selassie, 87
English, 11, 12, 14, 30, 32–4, 42, 49, 89, 90, 122, 126, 133, 181

Entoto, 15, 25, 40, 121, 161, 215, 216
Epiphany, 119, 121
Erer, 148, 151
Eritrea, 13, 14, 42, 48, 62, 65, 69, 75, 141
Eritrean Liberation Front, 65
Erythrean Sea, 69
Ethiopian Air Force, 135
Ethiopian Airlines, 13, 18
Ethiopian Army, 148
Ethiopian Herald, 12, 20, 46
Ethiopian Navy, 72
Ethiopian Tourist Organization, 47, 74, 75
Eto mountains, 88
Eucalyptus trees, 25, 31, 62, 67, 202, 212
Euphorbia cactus, 56, 141, 169
Europe, 18, 19, 60, 63, 69, 75, 90, 94, 135, 159
Ezana, King, 61, 78, 80

Falashas, 79, 82, 88
Fantale, Mount, 138
Faras Maghala, 148, 155
Fascists, 56, 62, 88
Fasildas, Emperor, 84, 90, 91, 94, 101
Ferenj, 24–6, 51, 52, 58, 70, 85, 111, 117, 118, 121, 187
Fiat, 16, 68, 109, 111
Fiche, 30
Figuier, 164
Finfini, 216
Fontanina, 51
France, 11, 134, 155, 156, 159, 212
French, 20, 69, 81, 135, 138, 142, 150, 152, 155
Frumentius, St., 78

Gabre Manfas Kiddus, St., 135
Gabre Maskal, King, 81
Gabriel, St., 126, 130, 132, 140, 141
Gallabat, 97
Gallas, 10, 42, 49, 50, 55, 90, 136, 141, 147, 149–51, 161, 167, 174, 215–17
Gallinya, 29
Ganges river, 83
Ge'ez, 78, 191
Gemu Gofa, 167, 170, 180, 185

Genna, 114
George, St., 19, 28
George VI, King, 16, 24
Germama, 216
Germans, 11, 85, 119, 134, 167, 169, 186
Ghibbi, 17, 22
Ghimjabet Mariam church, 91
Ghinda, 68
Gidole, 181
Gihon, 37
Giorgis, Beit, 125
Gishen Mariam, Beit, 191, 192, 196, 203
Gohatsion, 30
Gojjam, 25–31, 34, 39, 88, 99
Golgotha, 125, 126, 130, 131, 132
Gondar, 38, 47, 54, 65, 75, 79, 83, 84, 88–97, 101, 122, 186, 195, 207
Gorgora, 90, 91, 97
Gorkha, 83, 215
Gota, 139
Graziani, General, 24
Greece, 11, 97, 133
Greek, 69, 78, 114, 127
Greeks, 15, 22, 62, 82, 123, 138, 142
Green island, 69, 73, 74
Gura, 83
Gurages, 29, 151, 167, 187, 216
Gurkhas, 200

Haik lake, 54, 198
Haile Selassie I, Emperor, 13, 16–22, 25, 26, 28, 29, 33, 34, 42, 49, 71, 72, 74, 84, 175, 176, 191–3, 196, 214
Haile Selassie I University, 41, 146
Hailu, Ras, 27, 29–31
Haiti, 18
Hannah, 141
Harar, 44, 135, 138, 140, 146–3, 181, 185
—— Duke of, 148
Hararge, 141
Harris, Major, 215, 217
Hebrews, 79
Helena, St., 190
Hindus, 127, 128
Hirna, 139
Hirut Desta, Princess, 122

Historic Route, 47, 75
Hodeida, 147
Holland, 11, 135
Hosaina, 174

Ibis, 171
Ichege, 27
Ilg, Alfred, 153, 154
Imperial Guard, 18, 42
India, 15, 18, 58, 91, 127, 150
Indians, 34, 56, 57, 65, 67, 99, 142, 181
Injabara, 36, 37
Injera, 34–6, 44, 204, 209
Institute of Ethiopian Studies, 41, 192
Ishmael, Khedive, 83
Islam, 68
Israel, 11, 72, 79, 105, 106, 131, 135
Italian, 11, 14, 17, 69, 90, 111, 196, 211
Italians, 15, 20, 25–7, 29, 32, 33, 36, 48, 49, 51, 52, 56, 59–64, 68, 76, 77, 135, 138, 140, 154
Italy, 11, 59, 60, 64, 67, 69, 71, 97, 115, 134, 155, 196, 200
Itoos, 216
Iyakken, 141
Iyoas, 95

Janhoy Meda, 133
Jarosseau, Bishop, 150, 156, 161
Java, 160
Jerusalem, 21, 79, 84, 124, 190, 208
Jesuits, 90, 94, 99
Jesus Christ, 94, 96, 141, 208
Jews, 79, 84, 88, 105–10, 212
Jimma, 43, 141
John, St., 61, 125, 191
John I, King, 90, 91
John IV, Emperor, 53, 57, 59, 69, 83, 84
John the Baptist, 96, 129
Johnson, Dr., 37
Johnston, Charles, 217
Jordan, 65
Jordan river, 126, 129, 131
Joshua II, King, 91
Joshua the Great, 90, 91, 93, 95, 101
Jubilee Palace, 23

Somaliland, 26, 61, 140
Somalis, 50, 66, 104, 139, 142
Starkie, Dr Enid, 152–5
Stefanie lake, 175
Stephen, St., 101, 119, 191
Sudan, 10, 25, 26, 35, 37, 50, 65, 97, 191
Sudan Interior Mission, 183
Suez, 160
Susenyos, King, 90, 91
Sweden, 11, 135
Swedes, 30, 174
Swiss, 71, 153
Switzerland, 134
Syria, 65

Tabots, 128–31, 215
Taeca Mariam, 85
Taitu, Empress, 21, 43
Tajoura, 137
—— Gulf of, 142, 155
Takazze river, 61, 87, 88
Takele Wolde Hawariat, 46, 52
Talayyan, 199, 200, 209
Talla, 53, 115, 200, 201, 204, 209, 210
Tana lake, 25, 31, 37–9, 84, 88, 90, 95, 97, 99, 101
Tangkwas, 101
Taulud island, 69–71, 74
Teferi Makonnen, 21, 53
Teff, 36, 39, 199, 200
Tefut, 191, 208
Tej, 35, 43, 45, 176, 196, 198, 207
Tekle Haymanot, St., 27
Teleki, Count, 175
Tenta, 202
Teophilos, Abuna, 27, 193
Theodore, Emperor, 54, 59, 91, 92, 94, 202
Thessaly, 62
Tian, César, 152
Tigre, 42, 50, 53, 56–62, 75, 79, 121, 132, 156, 157, 194
Tigreans, 10, 58
Tigrinya, 29, 53, 58
Timkat, 94, 121–3, 132, 133, 207
Tisisat falls, 98–100
Trinity cathedral, 22, 27
Trinity church, 22
Troodos mountains, 160

Tsehai, Princess, 21
Tukuls, 10, 22, 36, 39, 137, 176–8, 199, 201–6, 209, 213
Turkey, 154
Turkish, 22, 69
Turks, 69, 147
Tuscany, 25

Ucciali, 60
United Nations, 11, 18, 103, 217
U.S.A., 11, 14, 30, 64, 73, 103
U.S. Peace Corps, 30, 45, 76, 180, 181
U.S.S.R., 11

Verlaine, Paul, 134, 159, 161

Waitos, 101
Wat, 34, 35, 44, 204, 208
Watet Abbai river, 37
Waugh, Evelyn, 156
Wavell, General, 15
Wichale, 54, 59
Wingate, General, 16, 26, 27, 33
Woldiya, 54, 121
Wolkefit pass, 88
Wollamo, 167, 170, 174–7
Wollo, 51, 53, 191, 192, 195
Wolseley, 18, 19
Wonji, 49, 135
Wukro, 61

Yekatit 12th Square, 24, 41
Yekuno Amlak, King., 27
Yemen, 81
Yerrur, Mount, 215
Y.M.C.A., 177
Yugoslavia, 11

Za Dengel, Emperor, 101
Zagwe, 123, 129, 131
Zangaros, 151
Zara Yakob, Emperor, 191, 207, 208
Zebegnas, 21, 193, 195
Zewditu, Empress, 21, 59
Zeyla, 155, 160
Ziganny, 57
Zimmermann, 154
Zuquala, Mount, 135, 215
Zwai lake, 168, 169, 188, 189

UNIVERSITY LIBRARY
NOTTINGHAM